# AN
# INCLUSIVE-LANGUAGE
# LECTIONARY

# AN INCLUSIVE-LANGUAGE LECTIONARY

## Readings for Year C

*Revised Edition*

*Prepared for voluntary use in churches by
the Inclusive-Language Lectionary Committee
appointed by the Division of Education and
Ministry, National Council of the Churches of
Christ in the U.S.A.*

*Published for*
The Cooperative Publication Association
*by*
John Knox Press, *Atlanta*
The Pilgrim Press, *New York*
The Westminster Press, *Philadelphia*

BOOK DESIGN BY ALICE DERR

PRINTED IN THE UNITED STATES OF AMERICA

**Library of Congress Cataloging-in-Publication Data**

An Inclusive-language lectionary.

  Includes bibliographical references and index.
  1. Bible—Liturgical lessons, English.
2. Lectionaries—Texts.   I. National Council of
the Churches of Christ in the United States of
America.   Inclusive Language Lectionary Committee.
II. Cooperative Publication Association.
BS391.2.I523     1988     264'.34     88-13799
ISBN 0-8298-0791-8 (pbk.: Pilgrim Press)

# Preface

All persons are equally loved, judged, and accepted by God. This belief has been promoted by the church and has its roots in the origins of the Judeo-Christian tradition. Young and old, male and female, and persons of every racial, cultural, and national background are included in the faith community. Basic to a sense of equality and inclusiveness is the recognition that God by nature transcends all human categories. God is more than male or female, and is more than can be described in historically and culturally limiting terms. Words and language, though inadequate and limited, are means by which we convey God's holiness and mystery. Seeking faithful expression about God and about God's inclusive love for all people, the Division of Education and Ministry of the National Council of the Churches of Christ authorized the preparation of *An Inclusive-Language Lectionary*.

A Task Force on Biblical Translation was appointed by the Division of Education and Ministry to investigate the way in which the language of the Bible presents the characteristics of God and of human beings. In 1980, after almost three years of study and discussion, the Task Force recommended to the Division the creation of an Inclusive-Language Lectionary Committee, which was then appointed. Members bring not only their personal commitment to the Christian faith and involvement in particular congregations but also their experience as pastors, teachers, and leaders who have relied on the Bible as their source of inspiration and basis for understanding God's word for the church today. They bring expertise in Hebrew, Greek, linguistics, English, worship, Old and New Testaments, theology, and education. In addition, the members come from a variety of denominations and liturgical traditions. The Inclusive-Language Lectionary Committee consists of Robert A. Bennett, Dianne Bergant, Victor Roland Gold (Chair), Thomas Hoyt, Jr., Kellie C. Jones, Patrick D. Miller, Jr., Virginia Ramey Mollenkott, Sharon H. Ringe (Vice-Chair), Susan Thistlethwaite, Burton H. Throckmorton, Jr., and

Barbara A. Withers (Editor). David Ng is the National Council of the Churches of Christ liaison to the Committee.

The Inclusive-Language Lectionary Committee followed the general guidelines provided by the Division of Education and Ministry to prepare lectionary readings for use in services of worship. These readings are based on the Revised Standard Version of the Bible, with the text revised primarily in those places where gender-specific or other exclusive language could be modified to reflect in English an inclusiveness of all persons. All modifications are supportable by the original Greek and Hebrew texts. The Committee worked on lectionary passages first in subcommittees, each committee consulting not only the original texts but also various translations and commentaries. All subcommittee work was submitted to an Editorial Committee which reviewed the texts for consistency of changes and agreement with guiding principles. The Editorial Committee consists of Barbara A. Withers (Editor), Burton H. Throckmorton, Jr. (Associate Editor), Patrick D. Miller, Jr., and Sharon H. Ringe. As the last step, the full Committee reviewed all work and made all final decisions.

Like most other lectionaries in use today, this lectionary follows the pattern of a three-year cycle beginning with the first Sunday in Advent. The readings for Year A were originally published in October of 1983 and followed the table of readings prepared by the Consultation on Church Union. The second and third volumes contained the readings from the Table of Readings and Psalms prepared for trial use by the North American Committee on Calendar and Lectionary. This revised edition of Year C follows the latter table of readings. A few additions and substitutions were made, consistent with the Committee's mandate (see Appendix, p. 263).

The Introduction which follows offers an explanation of what a lectionary is and discusses the need for inclusive language and how the Committee approached the gender-specific language of the Revised Standard Version. The lectionary passages, along with explanatory footnotes, form the major portion of this volume. An appendix stating a rationale for the major alternative words and phrases and an index of the biblical passages that appear in this lectionary complete this volume.

*An Inclusive-Language Lectionary* is offered to the church as a responsible attempt to represent the biblical writings in an inclusive manner. Respecting its commitment to be responsive to the interests and needs of the church for which the lectionary has been prepared, the Committee has put both the term "Lord" and its formal equivalent, "Sovereign," in the text. This revision was first made in Year C (1985) in an attempt to meet a concern of many persons throughout the church who had used Years A and B in which "Lord" does not appear. For example, "Give thanks to the SOVEREIGN [or LORD], call upon God's name" (Isa. 12:3). "Lord" is printed in this manner as an *alternate* or *substitute* for the word immediately preceding it. "Lord" is *not* to be read aloud *with* the word that precedes it.

*An Inclusive-Language Lectionary* is a major attempt to recast the language of scripture so that it addresses women and men equally. The church has never believed that God is male or that God speaks to the church in male-oriented language more relevant to men than to women. So the Committee submits this lectionary to the church, remembering the words of the apostle Paul: "There is neither Jew nor Greek, there is neither slave nor free, there is neither male nor female; for you are all one in Christ Jesus" (Gal. 3:28).

# Introduction

A lectionary is a fixed selection of readings, taken from both the Old and the New Testament, to be read and heard in the churches' services of worship. Most lectionaries are simply tables or lists of readings to be used in weekly worship; some include daily readings. They cite the biblical book from which the reading is taken, as well as the chapter and verses: for example, Christmas Day: *Luke 2:1–20*. By contrast, this lectionary contains the full text of each reading.

*Recent History of Lectionary Development.* The International Commission on English in the Liturgy created an ecumenical group known as the Consultation on Common Texts. One of the tasks of this Consultation was to explore the possibilities of creating a lectionary that would be acceptable to most English-speaking Christians: Anglican, Protestant, and Roman Catholic. To that end, a small working group known as the North American Committee on Calendar and Lectionary was formed. Over a period of five years a revised table of lections, or readings, was developed that took into account the critique of the Vatican II lectionary (early 1960s) and its subsequent adaptations by the major Protestant denominations. The report of the North American Committee was approved by the Consultation on Common Texts in 1982, and this "common texts" lectionary was recommended for trial use in the churches beginning with Advent 1983. It is this Table of Readings and Psalms which this lectionary follows, using the Revised Standard Version as its text.

*Function of the Lectionary in Congregational Worship.* In churches that use the lectionary every Sunday, congregations hear the same scriptures read. Thus the wider church, within denominations and across denominational lines, is united in its hearing, thinking, and praying. A lectionary provides a way for Christians to live out the church year, which begins on the first Sunday of Advent and proceeds through Christmas, Epiphany, Ash Wednesday, Lent, Passion (Palm) Sunday, Maundy Thursday, Good Friday, Easter, Ascension, and Pentecost. At least four readings are prescribed for each Sunday as well as for special days such as Christmas, Easter, All Saints, and Thanksgiving. The lectionary attempts to provide comprehensive and balanced coverage of the entire Bible. Over a three-year period about 95 percent of the New Testament is heard, as well as about 60 percent of the Old Testament.

It is apparent that any selection of scripture read in a service of worship has been lifted from its biblical context. In the study of the Bible, the context in which a biblical passage occurs is crucial to its interpretation. When passages are read in a service of worship, however, they are read in a new context, in relation to one another and to the church year. This radical change in the context of selections is a major fact that differentiates a lectionary from the Bible.

A lectionary thus has a special function in the worship of the church. It does not supplant the Bible. The Bible is the church's book—created by and for the church. A lectionary is also the church's book, being a prescribed set of readings selected by the church from its scripture for its own special use in worship. The unique feature of *An Inclusive-Language Lectionary* is that it recasts some of the wording of the Revised Standard Version in order to provide both to reader and to hearer a sense of belonging to a Christian faith community in which truly all are one in Christ.

*Why Inclusive Language?* The lectionary readings are based on the Revised Standard Version and original Greek and Hebrew texts, with the intent of reflecting the full humanity of women and men in the light of the gospel. A growing number of people feel they have been denied full humanity by a pattern of exclusion in English usage. Consider, for example, the traditional English use of the word "man." A man is a male human being, as opposed to a female human being. But in common usage "man" has also meant "human being," as opposed to "animal." On the other hand, "woman" means female, but never *human being*. No word that refers to a female person identifies her with humanity. So, in common English idiom, "man" has been defined by his humanity, but "woman" by her sex, by her relationship to man. "Woman" becomes a subgroup under "human." "Man" is the human race; "woman" is man's sexual partner in traditional English usage.

This is but one example of how language *reflects* the way in which we think but also *informs* the way in which we think. The mandate to the Lectionary Committee is to seek "language which expresses inclusiveness with regard to human beings and which attempts to expand the range of images beyond the masculine to assist the church in understanding the full nature of God." In the Appendix the reader will find specific examples of how these kinds of excluding language and imagery have been dealt with in this lectionary.

The RSV is highly respected by biblical scholars and is widely used in this country. However, in this lectionary the wording of the RSV has been recast to minimize the gender-specific language and other excluding imagery reflected in its language in reference to human beings, Christ, and God. Except for these changes the text of the RSV, for the most part, has been retained.

Gender-specific language, however, is not unique to English translations of the Bible; it is characteristic of the languages in which the Bible was written. Both the Old Testament and the New Testament were written in languages and in cultures that were basically patriarchal; and as the English language is also patriarchal, the patriarchal character of both Testaments has slipped easily into the great English versions of the Bible.

*Language About Human Beings.* In a few instances the RSV Bible committee has already avoided male-specific language in reference to human beings. For example, in Rom. 7:1 the RSV has used "person" ("the law is binding on a *person*") as a translation of the Greek word *anthropos* (meaning "man" or "person"). But most of the time *anthropos* is translated "man," or, in the plural, "men." For example, Matt. 5:16 in the RSV reads, "Let your light so shine before *men*" where the meaning of "men" is obviously "people," but not male people exclusively. This verse can be rendered: "Let your light so shine before *others*"—that is, men and women, which represents the clear intention of the words.

Excluding language also appears when masculine pronoun subjects are supplied with third person singular verbs when the context does not require them. Compare, for example, the RSV of John 6:35–37: "Jesus said to them, 'I am the bread of life; *he* who comes to me shall not hunger, and *he* who believes in me shall never thirst . . . ; and *him* who comes to me I will not cast out." What is the intention of this passage? It surely is not that only *men* come to Jesus and believe in Jesus. Why, then, does the RSV read "he" and "him"? It is because of the assumption that "he" also means "she," though we know that it does not.

In this lectionary all readings have been recast so that no masculine word pretends to include a woman. For example, the word "brethren" has been rendered in a variety of ways, including "sisters and brothers." Formal equivalents have been adopted for other male-specific words and phrases. For example, "kingdom" is usually rendered "realm" but also by other terms such as "reign" or "dominion"; "king" in reference to God or a messianic figure is rendered "ruler" and "monarch."

In a few instances, references to women have been added—for example, "Abraham [*and Sarah*]." Where the name of a person or details in the narrative make the gender clear, no change has been made. Thus, David is referred to as a "king," the wounded traveler in the parable of the Samaritan is a "man," and Jesus meets a "woman" by the well in Samaria. Where the gender of the person is not specified, the character is referred to as a "person" (e.g., John 9). Also, contemporary English usage suggests that we refer to a person as having a disabling condition, such as polio, rather than to a "cripple" or a "crippled person." So the biblical reference to "the blind and the lame" is rendered "those who are blind and those who are lame" (see Jer. 31:8). Where "darkness" is set in contrast with "light" and has a moral connotation, a substitute word for darkness is supplied—for example. "The light shines in the *deepest night*" (John 1:5).

*Language About Jesus Christ.* Jesus was a male human being. But when the Gospel of John says, "The Word became flesh" (John 1:14), it does not say or imply that the Word became *male* flesh, but simply *flesh.* Of course, to "become flesh," the one from God had to become male or female, but the language used in this lectionary tries to overcome the implication that in the incarnation Jesus' *maleness* is decisive—or even relevant—for the salvation of women and men who believe or for matters in which the imitation or model of Christ is a concern.

In this lectionary the fact of Jesus' maleness is taken for granted. The historical Jesus is referred to as a man, and the pronouns "he," "his," and "him" are used when the reference is to that historical person. These male-specific pronouns are not used to refer to the preexistent or post-crucifixion Jesus. They are replaced by proper names such as "Jesus," "Christ," and other words demanded by the context, so that in hearing the gospel the church may recognize the inclusiveness of all humankind in the incarnation.

Formal equivalents adopted in this lectionary for "the Son of man," "Son," and "Son of God" are, respectively, "the Human One," "Child," and "Child of God." (For a discussion of these terms, see the Appendix.)

*Language About God.* The God worshiped by the biblical authors and worshiped in the church today cannot be regarded as having gender, race, or color. Such attributes are used metaphorically or analogically. Father is only one metaphor for God in the Bible; other personal metaphors include mother, midwife, and breadmaker. Less familiar, but equally appropriate, are such impersonal images for God as love, rock, and light. Images for God in this lectionary are expressed in inclusive language so that when the church hears its scripture read, it is not overwhelmed by the male metaphors but is also enabled to hear female metaphors for God.

In the RSV Old Testament, the major names for God are "God" (*Elohim*), "LORD" (*Yahweh*), and "Lord" (*Adonai*), and several variations of these nouns—for example, "the LORD God" and "the Lord GOD." In this lectionary, "LORD (*Yahweh*) is rendered "GOD" or "SOVEREIGN," using an initial capital letter and small capitals, and "Lord" (*Adonai*) is rendered "God" or "Sovereign," using an initial capital letter and lower-case letters. (For a discussion of these terms, see the Appendix.)

In the New Testament lections, the formal equivalent adopted in this lectionary for "God the Father" or "the Father" is "God the Father [*and Mother*]" or "God the [*Mother and*] Father." The words that have been added to the text are italicized and in brackets. If the reader chooses to omit the bracketed words, the sentence will read exactly as rendered in the RSV. Where God is called "Father" several times in a single passage, as is often the case in the Gospel of John, the word "Father" is frequently rendered "God." (For an explanation of metaphor, and of specific ways in which this lectionary has recast scriptural language about God and images for God, see the Appendix.)

The terms "Sovereign" and "God" are used in this lectionary in place of the term "Lord"; but "Lord" appears in brackets as an *alternate* or *substitute reading*. So if one prefers, one may always read "Lord." "Lord" is not to be read aloud with the word that precedes it. See Appendix, pages 257–258.

# ADVENT 1

## Lesson 1 ~ Jeremiah 33:14-16

*God promises a ruler who will bring justice and righteousness.*

14 The days are coming, says the SOVEREIGN [*or* LORD], when I will fulfill the promise I made to the house of Israel and the house of Judah. 15 In those days and at that time I will cause a righteous Branch to spring forth for David, who shall execute justice and righteousness in the land. 16 In those days Judah will be saved and Jerusalem will dwell securely. And this is the name by which the city will be called: "The SOVEREIGN [*or* LORD] is our righteousness."

## Psalm 25:1-10

1 To you, O GOD [*or* LORD], I lift up my soul.
2 O my God, in you I trust,
    let me not be put to shame;
    let not my enemies exult over me.
3 Let none that wait for you be put to shame;
    let them be ashamed who are wantonly treacherous.
4 Make me to know your ways, O GOD [*or* LORD];
    teach me your paths.
5 Lead me in your truth, and teach me,
    for you are the God of my salvation;
    for you I wait all the day long.
6 Be mindful of your mercy, O GOD [*or* LORD], and of your steadfast love,
    for they have been from of old.
7 Remember not the sins of my youth, or my transgressions;
    according to your steadfast love remember me,
    for your goodness' sake, O GOD [*or* LORD]!
8 Good and upright is GOD [*or* the LORD],
    who therefore instructs sinners in the way.
9 God leads the humble in what is right,
    and teaches the humble God's way.
10 All the paths of GOD [*or* the LORD] are steadfast love and faithfulness,
    for those who keep God's covenant and testimonies.

## Lesson 2 ~ 1 Thessalonians 3:9-13

*Paul prays for the believers at Thessalonica.*

9 For what thanksgiving can we render to God for you, for all the joy which we feel for your sake before our God, 10 praying earnestly night and day that we may see you face to face and supply what is lacking in your faith?

11 Now may God, even God's self, our [*Mother and**] Father, and our Sovereign [*or* Lord] Jesus, direct our way to you; 12 and may the Sovereign [*or* Lord] make you increase and abound in love to one another and to all people, as we do to you, 13 in order to establish your hearts unblamable in holiness before God our Father [*and Mother**], at the coming of our Sovereign [*or* Lord] Jesus with all the saints.

## Gospel ~ Luke 21:25-36

*Jesus speaks about signs of the end.*

25 "And there will be signs in sun and moon and stars, and upon the earth distress of nations in perplexity at the roaring of the sea and the waves, 26 people fainting with fear and with foreboding of what is coming on the world; for the powers of the heavens will be shaken. 27 And then they will see the Human One○ coming in a cloud with power and great glory. 28 Now when these things begin to take place, look up and raise your heads, because your redemption is drawing near."

29 And Jesus told them a parable: "Look at the fig tree, and all the trees; 30 as soon as they come out in leaf, you see for yourselves and know that the summer is already near. 31 So also, when you see these things taking place, you know that the realm☆ of God is near. 32 Truly, I say to you, this generation will not pass away till all has taken place. 33 Heaven and earth will pass away, but my words will not pass away.

34 "But take heed to yourselves lest your hearts be weighed down with dissipation and drunkenness and cares of this life, and that day come upon you suddenly like a snare; 35 for it will come upon all who dwell upon the face of the whole earth. 36 But watch at all times, praying that you may have strength to escape all these things that will take place, and to stand before the Human One."○

---

*Addition to the text. RSV v. 11 *Now may our God and Father himself;* v. 13 *before our God and Father.* See "Metaphor" and "God the Father and Mother" in the Appendix.
○RSV *Son of man.* See Appendix.
☆RSV *kingdom.* See Appendix.

# ADVENT 2

## Lesson 1 ~ Baruch 5:1-9

*God's promised time of redemption draws near.*

<sup>1</sup> Take off the garment of your sorrow and affliction, O Jerusalem,
    and put on forever the beauty of the glory from God.
<sup>2</sup> Put on the robe of the righteousness from God;
    put on your head the diadem of the glory of the Everlasting.
<sup>3</sup> For God will show your splendor everywhere under heaven.
<sup>4</sup> For your name will forever be called by God,
    "Peace of righteousness and glory of godliness."
<sup>5</sup> Arise, O Jerusalem, stand upon the height
    and look toward the east,
and see your children gathered from west and east,
    at the word of the Holy One,
    rejoicing that God has remembered them.
<sup>6</sup> For they went forth from you on foot,
    led away by their enemies;
but God will bring them back to you,
    carried in glory, as on a royal throne.
<sup>7</sup> For God has ordered that every high mountain and the everlasting
        hills be made low,
    and the valleys filled up, to make level ground,
    so that Israel may walk safely in the glory of God.
<sup>8</sup> The woods and every fragrant tree
    have shaded Israel at God's command.
<sup>9</sup> For God will lead Israel with joy,
    in the light of God's glory,
    with the mercy and righteousness that come from God.

## Lesson 1 (alternate) ~ Malachi 3:1-4

*The messenger goes before God to bring judgment to the people.*

<sup>1</sup> I am sending my messenger to prepare the way before me, and God [[or the Lord]] whom you seek will suddenly come to the temple; the messenger of the covenant in whom you delight—that one is coming, says the GOD [[or LORD]] of hosts. <sup>2</sup> But who can endure the day of that coming, and who can stand when the messenger appears?

For my messenger is like a refiner's fire and like launderers' bleach, <sup>3</sup> who will sit as a refiner and purifier of silver, and will purify the tribe of

Levi and refine them like gold and silver, till they present right offerings to GOD [[*or* the LORD]]. <sup>4</sup> Then the offering of Judah and Jerusalem will be pleasing to GOD [[*or* the LORD]] as in the days of old and as in former years.

## Psalm 126

<sup>1</sup> When GOD [[*or* the LORD]] restored the fortunes of Zion,
    we were like those who dream.
<sup>2</sup> Then our mouth was filled with laughter,
    and our tongue with shouts of joy;
  then they said among the nations,
    "GOD [[*or* The LORD]] has done great things for them."
<sup>3</sup> GOD [[*or* The LORD]] has done great things for us;
    we are glad.
<sup>4</sup> Restore our fortunes, O GOD [[*or* LORD]],
    like the watercourses in the Negeb!
<sup>5</sup> May those who sow in tears
    reap with shouts of joy!
<sup>6</sup> Those who go forth weeping,
    bearing the seed for sowing,
  shall come home with shouts of joy,
    bringing their sheaves of grain.

## Lesson 2 ~ Philippians 1:3-11

*Paul thanks the Philippians for their partnership in the gospel.*

<sup>3</sup> I thank my God in all my remembrance of you, <sup>4</sup> always in every prayer of mine for you all making my prayer with joy, <sup>5</sup> thankful for your partnership in the gospel from the first day until now. <sup>6</sup> And I am sure that the one who began a good work in you will bring it to completion at the day of Jesus Christ. <sup>7</sup> It is right for me to feel thus about you all, because I hold you in my heart, for you are all partakers with me of grace, both in my imprisonment and in the defense and confirmation of the gospel. <sup>8</sup> For God is my witness, how I yearn for you all with the affection of Christ Jesus. <sup>9</sup> And it is my prayer that your love may abound more and more, with knowledge and all discernment, <sup>10</sup> so that you may approve what is excellent, and may be pure and blameless for the day of Christ, <sup>11</sup> filled with the fruits of righteousness which come through Jesus Christ, to the glory and praise of God.

# Gospel ~ Luke 3:1-6

*John the Baptist prepares the way of the Sovereign.*

¹ In the fifteenth year of the reign of Tiberius Caesar, Pontius Pilate being governor of Judea, and Herod being tetrarch of Galilee, and his brother Philip tetrarch of the region of Ituraea and Trachonitis, and Lysanias tetrarch of Abilene, ²in the high-priesthood of Annas and Caiaphas, the word of God came to John, the son of Zechariah [*and Elizabeth**], in the wilderness; ³and John went into all the region about the Jordan, preaching a baptism of repentance for the forgiveness of sins. ⁴As it is written in the book of the words of Isaiah the prophet,

> "The voice of one crying in the wilderness:
> Prepare the way of the Sovereign, [*or* Lord],
> make the paths of the Sovereign [*or* Lord] straight.
> ⁵ Every valley shall be filled,
> and every mountain and hill shall be brought low,
> and the crooked shall be made straight,
> and the rough ways shall be made smooth;
> ⁶ and all flesh shall see the salvation of God."

---

*Addition to the text. See "Addition of Women's Names to the Text" in the Appendix.

# ADVENT 3

### Lesson 1 ~ Zephaniah 3:14-20

*Israel hears the good news that God is in their midst.*

¹⁴ Sing aloud, beloved Zion;
  shout, O Israel!
 Rejoice and exult with all your heart,
  beloved Jerusalem!
¹⁵ The Sovereign [*or* Lord] has taken away the judgments against you,
  and has cast out your enemies.
 The Ruler◻ of Israel, the Sovereign [*or* Lord], is in your midst;
  you shall fear evil no more.
¹⁶ On that day it shall be said to Jerusalem:
 "Do not fear, O Zion;
  let not your hands grow weak.
¹⁷ The Sovereign [*or* Lord], your God, is in your midst,
  a warrior who gives victory,
 who will rejoice over you with gladness,
  who will renew you in God's love,
 and will exult over you with loud singing
¹⁸   as on a day of festival.
 I will remove disaster from you,
  so that you will not bear reproach for it.
¹⁹ At that time I will deal
  with all your oppressors.
 And I will save the one who is lame
  and gather the one who is outcast,
 and I will change their shame into praise
  and renown in all the earth.
²⁰ At that time I will bring you home,
  at the time when I gather you together;
 indeed, I will make you renowned and praised
  among all the peoples of the earth,
 when I restore your fortunes
  before your eyes," says the Sovereign [*or* Lord].

---

◻RSV *King*. See Appendix.

20

## Canticle ~ Isaiah 12:2-6

<sup>2</sup> "God is my salvation;
    I will trust, and will not be afraid;
  for the SOVEREIGN [or LORD] GOD is my strength and my song,
    and has become my salvation."

<sup>3</sup> With joy you will draw water from the wells of salvation. <sup>4</sup> And you will say in that day:

  "Give thanks to the SOVEREIGN [or LORD],
    call upon God's name;
  make known God's deeds among the nations,
    proclaim that God's name is exalted.
<sup>5</sup> Sing praises to the SOVEREIGN [or LORD], who has done gloriously;
    let this be known in all the earth.
<sup>6</sup> Shout, and sing for joy, O inhabitant of Zion,
    for great in your midst is the Holy One of Israel."

## Lesson 2 ~ Philippians 4:4-13

*Paul exhorts the Philippians to devote themselves to whatever is worthy of praise.*

<sup>4</sup> Rejoice in the Sovereign [or Lord] always; again I will say, Rejoice. <sup>5</sup> Let everyone know your forbearance. The Sovereign [or Lord] is at hand. <sup>6</sup> Have no anxiety about anything, but in everything, by prayer and supplication with thanksgiving, let your requests be made known to God. <sup>7</sup> And the peace of God, which passes all understanding, will keep your hearts and your minds in Christ Jesus.

<sup>8</sup> Finally, my friends, whatever is true, whatever is honorable, whatever is just, whatever is pure, whatever is lovely, whatever is gracious, if there is any excellence, if there is anything worthy of praise, think about these things. <sup>9</sup> What you have learned and received and heard and seen in me, do; and the God of peace will be with you.

<sup>10</sup> I rejoice in the Sovereign [or Lord] greatly that now at length you have revived your concern for me; you were indeed concerned for me, but had no opportunity. <sup>11</sup> Not that I complain of want; for I have learned, in whatever state I am, to be content. <sup>12</sup> I know how to be abased, and I know how to abound; in any and all circumstances I have learned the secret of facing plenty and hunger, abundance and want. <sup>13</sup> I can do all things in Christ who strengthens me.

## Gospel ~ Luke 3:7-18

*John the Baptist warns people of the imminent judgment, and denies that he is the Christ.*

⁷ John the Baptist said therefore to the multitudes that came out to be baptized by him, "You brood of vipers! Who warned you to flee from the wrath to come? ⁸ Bear fruits that befit repentance, and do not begin to say to yourselves, 'We have Abraham as our father'; for I tell you, God is able from these stones to raise up children to Abraham. ⁹ Even now the axe is laid to the root of the trees; every tree therefore that does not bear good fruit is cut down and thrown into the fire."

¹⁰ And the multitudes asked John, "What then shall we do?" ¹¹ And he answered them, "Let anyone who has two coats share with a person who has none; and let anyone who has food do likewise." ¹² Tax collectors also came to be baptized. and said to John, "Teacher, what shall we do?" ¹³ And he said to them, "Collect no more than is appointed you." ¹⁴ Soldiers also asked him, "And we, what shall we do?" And John said to them, "Rob no one by violence or by false accusation, and be content with your wages."

¹⁵ As the people were in expectation, all of them questioning in their hearts concerning John, whether perhaps he were the Christ, ¹⁶ John answered them all, "I baptize you with water; but the one who is mightier than I is coming, the thong of whose sandals I am not worthy to untie; that one will baptize you with the Holy Spirit and with fire. ¹⁷ With winnowing fork in hand, that one will clear the threshing floor, and gather the wheat into the granary, but will burn the chaff with unquenchable fire."

¹⁸ So, with many other exhortations, John preached good news to the people.

# ADVENT 4

## Lesson 1 ~ Micah 5:2-4

*Micah foretells the coming of a ruler who will bring peace.*

2 But you, O Bethlehem Ephrathah,
    who are little to be among the clans of Judah,
from you shall come forth for me
    one who is to be ruler in Israel,
whose origin is from of old,
    from ancient days.
3 Therefore God shall give them up until the time
    when she who is in travail has brought forth;
then the rest of the ruler's kindred shall return
    to the people of Israel.
4 And the ruler shall stand and feed the flock in the strength of the
        SOVEREIGN [or LORD],
in the majesty of the name of the SOVEREIGN [or LORD], the ruler's
        God.
And they shall dwell secure, for now the ruler shall be great
    to the ends of the earth.

## Psalm 80:1-7

1 Give ear, O Shepherd of Israel,
    you who lead Joseph like a flock!
You who are enthroned upon the cherubim, shine forth
2     before Ephraim and Benjamin and Manasseh!
Stir up your might,
    and come to save us!
3 Restore us, O God;
    let your face shine, that we may be saved!
4 O SOVEREIGN [or LORD] God of hosts,
    how long will you be angry with your people's prayers?
5 You have fed them with the bread of tears,
    and given them tears to drink in full measure.
6 You make us the scorn of our neighbors;
    and our enemies laugh among themselves.
7 Restore us, O God of hosts;
    let your face shine, that we may be saved!

## Lesson 2 ~ Hebrews 10:5-10

*Jesus Christ, the high priest, is the single sacrifice for sins.*

5 Christ, having come into the world, said,

"Sacrifices and offerings you have not desired,
but a body you have prepared for me;
6 in burnt offerings and sin offerings you have taken no pleasure.
7 Then I said, 'I have come to do your will, O God,'
as it is written of me in the scroll of the book."

8 When Christ said above, "You have neither desired nor taken pleasure in sacrifices and offerings and burnt offerings and sin offerings" (these are offered according to the law), 9 then Christ added, "I have come to do your will." Christ abolishes the first in order to establish the second. 10 And by that will we have been sanctified through the offering of the body of Jesus Christ once for all.

## Gospel ~ Luke 1:39-55

*Mary greets Elizabeth and sings a song of praise to God.*

39 In those days Mary arose and went with haste into the hill country, to a city of Judah, 40 and she entered the house of Zechariah and greeted Elizabeth. 41 And when Elizabeth heard the greeting of Mary, the baby leaped in her womb; and Elizabeth was filled with the Holy Spirit 42 and she exclaimed with a loud cry, "Blessed are you among women, and blessed is the fruit of your womb! 43 And why is this granted me, that the mother of my Sovereign [[or Lord]] should come to me? 44 For when the voice of your greeting came to my ears, the baby in my womb leaped for joy. 45 And blessed is she who believed that there would be a fulfillment of what was spoken to her from God [[or the Lord]]." 46 And Mary said,

"My soul magnifies the Sovereign [[or Lord]],
47 and my spirit rejoices in God my Savior,
48 who has regarded the low estate of God's servant.
For henceforth all generations will call me blessed;
49 for the one who is mighty has done great things for me,
and holy is God's name.
50 And God's mercy is on those who fear God
from generation to generation.
51 God has shown strength with God's arm,
and has scattered the proud in the imagination of their hearts,

<sup>52</sup> God has put down the mighty from their thrones,
  and exalted those of low degree;
<sup>53</sup> God has filled the hungry with good things,
  and has sent the rich empty away.
<sup>54</sup> God has helped God's servant Israel,
  in remembrance of God's mercy,
<sup>55</sup> as God spoke to our ancestors,
  to Abraham [*and Sarah*\*] and to their posterity forever."

---

*Addition to the text. RSV *to Abraham and to his posterity.* See "Addition of Women's Names to the Text" in the Appendix.

# CHRISTMAS EVE/DAY

## Lesson 1 ~ Isaiah 9:2-7

*An oracle points to the coming of one who brings a new age of peace and justice.*

2 The people who walked without light
    have seen a great light;
  those who dwelt in a land of deep shadows,
    on them has light shined.
3 You have multiplied the nation,
    you have increased its joy;
  they rejoice before you
    as with joy at the harvest,
    as victors rejoice when they divide the spoil.
4 For the yoke of Israel's burden,
    and the staff for its shoulder,
    the rod of its oppressor,
    you have broken as on the day of Midian.
5 For every boot of the tramping warrior in battle tumult
    and every garment rolled in blood
    will be burned as fuel for the fire.
6 For to us a child is born,
    to us an heir is given;
  and the government will be upon the shoulder
    of that one whose name will be called
  "Wonderful Counselor, Mighty God,
    Everlasting Father [*and Mother**], Prince of Peace."
7 Of the increase of that government and of peace
    there will be no end,
  upon the throne of David, and over David's kingdom,
    to establish it, and to uphold it
  with justice and with righteousness
    from this time forth and forevermore.
The zeal of the GOD [[*or* LORD]] of hosts will do this.

---

*Addition to the text. See "Metaphor" and "God the Father and Mother" in the Appendix.

[1] O sing to GOD [[or the LORD]] a new song;
    sing to GOD [[or the LORD]], all the earth!
[2] Sing to GOD [[or the LORD]], bless God's name.
    Tell of God's salvation from day to day.
[3] Declare God's glory among the nations,
    God's marvelous works among all people!
[4] For great is GOD [[or the LORD]], and greatly to be praised,
    indeed, to be feared above all gods.
[5] For all the gods of the nations are idols;
    but the SOVEREIGN [[or LORD]] made the heavens.
[6] Honor and majesty are before God;
    strength and beauty are in God's sanctuary.
[7] Ascribe to GOD [[or the LORD]], O families of nations,
    ascribe to GOD [[or the LORD]] glory and strength!
[8] Ascribe to GOD [[or the LORD]] the glory due God's name;
    bring an offering, and come into God's courts!
[9] Worship GOD [[or the LORD]] in holy array;
    tremble before God, all the earth!
[10] Say among the nations, "GOD [[or The LORD]] reigns!
    The world is established; it shall never be moved;
    God will judge the nations with equity."
[11] Let the heavens be glad, and let the earth rejoice;
    let the sea roar, and all that fills it;
[12]     let the field exult, and everything in it!
Then shall all the trees of the wood sing for joy
[13]     before GOD [[or the LORD]], who comes,
    who comes to judge the earth,
who will judge the world with righteousness,
    and the nations with truth.

## Lesson 2 ~ Titus 2:11-14

*The letter to Titus points to the meaning of Christ's appearance.*

[11] For the grace of God has appeared for the salvation of all, [12] training us to renounce irreligion and worldly passions, and to live sober, upright, and godly lives in this world, [13] awaiting our blessed hope, the appearing of the glory of our great God and Savior Jesus Christ, [14] who gave up Christ's self for us to redeem us from all iniquity and to purify for Christ's self a chosen people who are zealous for good deeds.

# Gospel ~ Luke 2:1-20

*Luke describes the birth of Jesus.*

[1] In those days a decree went out from Caesar Augustus that all the world should be enrolled. [2] This was the first enrollment, when Quirinius was governor of Syria. [3] And all went to be enrolled, each to their own city. [4] And Joseph also went up from Galilee, from the city of Nazareth, to Judea, to the city of David, which is called Bethlehem, because he was of the house and lineage of David, [5] to be enrolled with Mary, his betrothed, who was with child. [6] And while they were there, the time came for her to be delivered. [7] And she gave birth to her firstborn son, whom she wrapped in swaddling clothes and laid in a manger, because there was no place for them in the inn.

[8] And in that region there were shepherds out in the field, keeping watch over their flock by night. [9] And an angel of God [[*or* the Lord]] appeared to them, and the glory of God [[*or* the Lord]] shone around them, and they were filled with fear. [10] And the angel said to them, "Be not afraid; for I bring you good news of a great joy which will come to all the people; [11] for to you is born this day in the city of David a Savior, who is Christ the Sovereign [[*or* Lord]] [12] And this will be a sign for you: you will find a baby wrapped in swaddling clothes and lying in a manger." [13] And suddenly there was with the angel a multitude of the heavenly host praising God and saying,

[14] "Glory to God in the highest,
and on earth peace among those with whom God is pleased!"

[15] When the angels went away from them into heaven, the shepherds said to one another, "Let us go over to Bethlehem and see this thing that has happened, which God [[*or* the Lord]] has made known to us." [16] And they went with haste, and found Mary and Joseph, and the baby lying in a manger. [17] And when they saw it they made known the saying which had been told them concerning this child; [18] and all who heard it wondered at what the shepherds told them. [19] But Mary kept all these things, pondering them in her heart. [20] And the shepherds returned, glorifying and praising God for all they had heard and seen, as it had been told them.

# CHRISTMAS DAY, Additional Lections, First Set

## Lesson 1 ~ Isaiah 62:6-7, 10-12

*God sets watchers on the walls of Zion to contemplate the return of the exiles to the holy city.*

6 Upon your walls, O Jerusalem,
    I have set watchers;
  all the day and all the night
    they shall never be silent.
  You who put GOD [[or the LORD]] in remembrance,
    take no rest,
7 and give God no rest
    until Jerusalem is established
    and is made an object of praise on the earth.
10 Go through, go through the gates,
    prepare the way for the people;
  build up, build up the highway,
    clear it of stones,
    lift up an ensign over the peoples.
11 GOD [[or The LORD]] has proclaimed
    to the end of the earth:
  Say to the children of Zion,
    "Your salvation comes;
  God's reward is with God,
    and God's recompense goes before God."
12 And they shall be called The holy people,
    The redeemed of GOD [[or the LORD]];
  and you shall be called Sought out,
    a city not forsaken.

## Psalm 97

1 GOD [[or The LORD]] reigns; let the earth rejoice;
    let the many coastlands be glad!
2 Clouds and thick darkness are round about God;
    righteousness and justice are the foundation of God's throne.
3 Fire goes before God,
    and burns up God's adversaries round about.
4 God's lightnings lighten the world;
    the earth sees and trembles.

⁵ The mountains melt like wax before the SOVEREIGN [[*or* LORD]],
   before the God [[*or* Lord]] of all the earth.
⁶ The heavens proclaim God's righteousness;
   and all people behold God's glory.
⁷ All worshipers of images are put to shame,
   who make their boast in worthless idols;
   all gods bow down before God.
⁸ Zion hears and is glad,
   and the daughters of Judah rejoice,
   because of your judgments, O GOD [[*or* LORD]].
⁹ For you, O GOD [[*or* LORD]], are most high over all the earth;
   you are exalted far above all gods.
¹⁰ GOD [[*or* The LORD]] loves those who hate evil,
   preserves the lives of the saints,
   and delivers them from the hand of the wicked.
¹¹ Light dawns for the righteous,
   and joy for the upright in heart.
¹² Rejoice in GOD [[*or* the LORD]], O you righteous,
   and give thanks to God's holy name!

### Lesson 2 ~ Titus 3:4-7

*In the letter to Titus we are told that all things are changed because of the mercy of God.*

⁴ When the goodness and loving kindness of God our Savior appeared, ⁵ we were saved, not because of deeds done by us in righteousness, but in virtue of God's own mercy, by the washing of regeneration and renewal in the Holy Spirit, ⁶ which God poured out upon us richly through Jesus Christ our Savior, ⁷ so that we might be justified by God's grace and become heirs in hope of eternal life.

## Gospel ~ Luke 2:8-20

*Luke describes the birth of Jesus.*

[8] And in that region there were shepherds out in the field, keeping watch over their flock by night. [9] And an angel of God [[*or* the Lord]] appeared to them, and the glory of God [[*or* the Lord]] shone around them, and they were filled with fear. [10] And the angel said to them, "Be not afraid; for I bring you good news of a great joy which will come to all the people; [11] for to you is born this day in the city of David a Savior, who is Christ the Sovereign [[*or* Lord]]. [12] And this will be a sign for you: you will find a baby wrapped in swaddling clothes and lying in a manger." [13] And suddenly there was with the angel a multitude of the heavenly host praising God and saying,

[14] "Glory to God in the highest,
  and on earth peace among those with whom God is pleased!"

[15] When the angels went away from them into heaven, the shepherds said to one another, "Let us go over to Bethlehem and see this thing that has happened, which God [[*or* the Lord]] has made known to us." [16] And they went with haste, and found Mary and Joseph, and the baby lying in a manger. [17] And when they saw it they made known the saying which had been told them concerning this child; [18] and all who heard it wondered at what the shepherds told them. [19] But Mary kept all these things, pondering them in her heart. [20] And the shepherds returned, glorifying and praising God for all they had heard and seen, as it had been told them.

# CHRISTMAS DAY, Additional Lections, Second Set

## Lesson 1 ~ Isaiah 52:7-10

*Isaiah proclaims God's word of comfort.*

7 How beautiful upon the mountains
    are the feet of the one who brings good tidings,
  who publishes peace, who brings good tidings of good,
    who publishes salvation,
    who says to Zion, "Your God reigns."
8 Hark, your watchers lift up their voice,
    together they sing for joy;
  for eye to eye they see
    the return of GOD [[*or* the LORD]] to Zion.
9 Break forth together into singing,
    you waste places of Jerusalem;
  for GOD [[*or* the LORD]] has comforted God's people,
    and has redeemed Jerusalem.
10 GOD [[*or* The LORD]] has bared God's holy arm
    before the eyes of all the nations;
  and all the ends of the earth shall see
    the salvation of our God.

## Psalm 98

1 O sing a new song to GOD [[*or* the LORD]],
    who has done marvelous things,
  whose right hand and holy arm
    have gained the victory!
2 GOD [[*or* The LORD]] has made known the victory,
    and has revealed God's vindication in the sight of the nations.
3 God has remembered God's steadfast love and faithfulness
    to the house of Israel.
  All the ends of the earth have seen
    the victory of our God.
4 Make a joyful noise to GOD [[*or* the LORD]], all the earth;
    break forth into joyous song and sing praises!
5 Sing praises to GOD [[*or* the LORD]] with the lyre,
    with the lyre and the sound of melody!
6 With trumpets and the sound of the horn
    make a joyful noise before the Ruler,□ the SOVEREIGN [[*or* LORD]]!

---

□RSV *King*. See Appendix.

⁷ Let the sea roar, and all that fills it;
    the world and those who dwell in it!
⁸ Let the floods clap their hands;
    let the hills sing together for joy
⁹ before GOD [[*or* the LORD]], who comes
        to judge the earth,
    to judge the world with righteousness,
    and the nations with equity.


### Lesson 2 ~ Hebrews 1:1-12

*The letter to the Hebrews begins by emphasizing that Jesus Christ is greater than the prophets and the angels.*

¹ In many and various ways God spoke of old to our forebears by the prophets; ² but in these last days God has spoken to us by a Child, ◇ whom God appointed the heir of all things, through whom also God created the world. ³ This Child, by whose word of power the universe is upheld, reflects the glory of God and bears the very stamp of God's nature. Having made purification for sins, the Child sat down at the right hand of the Majesty on high, ⁴ having become as much superior to angels as the name the Child has obtained is more excellent than theirs.

⁵ For to what angel did God ever say,

"You are my Child, ◇
today I have begotten you"?

Or again,

"I will be to the Child a parent,
and the Child shall be my very own"?

⁶ And again, when bringing the firstborn into the world, God says,

"Let all the angels of God worship this Child."

⁷ Of the angels it is said,

"God makes the angels into winds,
and the servants of God into flames of fire."

⁸ But of the Child◇ it is said,

"Your throne, O God, is forever and ever,
the righteous scepter is the scepter of your dominion. ☆

---

◇RSV *Son*. See Appendix
☆RSV *kingdom*. See Appendix.

$^9$ You have loved righteousness and hated lawlessness;
   therefore God, your God, has anointed you
   with the oil of gladness beyond your comrades."

$^{10}$ And,

   "You, Sovereign [[or Lord]], founded the earth in the beginning,
   and the heavens are the work of your hands;
$^{11}$ they will perish, but you remain;
   they will all grow old like a garment,
$^{12}$ like a mantle you will roll them up,
   and they will be changed.
   But you are the same,
   and your years will never end."

### Gospel ~ John 1:1-14

*The author of the Gospel of John unfolds the mystery of the incarnation.*

$^1$ In the beginning was the Word, and the Word was with God, and the Word was God. $^2$ The Word was in the beginning with God; $^3$ all things were made through the Word, and without the Word was not anything made that was made. $^4$ In the Word was life, and the life was the light of all. $^5$ The light shines in the deepest night, and the night has not overcome it.

$^6$ There was a man sent from God, whose name was John. $^7$ John came for testimony, to bear witness to the light, that all might believe through him. $^8$ John was not the light, but came to bear witness to the light.

$^9$ The true light that enlightens everyone was coming into the world. $^{10}$ The Word was in the world, and the world was made through the Word, yet the world did not know the Word. $^{11}$ The Word came to the Word's own home, but those to whom the Word came did not receive the Word. $^{12}$ But to all who received the Word, who believed in the name of the Word, power was given to become children of God; $^{13}$ who were born, not of blood nor of the will of the flesh nor of human will, but of God.

$^{14}$ And the Word became flesh and dwelt among us, full of grace and truth; we have beheld the Word's glory, glory as of the only Child$^\diamond$ from [*God*] the Father [*and Mother**].

---

$^\diamond$RSV *Son*. See Appendix.
*Addition to the text. See "Metaphor" and "God the Father and Mother" in the Appendix.

# CHRISTMAS 1

## Lesson 1 ~ 1 Samuel 2:18-20, 26

*The young Samuel ministers before God.*

¹⁸ Samuel, a boy girded with a linen ephod, was ministering before GOD [[*or* the LORD]]. ¹⁹ And Samuel's mother used to make for him a little robe and take it to him each year, when she went up with her husband to offer the yearly sacrifice. ²⁰ Then Eli would bless Elkanah and his wife, and say, "May GOD [[*or* the LORD]] give you children by this woman for the loan which she lent to GOD [[*or* the LORD]]"; so then they would return to their home.

²⁶ Now the boy Samuel continued to grow both in stature and in favor with GOD [[*or* the LORD]] and with humankind.

## Lesson 1 (alternate) ~ Ecclesiasticus (Sirach) 3:3-7, 14-17

*Children are urged to honor their parents.*

³ Those who honor their father atone for sins,
⁴ and those who glorify their mother are like those who lay up treasure.
⁵ Those who honor their parents will be gladdened by their own children;
and when they pray, they will be heard.
⁶ Those who glorify their father will have long life,
and those who obey God [[*or* the Lord]] will refresh their mother;
⁷ they will serve their parents as their rulers.
¹⁴ For kindness to a parent will not be forgotten,
and against your sins it will be credited to you;
¹⁵ in the day of your affliction it will be remembered in your favor;
as frost in fair weather, your sins will melt away.
¹⁶ Those who forsake their father are like blasphemers,
and those who anger their mother are cursed by God [[*or* the Lord]].
¹⁷ My child, perform your tasks in meekness;
then you will be loved by those whom God accepts.

# Psalm 111

1 Praise GOD [[*or* the LORD]]!
  I will give thanks to GOD [[*or* the LORD]] with my whole heart,
    in the company of the upright, in the congregation.
2 Great are the works of GOD [[*or* the LORD]],
    studied by all who have pleasure in them.
3 Full of honor and majesty is God's work,
    and God's righteousness endures forever.
4 God has caused God's wonderful works to be remembered,
    and is gracious and merciful,
5 providing food for those who fear God
    and being ever mindful of the covenant.
6 God has shown God's people the power of God's works,
    in giving them the heritage of the nations.
7 The works of God's hands are faithful and just;
    all God's precepts are trustworthy,
8 they are established forever and ever,
    to be performed with faithfulness and uprightness.
9 God sent redemption to God's people,
    and has commanded the covenant forever.
    Holy and terrible is God's name!
10 The fear of GOD [[*or* the LORD]] is the beginning of wisdom;
    a good understanding have all those who practice it.
    God's praise endures forever!

## Lesson 2 ~ Colossians 3:12-17

*The Colossians are encouraged to live lives appropriate to God's chosen ones.*

¹² Put on then, as God's chosen ones, holy and beloved, compassion, kindness, lowliness, meekness, and patience, ¹³ forbearing one another and, if one has a complaint against another, forgiving each other; as the Sovereign [or Lord] has forgiven you, so you also must forgive. ¹⁴ And above all these put on love, which binds everything together in perfect harmony. ¹⁵ And let the peace of Christ rule in your hearts, to which indeed you were called in the one body. And be thankful. ¹⁶ Let the word of Christ dwell in you richly, teach and admonish one another in all wisdom, and sing psalms and hymns and spiritual songs with thankfulness in your hearts to God. ¹⁷ And whatever you do, in word or deed, do everything in the name of the Sovereign [or Lord] Jesus, giving thanks to God the Father [and Mother*] through Jesus Christ.

## Gospel ~ Luke 2:41-52

*The young Jesus is brought to the temple and talks with the teachers.*

⁴¹ Now Jesus' parents went to Jerusalem every year at the feast of the Passover. ⁴² And when he was twelve years old, they went up according to custom; ⁴³ and when the feast was ended, as they were returning, the boy Jesus stayed behind in Jerusalem. His parents did not know it, ⁴⁴ but supposing him to be in the company they went a day's journey, and they sought him among their kinsfolk and acquaintances; ⁴⁵ and when they did not find him, they returned to Jerusalem, seeking him. ⁴⁶ After three days they found Jesus in the temple, sitting among the teachers, listening to them and asking them questions; ⁴⁷ and all who heard him were amazed at his understanding and his answers. ⁴⁸ And when they saw him they were astonished; and his mother said, "Son, why have you treated us so? Your father and I have been looking for you anxiously." ⁴⁹ And Jesus said to them, "How is it that you sought me? Did you not know that I must be in the house of [God,] my Father [and Mother*]?" ⁵⁰ And they did not understand the saying which Jesus spoke to them. ⁵¹ And he went down with them and came to Nazareth, and was obedient to them; and his mother kept all these things in her heart.

⁵² And Jesus increased in wisdom and in stature, and in favor with God and humankind.

---

*Addition to the text. RSV v. 17 *God the Father*; v. 49 *in my Father's house.* See "Metaphor" and "God the Father and Mother" in the Appendix.

# JANUARY 1 (New Year)

*The prophet Isaiah speaks of the servant of God.*

¹ Listen to me, O coastlands,
    and hearken, you nations from afar.
GOD [*or* The LORD] called me from the womb,
    and from the body of my mother God named my name.
² God made my mouth like a sharp sword,
    in the shadow of God's hand I was hidden;
God made me a polished arrow,
    in the quiver I was hidden away.
³ And God said to me, "You are my servant,
    Israel, in whom I will be glorified."
⁴ But I said, "I have labored in vain,
    I have spent my strength for nothing and vanity;
yet surely my right is with the SOVEREIGN [*or* LORD],
    and my recompense with my God."
⁵ And now GOD [*or* the LORD] says,
    who formed me from the womb to be God's servant,
to bring Jacob back to God,
    and that Israel might be gathered to God,
for I am honored in the eyes of the SOVEREIGN [*or* LORD],
    and my God has become my strength—
⁶ God says:
"It is too light a thing that you should be my servant
    to raise up the tribes of Jacob
    and to restore the preserved of Israel;
I will give you as a light to the nations,
    that my salvation may reach to the end of the earth."
⁷ Thus says the SOVEREIGN [*or* LORD],
    the Redeemer of Israel and Israel's Holy One,
to one deeply despised, abhorred by the nations,
    the servant of rulers:
"Monarchs□ shall see and arise;
    rulers, and they shall prostrate themselves;
because of the SOVEREIGN [*or* LORD], who is faithful,
    the Holy One of Israel, who has chosen you."

---

□RSV *Kings*. See Appendix.

[8] Thus says the SOVEREIGN [[or LORD]]:
   "In a time of favor I have answered you,
      in a day of salvation I have helped you;
   I have kept you and given you
      as a covenant to the people,
   to establish the land,
      to apportion the desolate heritages;
[9] saying to the prisoners, 'Come forth,'
      to those who are in dungeons, 'Appear.'
   They shall feed along the ways,
      on all bare heights shall be their pasture;
[10] they shall not hunger or thirst,
      neither scorching wind nor sun shall smite them,
   for the one who has pity on them will lead them,
      and by springs of water will guide them."


## Psalm 90:1-12

[1] God [[or Lord]], you have been our dwelling place
      in all generations.
[2] Before the mountains were brought forth,
      or ever you had formed the earth and the world,
      from everlasting to everlasting you are God.
[3] You turn people back to the dust,
      and say, "Turn back, O mortals!"
[4] For a thousand years in your sight
      are but as yesterday when it is past,
      or as a watch in the night.
[5] You sweep people away; they are like a dream,
      like grass which is renewed in the morning:
[6] in the morning it flourishes and is renewed;
      in the evening it fades and withers.
[7] For we are consumed by your anger;
      by your wrath we are overwhelmed.
[8] You have set our iniquities before you,
      our secret sins in the light of your countenance.
[9] For all our days pass away under your wrath,
      our years come to an end like a sigh.
[10] The years of our life are threescore and ten,
      or even by reason of strength fourscore;

> yet their span is but toil and trouble;
>> they are soon gone, and we fly away.
> [11] Who considers the power of your anger,
>> and your wrath according to the fear of you?
> [12] So teach us to number our days
>> that we may get a heart of wisdom.

### Lesson 2 ~ Ephesians 3:1-10

*The Ephesians learn about ministry that is rooted in Christ.*

[1] For this reason I, Paul, a prisoner for Christ Jesus on behalf of you Gentiles— [2] assuming that you have heard of the stewardship of God's grace that was given to me for you, [3] how the mystery was made known to me by revelation, as I have written briefly. [4] When you read this you can perceive my insight into the mystery of Christ, [5] which was not made known to the human race in other generations as it has now been revealed to Christ's holy apostles and prophets by the Spirit; [6] that is, how the Gentiles are joint heirs, members of the same body, and partakers of the promise in Christ Jesus through the gospel.

[7] Of this gospel I was made a minister according to the gift of God's grace which was given me by the working of God's power. [8] To me, though I am the very least of all the saints, this grace was given, to preach to the Gentiles the unsearchable riches of Christ, [9] and to make everyone see what is the plan of the mystery hidden for ages in God who created all things; [10] that through the church the manifold wisdom of God might now be made known to the principalities and powers in the heavenly places.

## Gospel ~ Luke 14:16-24

*Jesus tells the parable about a great banquet.*

[16] Jesus said, "A person once gave a great banquet, and invited many; [17] and at the time for the banquet the host sent a servant to say to those who had been invited, 'Come; for all is now ready.' [18] But they all alike began to make excuses. The first said, 'I have bought a field, and I must go out and see it; please have me excused.' [19] And another said, 'I have bought five yoke of oxen, and I go to examine them; please have me excused.' [20] And another said, 'I have married a wife, and therefore I cannot come.' [21] So the servant came and reported this to the householder. Then the householder in anger said to the servant, 'Go out quickly to the streets and lanes of the city, and bring in the people who are poor and maimed and blind and lame.' [22] And the servant said, 'What you commanded has been done, and still there is room.' [23] And the householder said to the servant, 'Go out to the highways and hedges, and compel people to come in, that my house may be filled. [24] For I tell you, none of those who were invited shall taste my banquet.'"

# JANUARY 1 Holy Name of Jesus; Solemnity of Mary, Mother of God

## Lesson 1 ~ Numbers 6:22-27

*Moses learns how Aaron is to bless the people of Israel.*

22 GOD [[*or* The LORD]] said to Moses, 23 "Say to Aaron and his offspring, Thus you shall bless the people of Israel: you shall say to them,

24 GOD [[*or* The LORD]] bless you and keep you:

25 GOD [[*or* The LORD]] make God's face to shine upon you, and be gracious to you:

26 GOD [[*or* The LORD]] lift up God's countenance upon you, and give you peace.

27 "So shall they put my name upon the people of Israel, and I will bless them."

## Psalm 67

1 May God be gracious to us and bless us
    and make God's face to shine upon us,
2 that your way may be known upon earth,
    your saving power among all nations.
3 Let the people praise you, O God;
    let all the people praise you!
4 Let the nations be glad and sing for joy,
    for you judge the people with equity
    and guide the nations upon earth.
5 Let the people praise you, O God;
    let all the people praise you!
6 The earth has yielded its increase;
    God, our God, has blessed us.
7 God has blessed us;
    let all the ends of the earth fear God!

## Lesson 2 ∼ Galatians 4:4-7

*Paul writes to the Galatians about the time of Christ's coming.*

[4] But when the time had fully come, God sent forth God's Child,◇ born of woman, born under the law, [5] to redeem those who were under the law, so that we might receive adoption as children of God. [6] And because you are children, God has sent the Spirit of the Child◇ into our hearts, crying, "[*God! my Mother and*\*] Father!" [7] So through God you are no longer a slave but a child, and if a child then an heir.

## Lesson 2 (alternate) ∼ Philippians 2:9-13

*Paul reflects on Christ's example of humility.*

[9] Therefore God has highly exalted Jesus and bestowed on Jesus the name which is above every name, [10] that at the name of Jesus every knee should bow, in heaven and on earth and under the earth, [11] and every tongue confess that Jesus Christ is Sovereign [[*or* Lord]], to the glory of God the Father [*and Mother*\*].

[12] Therefore, my beloved, as you have always obeyed, so now, not only as in my presence but much more in my absence, work out your own salvation with fear and trembling; [13] for God is at work in you, both to will and to work for God's good pleasure.

## Gospel ∼ Luke 2:15-21

*Luke describes the shepherds' visit to Bethlehem.*

[15] When the angels went away from them into heaven, the shepherds said to one another, "Let us go over to Bethlehem and see this thing that has happened, which God [[*or* the Lord]] has made known to us." [16] And they went with haste, and found Mary and Joseph, and the baby lying in a manger. [17] And when they saw it they made known the saying which had been told them concerning this child; [18] and all who heard it wondered at what the shepherds told them. [19] But Mary kept all these things, pondering them in her heart. [20] And the shepherds returned, glorifying and praising God for all they had heard and seen, as it had been told them.

[21] And at the end of eight days, the child was circumcised and was called Jesus, the name given by the angel before the child was conceived in the womb.

---

◇RSV *his Son.* See Appendix.

\*Addition to the text. RSV Gal. 4:6 *"Abba!"*; Phil. 2:11 *God the Father.* See "Metaphor" and "God the Father and Mother" in the Appendix.

# CHRISTMAS 2

*(Or the lections for Epiphany if not otherwise used)*

### Lesson 1 ~ Jeremiah 31:7-14

*The prophet Jeremiah assures Israel that their despair shall be turned to joy.*

⁷ For thus says the SOVEREIGN [[*or* LORD]]:
"Sing aloud with gladness for Jacob,
 and raise shouts for the chief of the nations;
proclaim, give praise, and say,
 'GOD [[*or* The LORD]] has saved the people,
the remnant of Israel.'
⁸ I will bring them from the north country,
 and gather them from the farthest parts of the earth,
among them those who are blind and those who are lame,
 the woman with child and the woman in travail, together;
 a great company, they shall return here.
⁹ With weeping they shall come,
 and with consolations I will lead them back,
I will make them walk by brooks of water,
 in a straight path in which they shall not stumble;
for I am a father [*and a mother**] to Israel,
 and Ephraim is my firstborn.
¹⁰ Hear the word of GOD [[*or* the LORD]], O nations,
 and declare it in the coastlands afar off;
say, 'The one who scattered Israel will gather them,
 and will keep them as a shepherd keeps a flock.'
¹¹ For GOD [[*or* the LORD]] has ransomed Jacob,
 and has redeemed them from hands too strong for them.
¹² They shall come and sing aloud on the height of Zion,
 and they shall be radiant over the goodness of GOD [[*or* the LORD]],
over the grain, the wine, and the oil,
 and over the young of the flock and the herd;
their life shall be like a watered garden,
 and they shall languish no more.
¹³ Then shall the women rejoice in the dance,
 and the young men and the old shall be merry.

---

*Addition to the text.

I will turn their mourning into joy,
    I will comfort them, and give them gladness for sorrow.
14 I will feast the soul of the priests with abundance,
    and my people shall be satisfied with my goodness,
                        says the SOVEREIGN [[or LORD]]."


### Lesson 1 (alternate) ~ Ecclesiasticus (Sirach) 24:1-4, 12-16

*Sirach sings the praises of Wisdom.*

1 Wisdom will praise herself,
    and will glory in the midst of her people.
2 In the assembly of the Most High she will open her mouth,
    and in the presence of the host of the Most High she will glory:
3 "I came forth from the mouth of the Most High,
    and covered the earth like a mist.
4 I dwelt in high places,
    and my throne was in a pillar of cloud.
12 So I took root in an honored people,
    in the portion of God [[or the Lord]], who is their inheritance.
13 I grew tall like a cedar in Lebanon,
    and like a cypress on the heights of Hermon.
14 I grew tall like a palm tree in En-gedi,
    and like rose plants in Jericho;
  like a beautiful olive tree in the field,
    and like a plane tree I grew tall.
15 Like cassia and camel's thorn I gave forth the aroma of spices,
    and like choice myrrh I spread a pleasant odor,
  like galbanum, onycha, and stacte,
    and like the fragrance of frankincense in the tabernacle.
16 Like a terebinth I spread out my branches,
    and my branches are glorious and graceful."


### Psalm 147:12-20

12 Praise GOD [[or the LORD]], O Jerusalem!
    Praise your God, O Zion,
13 for God strengthens the bars of your gates,
    and blesses your children within you,
14 making peace in your borders,
    and filling you with the finest of the wheat.

<sup>15</sup> God sends forth a command to the earth;
  God's word runs swiftly.
<sup>16</sup> God gives snow like wool,
  scattering hoarfrost like ashes,
<sup>17</sup> and casting forth ice like morsels;
  who can stand before God's cold?
<sup>18</sup> God sends forth God's word, and melts them,
  making the wind blow, and the waters flow.
<sup>19</sup> God declares God's word to Jacob,
  God's statutes and ordinances to Israel.
<sup>20</sup> God has not dealt thus with any other nation;
  they do not know the ordinances.
  Praise GOD [[or the LORD]]!

## Lesson 2 ~ Ephesians 1:3-6, 15-18

*The writer of the letter to the Ephesians begins by praising God's grace in Jesus Christ.*

<sup>3</sup> Blessed be God the Father [and Mother*] of our Sovereign [[or Lord]] Jesus Christ, who has blessed us in Christ with every spiritual blessing in the heavenly places, <sup>4</sup> even as God chose us in Christ before the foundation of the world, that we should be holy and blameless before God, <sup>5</sup> who destined us in love to be God's children through Jesus Christ, according to the purpose of God's will, <sup>6</sup> to the praise of God's glorious grace freely bestowed on us in the Beloved.

<sup>15</sup> For this reason, because I have heard of your faith in the Sovereign [[or Lord]] Jesus and your love toward all the saints, <sup>16</sup> I do not cease to give thanks for you, remembering you in my prayers, <sup>17</sup> that the God of our Sovereign [[or Lord]] Jesus Christ, the Father [and Mother*] of glory, may give you a spirit of wisdom and of revelation in the knowledge of God, <sup>18</sup> having the eyes of your hearts enlightened, that you may know what is the hope to which you have been called, what are the riches of God's glorious inheritance in the saints.

---

*Addition to the text. RSV v.3 *the God and Father;* v.17 *the Father of glory.* See "Metaphor" and "God the Father and Mother" in the Appendix.

## Gospel ~ John 1:1-18

*The author of the Gospel of John unfolds the mystery of the incarnation.*

¹ In the beginning was the Word, and the Word was with God, and the Word was God. ² The Word was in the beginning with God; ³ all things were made through the Word, and without the Word was not anything made that was made. ⁴ In the Word was life, and the life was the light of all. ⁵ The light shines in the deepest night, and the night has not overcome it.

⁶ There was a man sent from God, whose name was John. ⁷ John came for testimony, to bear witness to the light, that all might believe through him. ⁸ John was not the light, but came to bear witness to the light.

⁹ The true light that enlightens everyone was coming into the world. ¹⁰ The Word was in the world, and the world was made through the Word, yet the world did not know the Word. ¹¹ The Word came to the Word's own home, but those to whom the Word came did not receive the Word. ¹² But to all who received the Word, who believed in the name of the Word, power was given to become children of God; ¹³ who were born, not of blood nor of the will of the flesh nor of human will, but of God.

¹⁴ And the Word became flesh and dwelt among us, full of grace and truth; we have beheld the Word's glory, glory as of the only Child◇ from [*God*] the Father [*and Mother**]. ¹⁵ (John bore witness to the Child, and cried, "This was the person of whom I said, "The one who comes after me ranks before me, for that one was before me.'") ¹⁶ And from the fullness of the Child have we all received, grace upon grace. ¹⁷ For the law was given through Moses; grace and truth came through Jesus Christ. ¹⁸ No one has ever seen God; the only Child,◇ who is in the bosom of [*God*] the [*Mother and**] Father, that one has made God known.

---

◇RSV *Son*. See Appendix.
*Addition to the text. See "Metaphor" and "God the Father and Mother" in the Appendix.

# EPIPHANY

## Lesson 1 ~ Isaiah 60:1-6

*Isaiah tells of the coming of God's glory to the people.*

<sup>1</sup> Arise, shine; for your light has come,
  and the glory of GOD [[*or* the LORD]] has risen upon you.
<sup>2</sup> For shadows shall cover the earth,
  and thick shadow the nations;
 but GOD [[*or* the LORD]] will arise upon you,
  and the glory of God will be seen upon you.
<sup>3</sup> And nations shall come to your light,
  and rulers□ to the brightness of your rising.
<sup>4</sup> Lift up your eyes round about, and see;
  they all gather together, they come to you;
 your sons shall come from afar,
  and your daughters shall be carried in the arms.
<sup>5</sup> Then you shall see and be radiant,
  your heart shall thrill and rejoice;
 because the abundance of the sea shall be turned to you,
  the wealth of the nations shall come to you.
<sup>6</sup> A multitude of camels shall cover you,
  the young camels of Midian and Ephah;
  all those from Sheba shall come.
 They shall bring gold and frankincense,
  and shall proclaim the praise of GOD [[*or* the LORD]].

## Psalm 72:1-14

<sup>1</sup> Give the ruler□ your justice, O God,
  and your righteousness to the royal heir!
<sup>2</sup> May the ruler judge your people with righteousness,
  and your poor with justice!
<sup>3</sup> Let the mountains bear prosperity for the people,
  and the hills, in righteousness!
<sup>4</sup> May the ruler defend the cause of the poor of the people,
  give deliverance to the needy,
  and crush the oppressor!
<sup>5</sup> May the ruler live while the sun endures,
  and as long as the moon, throughout all generations!

---

□ RSV Isa. 60:3 *kings*; Ps. 72:1 *king*. See Appendix.

⁶ May the ruler be like rain that falls on the mown grass,
  like showers that water the earth!
⁷ In the ruler's days may righteousness flourish,
  and peace abound, till the moon be no more!
⁸ May the ruler have dominion from sea to sea,
  and from the River to the ends of the earth!
⁹ May the foes of the ruler bow down,
  and the enemies lick the dust!
¹⁰ May the kings of Tarshish and of the isles
  render tribute,
  may the kings of Sheba and Seba
  bring gifts!
¹¹ May all kings bow down
  and all nations serve the ruler!
¹² For the ruler delivers the needy when they call,
  the poor and those who have no helper,
¹³ and has pity on the weak and the needy,
  and saves the lives of the needy.
¹⁴ The ruler redeems their lives from oppression and violence,
  and their blood is precious in the ruler's sight.

## Lesson 2 ~ Ephesians 3:1-12

*The Ephesians learn about ministry that is rooted in Christ.*

¹ For this reason I, Paul, a prisoner for Christ Jesus on behalf of you Gentiles— ² assuming that you have heard of the stewardship of God's grace that was given to me for you, ³ how the mystery was made known to me by revelation, as I have written briefly. ⁴ When you read this you can perceive my insight into the mystery of Christ, ⁵ which was not made known to the human race in other generations as it has now been revealed to Christ's holy apostles and prophets by the Spirit; ⁶ that is, how the Gentiles are joint heirs, members of the same body, and partakers of the promise in Christ Jesus through the gospel.

⁷ Of this gospel I was made a minister according to the gift of God's grace which was given me by the working of God's power. ⁸ To me, though I am the very least of all the saints, this grace was given, to preach to the Gentiles the unsearchable riches of Christ, ⁹ and to make everyone see what is the plan of the mystery hidden for ages in God who created all things; ¹⁰ that through the church the manifold wisdom of God might now be made known to the principalities and powers in the heavenly places.

[11]This was according to the eternal purpose which God has realized in Christ Jesus our Sovereign [[or Lord]], [12]in whom we have boldness and confidence of access through our faith in Christ.

### Gospel ~ Matthew 2:1-12

*Matthew describes the visit of the magi to the child.*

[1]Now when Jesus was born in Bethlehem of Judea in the days of Herod the king, magi from the East came to Jerusalem, saying, [2]"Where is the one who has been born king of the Jews? For we have seen his star in the East, and have come to worship him. [3]And hearing this, Herod the king was troubled, and all Jerusalem as well; [4]and assembling all the chief priests and scribes of the people, he inquired of them where the Christ was to be born. [5]They told Herod, "In Bethlehem of Judea; for so it is written by the prophet:

[6]'And you, O Bethlehem, in the land of Judah,
are by no means least among the rulers of Judah;
for from you shall come a ruler
who will govern my people Israel.'"

[7]Then Herod summoned the magi secretly, ascertained from them what time the star appeared, and [8]sent them to Bethlehem, saying, "Go and search diligently for the child, and when you have found him bring me word, that I too may come and worship him." [9]When they had heard the king they went their way; and the star which they had seen in the East went before them, till it came to rest over the place where the child was. [10]When they saw the star, they rejoiced exceedingly with great joy; [11]and going into the house they saw the child with Mary his mother, and they fell down and worshiped him. Then, opening their treasures, they offered the child gifts, gold and frankincense and myrrh. [12]And being warned in a dream not to return to Herod, they departed to their own country by another way.

# BAPTISM OF JESUS

## Lesson 1 ~ Isaiah 61:1-4

*The one whom God has anointed proclaims good news.*

<sup>1</sup> The spirit of the Sovereign [[*or* Lord]] GOD is upon me,
    because GOD [[*or* the LORD]] has anointed me
to bring good tidings to those who are afflicted;
    God has sent me to bind up the brokenhearted,
to proclaim liberty to the captives,
    and the opening of the prison to those who are bound;
<sup>2</sup> to proclaim the year of GOD's [[*or* the LORD's]] favor,
    and the day of vengeance of our God;
to comfort all who mourn;
<sup>3</sup> to grant to those who mourn in Zion—
    to give them a garland instead of ashes,
the oil of gladness instead of mourning,
    the mantle of praise instead of a faint spirit;
that they may be called oaks of righteousness,
    the planting of GOD [[*or* the LORD]], that God may be glorified.
<sup>4</sup> They shall build up the ancient ruins,
    they shall raise up the former devastations;
they shall repair the ruined cities,
    the devastations of many generations.

## Psalm 29

<sup>1</sup> Ascribe to GOD [[*or* the LORD]], O heavenly beings,
    ascribe to GOD [[*or* the LORD]] glory and strength.
<sup>2</sup> Ascribe to GOD [[*or* the LORD]] the glory of God's name;
    worship GOD [[*or* the LORD]] in holy array.
<sup>3</sup> The voice of GOD [[*or* the LORD]] is upon the waters;
    the God of glory thunders,
GOD [[*or* the LORD]], upon many waters.
<sup>4</sup> The voice of GOD [[*or* the LORD]] is powerful,
    the voice of GOD [[*or* the LORD]] is full of majesty.
<sup>5</sup> The voice of GOD [[*or* the LORD]] breaks the cedars,
    GOD [[*or* the LORD]] breaks the cedars of Lebanon,
<sup>6</sup> making Lebanon to skip like a calf,
    and Sirion like a young wild ox.
<sup>7</sup> The voice of GOD [[*or* the LORD]] flashes forth flames of fire.
<sup>8</sup> The voice of GOD [[*or* the LORD]] shakes the wilderness,
    GOD [[*or* the LORD]] shakes the wilderness of Kadesh.

<sup> </sup>⁹ The voice of GOD [[*or* the LORD]] makes the oaks to whirl,
    and strips the forests bare;
    and in God's temple all cry, "Glory!"
¹⁰ GOD [[*or* The LORD]] sits enthroned over the flood;
    GOD [[*or* the LORD]] sits enthroned as ruler⊡ forever.
¹¹ May GOD [[*or* the LORD]] give strength to the people!
    May GOD [[*or* the LORD]] bless the people with peace!

### Lesson 2 ~ Acts 8:14-17

*Peter and John laid their hands on the Samaritans, so that they might receive the Holy Spirit.*

¹⁴ Now when the apostles at Jerusalem heard that Samaria had received the word of God, they sent to them Peter and John, ¹⁵ who came down and prayed for them that they might receive the Holy Spirit; ¹⁶ for the Spirit had not yet fallen on any of them, but they had only been baptized in the name of the Sovereign [[*or* Lord]] Jesus. ¹⁷ Then Peter and John laid their hands on them and they received the Holy Spirit.

### Gospel ~ Luke 3:15-17, 21-22

*Luke tells of Jesus' baptism.*

¹⁵ As the people were in expectation, all of them questioning in their hearts concerning John, whether perhaps he were the Christ, ¹⁶ John answered them all, "I baptize you with water; but the one who is mightier than I is coming, the thong of whose sandals I am not worthy to untie; that one will baptize you with the Holy Spirit and with fire. ¹⁷ With winnowing fork in hand, that one will clear the threshing floor, and gather the wheat into the granary, but will burn the chaff with unquenchable fire."
²¹ Now when all the people were baptized, and when Jesus also had been baptized and was praying, the heaven was opened, ²² and the Holy Spirit descended upon Jesus in bodily form, as a dove, and a voice came from heaven, "You are my beloved Child;◇ with you I am well pleased."

---

⊡RSV *king*. See Appendix.
◇RSV *Son*. See Appendix.

# EPIPHANY 2

## Lesson 1 ~ Isaiah 62:1-5

*Israel is given a new name to mark its redemption by God.*

1 For Zion's sake I will not keep silent,
    and for Jerusalem's sake I will not rest,
until its vindication goes forth as brightness,
    and its salvation as a burning torch.
2 The nations shall see your vindication,
    and all the rulers⬜ your glory;
and you shall be called by a new name
    which the mouth of GOD [[*or* the LORD]] will give.
3 You shall be a crown of beauty in the hand of the SOVEREIGN [[*or*
    LORD]],
    and a royal diadem in the hand of your God.
4 You shall no more be termed Forsaken,
    and your land shall no more be termed Desolate;
but you shall be called My delight is in her,
    and your land Married;
for GOD [[*or* the LORD]] delights in you,
    and your land shall be married.
5 For as a young man marries a young woman,
    so shall your children marry you,
and as the bridegroom rejoices in the bride,
    so shall your God rejoice in you.

## Psalm 36:5-10

5 Your steadfast love, O GOD [[*or* LORD]], extends to the heavens,
    your faithfulness to the clouds.
6 Your righteousness is like the mountains of God,
    your judgments are like the great deep;
all living things you save, O GOD [[*or* LORD]].
7 How precious is your steadfast love, O God!
    All people may take refuge in the shadow of your wings.
8 They feast on the abundance of your house,
    and you give them drink from the river of your delights.
9 For with you is the fountain of life;
    in your light do we see light.
10 O continue your steadfast love to those who know you,
    and your salvation to the upright of heart!

---

⬜RSV *kings*. See Appendix.

## Lesson 2 ~ 1 Corinthians 12:1-11

*Paul writes to the Corinthians about spiritual gifts.*

[1] Now concerning spiritual gifts, brothers and sisters, I do not want you to be uninformed. [2] You know that when you were heathen, you were led astray to speechless idols, however you may have been moved. [3] Therefore I want you to understand that no one speaking by the Spirit of God ever says "Jesus be cursed!" and no one can say "Jesus is Sovereign [*or* Lord] except by the Holy Spirit.

[4] Now there are varieties of gifts, but the same Spirit; [5] and there are varieties of service, but the same Sovereign [*or* Lord]; [6] and there are varieties of working, but it is the same God who inspires them all in everyone. [7] To each is given the manifestation of the Spirit for the common good. [8] To one is given through the Spirit the utterance of wisdom, and to another the utterance of knowledge according to the same Spirit, [9] to another faith by the same Spirit, to another gifts of healing by the one Spirit, [10] to another the working of miracles, to another prophecy, to another the ability to distinguish between spirits, to another various kinds of tongues, to another the interpretation of tongues. [11] All these are inspired by one and the same Spirit, who apportions to each one individually as the Spirit wills.

## Gospel ~ John 2:1-11

*Jesus' first sign is performed at the wedding in Cana.*

[1] On the third day there was a marriage at Cana in Galilee, and the mother of Jesus was there; [2] Jesus also was invited to the marriage, with the disciples. [3] When the wine gave out, the mother of Jesus said to him, "They have no wine." [4] And Jesus said to her, "O woman, what have you to do with me? My hour has not yet come." [5] His mother said to the servants, "Do whatever he tells you." [6] Now six stone jars for the Jewish rites of purification were standing there, each holding twenty or thirty gallons. [7] Jesus said to the servants, "Fill the jars with water." And they filled them up to the brim. [8] He said to them, "Now draw some out, and take it to the steward of the feast." So they took it. [9] When the steward of the feast tasted the water now become wine, and did not know where it came from (though the servants who had drawn the water knew), the steward of the feast called the bridegroom [10] and said to him, "Everyone serves the good wine first; and when people have drunk freely, then the poor wine; but you have kept the good wine until now." [11] This, the first of his signs, Jesus did at Cana in Galilee, and manifested his glory; and the disciples believed in Jesus.

# EPIPHANY 3

## Lesson 1 ~ Nehemiah 8:1-4a, 5-6, 8-10

*Ezra reads from the book of the law of Moses.*

¹ And all the people gathered as one into the square before the Water Gate; and they told Ezra the scribe to bring the book of the law of Moses which GOD [[*or* the LORD]] had given to Israel. ² And Ezra the priest brought the law before the assembly, both men and women and all who could hear with understanding, on the first day of the seventh month. ³ And Ezra read from it facing the square before the Water Gate from early morning until midday, in the presence of the men and the women and those who could understand; and the ears of all the people were attentive to the book of the law. ⁴ And Ezra the scribe stood on a wooden pulpit which they had made for the purpose. ⁵ And Ezra opened the book in the sight of all the people, for he was above all the people; and when he opened it all the people stood. ⁶ And Ezra blessed the SOVEREIGN [[*or* LORD]], the great God; and all the people answered, "Amen, Amen," lifting up their hands; and they bowed their heads and worshiped GOD [[*or* the LORD]] with their faces to the ground. ⁸ And they read from the book, from the law of God, clearly; and they gave the sense, so that the people understood the reading.

⁹ And Nehemiah, who was the governor, and Ezra the priest and scribe, and the Levites who taught the people said to all the people, "This day is holy to the SOVEREIGN [[*or* LORD]] your God; do not mourn or weep." For all the people wept when they heard the words of the law. ¹⁰ Then Ezra said to them, "Go your way, eat the fat and drink sweet wine and send portions to the one for whom nothing is prepared; for this day is holy to our God [[*or* Lord]]; and do not be grieved, for the joy of GOD [[*or* the LORD]] is your strength."

## Psalm 19:7-14

⁷ The law of GOD [[*or* the LORD]] is perfect,
    reviving the soul;
  the testimony of GOD [[*or* the LORD]] is sure,
    making wise the simple;
⁸ the precepts of GOD [[*or* the LORD]] are right,
    rejoicing the heart;
  the commandment of GOD [[*or* the LORD]] is pure,
    enlightening the eyes;

$^9$ the fear of GOD [[or the LORD]] is clean,
  enduring forever;
  the ordinances of GOD [[or the LORD]] are true,
  and righteous altogether.
$^{10}$ More to be desired are they than gold,
  even much fine gold;
  sweeter also than honey
  and drippings of the honeycomb.
$^{11}$ Moreover by them is your servant warned;
  in keeping them there is great reward.
$^{12}$ But who can discern one's errors?
  Clear me from hidden faults.
$^{13}$ Keep back your servant also from presumptuous sins;
  let them not have dominion over me!
  Then I shall be blameless,
  and innocent of great transgression.
$^{14}$ Let the words of my mouth and the meditation of my heart
  be acceptable in your sight,
  O GOD [[or LORD]], my rock and my redeemer.

## Lesson 2 ∼ 1 Corinthians 12:12-30

*The body of Christ, though one, has many members.*

$^{12}$ For just as the body is one and has many members, and all the members of the body, though many, are one body, so it is with Christ. $^{13}$ For by one Spirit we were all baptized into one body—Jews or Greeks, slaves or free—and all were made to drink of one Spirit.

$^{14}$ For the body does not consist of one member but of many. $^{15}$ If the foot should say, "Because I am not a hand, I do not belong to the body," that would not make it any less a part of the body. $^{16}$ And if the ear should say, "Because I am not an eye, I do not belong to the body," that would not make it any less a part of the body. $^{17}$ If the whole body were an eye, where would be the hearing? If the whole body were an ear, where would be the sense of smell? $^{18}$ But as it is, God arranged the organs in the body, each one of them, as God chose. $^{19}$ If all were a single organ, where would the body be? $^{20}$ As it is, there are many parts, yet one body. $^{21}$ The eye cannot say to the hand, "I have no need of you," nor again the head to the feet, "I have no need of you." $^{22}$ On the contrary, the parts of the body which seem to be weaker are indispensable, $^{23}$ and those parts of the body which we think less honorable we invest with the greater honor, and our unpresentable parts are treated with greater modesty, $^{24}$ which our more presentable parts do not require. But God has so composed the body, giving the greater honor to the inferior part, <sup>25</sup>that there may be no discord in the body, but that the members may have the same care for one another. <sup>26</sup>If one member suffers, all suffer together; if one member is honored, all rejoice together.

<sup>27</sup>Now you are the body of Christ and individually members of it. <sup>28</sup>And God has appointed in the church first apostles, second prophets, third teachers, then workers of miracles, then healers, helpers, administrators, speakers in various kinds of tongues. <sup>29</sup>Are all apostles? Are all prophets? Are all teachers? Do all work miracles? <sup>30</sup>Do all possess gifts of healing? Do all speak with tongues? Do all interpret?

## Gospel ~ Luke 4:14-21

*Jesus preaches in the synagogue at Nazareth.*

<sup>14</sup>And Jesus returned in the power of the Spirit into Galilee, and a report concerning him went out through all the surrounding country. <sup>15</sup>And he taught in their synagogues, being glorified by all.

<sup>16</sup>And Jesus came to Nazareth, where he had been brought up, and went to the synagogue, as his custom was, on the sabbath day. And he stood up to read; <sup>17</sup>and being given the book of the prophet Isaiah, Jesus opened the book and found the place where it was written,

<sup>18</sup>"The Spirit of God [[*or* the Lord]] is upon me,
   because God has anointed me to preach good news to the poor,
   and has sent me to proclaim release to the captives
   and recovering of sight to those who are blind,
   to set at liberty those who are oppressed,
<sup>19</sup>to proclaim the acceptable year of the Sovereign [[*or* Lord]]."

<sup>20</sup>And Jesus closed the book, and gave it back to the attendant, and sat down; and the eyes of all in the synagogue were fixed on Jesus, <sup>21</sup>who began to say to them, "Today this scripture has been fulfilled in your hearing."

# EPIPHANY 4

## Lesson 1 ~ Jeremiah 1:4-10

*Jeremiah tells of being called by God to be a prophet.*

⁴ Now the word of GOD [[*or* the LORD]] came to me saying,

⁵ "Before I formed you in the womb I knew you,
    and before you were born I consecrated you;
    I appointed you a prophet to the nations."

⁶ Then I said, "Ah, Sovereign [[*or* Lord]] GOD! I do not know how to speak, for I am only a youth." ⁷ But GOD [[*or* the LORD]] said to me,

    "Do not say, 'I am only a youth';
    for to all to whom I send you you shall go,
    and whatever I command you you shall speak.
⁸ Be not afraid of them,
    for I am with you to deliver you,

                says the SOVEREIGN [[*or* LORD]]."

⁹ Then GOD [[*or* the LORD]] stretched out a hand and touched my mouth and said to me,

    "I have put my words in your mouth.
¹⁰ See, I have set you this day over nations and over kingdoms,
    to pluck up and to break down,
    to destroy and to overthrow,
    to build and to plant."

## Psalm 71:1-6

¹ In you, O GOD [[*or* LORD]], do I take refuge;
    let me never be put to shame!
² In your righteousness deliver me and rescue me;
    incline your ear to me, and save me!
³ Be to me a rock of refuge,
    a strong fortress, to save me,
    for you are my rock and my fortress.
⁴ Rescue me, O my God, from the hand of the wicked,
    from the grasp of the unjust and the cruel.
⁵ For you, O God [[*or* Lord]], are my hope,
    my trust, O GOD [[*or* LORD]], from my youth.
⁶ Upon you I have leaned from my birth;
    you are the one who took me from my mother's womb.
    My praise is continually of you.

## Lesson 2 ~ 1 Corinthians 13:1-13

*Paul teaches the Corinthians that love is the greatest gift.*

¹ If I speak in human tongues or the tongues of angels, but have not love, I am a noisy gong or a clanging cymbal. ² And if I have prophetic powers, and understand all mysteries and all knowledge, and if I have all faith, so as to remove mountains, but have not love, I am nothing. ³ If I give away all I have, and if I deliver my body to be burned, but have not love, I gain nothing.

⁴ Love is patient and kind; love is not jealous or boastful; ⁵ it is not arrogant or rude. Love does not insist on its own way; it is not irritable or resentful; ⁶ it does not rejoice at wrong, but rejoices in the right. ⁷ Love bears all things, believes all things, hopes all things, endures all things.

⁸ Love never ends; as for prophecies, they will pass away; as for tongues, they will cease; as for knowledge, it will pass away. ⁹ For our knowledge is imperfect and our prophecy is imperfect; ¹⁰ but when the perfect comes, the imperfect will pass away. ¹¹ When I was a child, I spoke like a child, I thought like a child, I reasoned like a child; when I became an adult, I gave up childish ways. ¹² For now we see in a mirror dimly, but then face to face. Now I know in part; then I shall understand fully, even as I have been fully understood. ¹³ So faith, hope, love abide, these three; but the greatest of these is love.

## Gospel ~ Luke 4:21-30

*Jesus is rejected by the people of Nazareth.*

²¹ And Jesus began to say to them, "Today this scripture has been fulfilled in your hearing." ²² And all spoke well of him, and wondered at the gracious words which proceeded out of his mouth; and they said, "Is not this Joseph's son?" ²³ And Jesus said to them, "Doubtless you will quote to me this proverb, 'Physician, heal yourself; what we have heard you did at Capernaum, do here also in your own country.'" ²⁴ And Jesus said, "Truly, I say to you, no prophet is acceptable in the prophet's own country. ²⁵ But in truth, I tell you, there were many widows in Israel in the days of Elijah, when the heaven was shut up three years and six months, when there came a great famine over all the land; ²⁶ and Elijah was sent to none of them but only to Zarephath, in the land of Sidon, to a woman who was a widow. ²⁷ And there were many people with leprosy in Israel in the time of the prophet Elisha; and none of them was cleansed, but only Naaman the Syrian." ²⁸ When they heard this, all in the synagogue were filled with wrath. ²⁹ And they rose up and put Jesus out of the city, and led him to the brow of the hill on which their city was built, that they might throw him down headlong. ³⁰ But passing through the midst of them he went away.

# EPIPHANY 5

## Lesson 1 ~ Isaiah 6:1-8 (9-13)

*Isaiah is called to be a prophet.*

[1] In the year that King Uzziah died I saw God [[*or* the Lord]] sitting upon a throne, high and lifted up, whose train filled the temple. [2] Above God stood the seraphim; each had six wings: with two they covered their faces, and with two they covered their feet, and with two they flew. [3] And one called to another and said:

> "Holy, holy, is the GOD [[*or* LORD]] of hosts;
> the whole earth is full of God's glory."

[4] And the foundations of the thresholds shook at the voice of the one who called, and the house was filled with smoke. [5] And I said: "Woe is me! For I am lost; for I am a person of unclean lips, and I dwell in the midst of a people of unclean lips; for my eyes have seen the Ruler,[□] the GOD [[*or* LORD]] of hosts!"

[6] Then one of the seraphim flew to me, having in its hand a burning coal which it had taken with tongs from the altar. [7] And the seraph touched my mouth, and said: "This has touched your lips; your guilt is taken away, and your sin forgiven." [8] And I heard the voice of God [[*or* the Lord]] saying, "Whom shall I send, and who will go for us?" Then I said "Here am I! Send me." [9] And God said, "Go, and say to this people:

> 'Hear and hear, but do not understand;
> see and see, but do not perceive.'
> [10] Make the heart of this people fat,
> and their ears heavy,
> and shut their eyes;
> lest they see with their eyes,
> and hear with their ears,
> and understand with their hearts,
> and turn and be healed."

[11] Then I said, "How long, O God [[*or* Lord]]?" And God said:

> "Until cities lie waste
> without inhabitant,
> and houses without people,
> and the land is utterly desolate,
> [12] and GOD [[*or* the LORD]] removes people far away,
> and the forsaken places are many in the midst of the land.

---

[□]RSV *King*. See Appendix.

<sup>13</sup> And though a tenth remain in the land,
    the land will be burned again.
  Like a terebinth or an oak,
    whose stump remains standing
    when the tree is felled,
  the holy seed is the stump in the land."

## Psalm 138

<sup>1</sup> I give you thanks, O GOD [[or LORD]], with my whole heart;
    before the gods I sing your praise;
<sup>2</sup> I bow down toward your holy temple
      and give thanks to your name for your steadfast love and your
        faithfulness;
  for you have exalted above everything
    your name and your word.
<sup>3</sup> On the day I called you, you answered me,
    my strength of soul you increased.
<sup>4</sup> All the rulers□ of the earth shall praise you, O GOD [[or LORD]],
    for they have heard the words of your mouth;
<sup>5</sup> and they shall sing of the ways of GOD [[or the LORD]],
    for great is the glory of GOD [[or the LORD]].
<sup>6</sup> For GOD [[or the LORD]], though high, regards the lowly,
    but knows the haughty from afar.
<sup>7</sup> Though I walk in the midst of trouble,
    you preserve my life;
  you stretch out your hand against the wrath of my enemies,
    and your right hand delivers me.
<sup>8</sup> GOD's [[or The LORD's]] purpose for me will be fulfilled;
    your steadfast love, O GOD [[or LORD]], endures forever.
    Do not forsake the work of your hands.

---

□RSV *kings*. See Appendix.

## Lesson 2 ~ 1 Corinthians 15:1-11

*Paul recalls the tradition of the appearances of the risen Christ.*

[1] Now I would remind you, sisters and brothers, in what terms I preached to you the gospel, which you received, in which you stand, [2] by which you are saved, if you hold it fast—unless you believed in vain.

[3] For I delivered to you as of first importance what I also received, that Christ died for our sins in accordance with the scriptures, [4] that Christ was buried, and was raised on the third day in accordance with the scriptures, [5] and that Christ appeared to Cephas, then to the twelve. [6] Then Christ appeared to more than five hundred followers at one time, most of whom are still alive, though some have fallen asleep. [7] Then Christ appeared to James, then to all the apostles. [8] Last of all, as to one untimely born, Christ appeared also to me. [9] For I am least of the apostles, unfit to be called an apostle, because I persecuted the church of God. [10] But by the grace of God I am what I am, and God's grace toward me was not in vain. On the contrary, I worked harder than any of them, though it was not I, but the grace of God which is with me. [11] Whether then it was I or they, so we preach and so you believed.

## Gospel ~ Luke 5:1-11

*Simon Peter, James, and John leave their nets to follow Jesus.*

[1] While the people pressed upon him to hear the word of God, Jesus was standing by the lake of Gennesaret. [2] And he saw two boats by the lake; but those who were fishing had gone out of them and were washing their nets. [3] Getting into one of the boats, which was Simon's, Jesus asked Simon to put out a little from the land. And Jesus sat down and taught the people from the boat. [4] And when he had ceased speaking, he said to Simon, "Put out into the deep and let down your nets for a catch." [5] And Simon answered, "Teacher,[†] we toiled all night and took nothing! But at your word I will let down the nets." [6] And when they had done this, they enclosed a great shoal of fish; and as their nets were breaking, [7] they beckoned to their partners in the other boat to come and help them. And they came and filled both the boats, so that they began to sink. [8] But when Simon Peter saw it, he fell down at Jesus' knees, saying, "Depart from me, O Sovereign [[or Lord]], for I am a sinful person." [9] For Simon was astonished, and all that were with him, at the catch of fish which they had taken; [10] and so also were James and John, sons of Zebedee, who were partners with Simon. And Jesus said to Simon, "Do not be afraid; henceforth you will be catching human beings." [11] And when they had brought their boats to land, they left everything and followed Jesus.

---

[†]RSV *Master*. See Appendix.

# EPIPHANY 6

## Lesson 1 ~ Jeremiah 17:5-10

*Those who trust in God are blessed.*

5 Thus says the SOVEREIGN [[or LORD]]:
"Cursed are those who trust in human beings
and make flesh their arm,
whose hearts turn away from GOD [[or the LORD]].
6 They are like a shrub in the desert,
and shall not see any good come.
They shall dwell in the parched places of the wilderness,
in an uninhabited salt land.
7 Blessed are those who trust in GOD [[or the LORD]],
whose trust is GOD [[or the LORD]].
8 They are like a tree planted by water,
that sends out its roots by the stream,
and does not fear when heat comes,
for its leaves remain green,
and is not anxious in the year of drought,
for it does not cease to bear fruit."
9 The heart is deceitful above all things,
and desperately corrupt;
who can understand it?
10 "I the SOVEREIGN [[or LORD]] search the mind
and try the heart,
to give to everyone according to their ways,
according to the fruit of their doings."

## Psalm 1

1 Blessed are those
who walk not in the counsel of the wicked,
nor stand in the way of sinners,
nor sit in the seat of scoffers;
2 but whose delight is in the law of GOD [[or the LORD]],
and who meditate on that law day and night.
3 They are like a tree
planted by streams of water,
that yields its fruit in its season,
and its leaf does not wither.
In all that they do, they prosper.

4 The wicked are not so,
   but are like chaff which the wind drives away.
5 Therefore the wicked will not stand in the judgment,
   nor sinners in the congregation of the righteous;
6 for GOD [or the LORD] knows the way of the righteous,
   but the way of the wicked will perish.


## Lesson 2 ~ 1 Corinthians 15:12-20

*Paul affirms the resurrection of Christ.*

12 Now if Christ is preached as raised from the dead, how can some of you say that there is no resurrection of the dead? 13 But if there is no resurrection of the dead, then Christ has not been raised; 14 if Christ has not been raised, then our preaching is in vain and your faith is in vain. 15 We are even found to be misrepresenting God, because we testified of God that God raised Christ, whom God did not raise if it is true that the dead are not raised. 16 For if the dead are not raised, then Christ has not been raised. 17 If Christ has not been raised, your faith is futile and you are still in your sins. 18 Then those also who have fallen asleep in Christ have perished. 19 If for only this life we have hoped in Christ, we are of all people most to be pitied.

20 But in fact Christ has been raised from the dead, the firstfruits of those who have fallen asleep.

## Gospel ~ Luke 6:17-26

*Jesus begins the Sermon on the Plain.*

<sup>17</sup> And Jesus came down with them and stood on a level place, with a great crowd of disciples and a great multitude of people from all Judea and Jerusalem and the seacoast of Tyre and Sidon, who came to hear him and to be healed of their diseases; <sup>18</sup> and those who were troubled with unclean spirits were cured. <sup>19</sup> And all the crowd sought to touch Jesus, for power came forth from him and healed them all.

<sup>20</sup> And Jesus lifted up his eyes on the disciples, and said:

"Blessed are you poor, for yours is the realm☆ of God.

<sup>21</sup> "Blessed are you that hunger now, for you shall be satisfied.

"Blessed are you that weep now, for you shall laugh.

<sup>22</sup> "Blessed are you when people hate you, and when they exclude you and revile you, and cast out your name as evil, on account of the Human One!○ <sup>23</sup> Rejoice in that day, and leap for joy, for your reward is great in heaven; for so their ancestors did to the prophets.

<sup>24</sup> "But woe to you that are rich, for you have received your consolation.

<sup>25</sup> "Woe to you that are full now, for you shall hunger.

"Woe to you that laugh now, for you shall mourn and weep.

<sup>26</sup> "Woe to you, when all speak well of you, for so their ancestors did to the false prophets."

---

☆RSV *kingdom*. See Appendix.
○RSV *Son of man*. See Appendix.

# EPIPHANY 7

## Lesson 1 ~ Genesis 45:3-11, 15

*Joseph is reconciled with his brothers.*

[3] And Joseph said to his brothers, "I am Joseph; is my father still alive?" But his brothers could not answer him, for they were dismayed at his presence.

[4] So Joseph said to his brothers, "Come near to me, please." And they came near. And he said, "I am your brother, Joseph, whom you sold into Egypt. [5] And now do not be distressed, or angry with yourselves, because you sold me here; for God sent me before you to preserve life. [6] For the famine has been in the land these two years; and there are yet five years in which there will be neither plowing nor harvest. [7] And God sent me before you to preserve for you a remnant on earth, and to keep alive for you many survivors. [8] So it was not you who sent me here, but God; and God has made me a father to Pharaoh, and ruler of all his house and over all the land of Egypt. [9] Make haste and go up to my father and say to him, 'Thus says your son Joseph, God has made me ruler of all Egypt; come down to me, do not delay; [10] you shall dwell in the land of Goshen, and you shall be near me, you and your children and your children's children, and your flocks, your herds, and all that you have; [11] and there I will provide for you, for there are yet five years of famine to come; lest you and your household, and all that you have, come to poverty.'"

[15] And Joseph kissed all his brothers and wept upon them; and after that his brothers talked with him.

## Psalm 37:1-11

[1] Fret not yourself because of the wicked,
    be not envious of wrongdoers!
[2] For they will soon fade like the grass,
    and wither like the green herb.
[3] Trust in GOD [or the LORD], and do good;
    so you will dwell in the land, and enjoy security.
[4] Take delight in GOD [or the LORD],
    who will give you the desires of your heart.
[5] Commit your way to GOD [or the LORD];
    trust in God, and God will act,
[6] and will bring forth your vindication as the light,
    and your right as the noonday.

⁷ Be still before GOD [[or the LORD]], and wait patiently for God;
    fret not yourself over those who prosper in their way,
    over those who carry out evil devices!
⁸ Refrain from anger, and forsake wrath!
    Fret not yourself; it tends only to evil.
⁹ For the wicked shall be cut off;
    but those who wait for GOD [[or the LORD]] shall possess the land.
¹⁰ Yet a little while, and the wicked will be no more;
    though you look well at their place, they will not be there.
¹¹ But the meek shall possess the land,
    and delight themselves in abundant prosperity.


### Lesson 2 ~ 1 Corinthians 15:35-38, 42-50

*Paul answers questions about the resurrection of the dead.*

³⁵ But someone will ask, "How are the dead raised? With what kind of body do they come?" ³⁶ You fool! What you sow does not come to life unless it dies. ³⁷ And what you sow is not the body which is to be, but a bare kernel, perhaps of wheat or of some other grain. ³⁸ But God gives it a body as God has chosen, and to each kind of seed its own body.

⁴² So is it with the resurrection of the dead. What is sown is perishable, what is raised is imperishable. ⁴³ It is sown in dishonor, it is raised in glory. It is sown in weakness, it is raised in power. ⁴⁴ It is sown a physical body, it is raised a spiritual body. If there is a physical body, there is also a spiritual body. ⁴⁵ Thus it is written, "The first Adam became a living being"; the last Adam became a life-giving spirit. ⁴⁶ But it is not the spiritual which is first but the physical, and then the spiritual. ⁴⁷ The first was from the earth, made of dust; the second is from heaven. ⁴⁸ As was the one made of dust, so are those who are of the dust; and as is the one of heaven, so are those who are of heaven. ⁴⁹ Just as we have borne the image of the one of dust, we shall also bear the image of the one of heaven. ⁵⁰ I tell you this, friends: flesh and blood cannot inherit the realm☆ of God, nor does the perishable inherit the imperishable.

---

☆RSV *kingdom*. See Appendix.

*Jesus teaches about the measure of love.*

²⁷ But I say to you that hear, Love your enemies, do good to those who hate you, ²⁸ bless those who curse you, pray for those who abuse you. ²⁹ To a person who strikes you on the cheek, offer the other also; and from a person who takes away your coat, do not withhold even your shirt. ³⁰ Give to everyone who begs from you; and of anyone who takes away your goods do not ask them again. ³¹ And as you wish that people would do to you, do so to them.

³² If you love those who love you, what credit is that to you? For even sinners love those who love them. ³³ And if you do good to those who do good to you, what credit is that to you? For even sinners do the same. ³⁴ And if you lend to those from whom you hope to receive, what credit is that to you? Even sinners lend to sinners, to receive as much again. ³⁵ But love your enemies, and do good, and lend, expecting nothing in return; and your reward will be great, and you will be children of the Most High; for God is kind to the ungrateful and the selfish. ³⁶ Be merciful, even as [God] your Father [and Mother*] is merciful.

³⁷ Judge not, and you will not be judged; condemn not, and you will not be condemned; forgive, and you will be forgiven; ³⁸ give, and it will be given to you; good measure, pressed down, shaken together, running over, will be put into your lap. For the measure you give will be the measure you get back.

---

*Addition to the text. See "Metaphor" and "God the Father and Mother" in the Appendix.

# EPIPHANY 8

## Lesson 1 ~ Ecclesiasticus (Sirach) 27:4-7

*Our thoughts are to be tested.*

4 When a sieve is shaken, the refuse remains;
  so one's filth remains in one's thoughts.
5 The kiln tests the potter's vessels;
  so one is tested by one's reasoning.
6 The fruit discloses the cultivation of a tree;
   so the expression of a thought discloses the cultivation of one's
   mind.
7 Do not praise anyone before you hear them reason,
  for this is the way people are tested.

## Lesson 1 (alternate) ~ Isaiah 55:10-13

*The prophet Isaiah speaks of the power of God's word.*

10 As the rain and the snow come down from heaven,
   and do not return but water the earth,
 making it bring forth and sprout,
   giving seed to the sower and bread to the eater,
11 so shall my word be that goes forth from my mouth;
   it shall not return to me empty,
 but it shall accomplish that which I purpose,
   and prosper in the thing for which I sent it.
12 For you shall go out in joy,
   and be led forth in peace;
 the mountains and the hills before you
   shall break forth into singing,
   and all the trees of the field shall clap their hands.
13 Instead of the thorn shall come up the cypress;
   instead of the brier shall come up the myrtle;
 and it shall be to GOD [[*or* the LORD]] for a memorial,
   for an everlasting sign which shall not be cut off.

## Psalm 92:1-4, 12-15

1 It is good to give thanks to GOD [or the LORD],
   to sing praises to your name, O Most High;
2 to declare your steadfast love in the morning,
   and your faithfulness by night,
3 to the music of the lute and the harp,
   to the melody of the lyre.
4 For you, O GOD [or LORD], have made me glad by your work;
   at the works of your hands I sing for joy.
12 The righteous flourish like the palm tree,
   and grow like a cedar in Lebanon.
13 They are planted in the house of the SOVEREIGN [or LORD],
   they flourish in the courts of our God.
14 They still bring forth fruit in old age,
   they are ever full of sap and green,
15 to show that GOD [or the LORD] is upright,
   my rock, in whom there is no unrighteousness.

## Lesson 2 ~ 1 Corinthians 15:51-58

*Paul assures the Corinthians of their victory over death through Jesus Christ.*

51 I tell you a mystery. We shall not all sleep, but we shall all be changed, 52 in a moment, in the twinkling of an eye, at the last trumpet. For the trumpet will sound, and the dead will be raised imperishable, and we shall be changed. 53 For this perishable nature must put on the imperishable, and this mortal nature must put on immortality. 54 When the perishable puts on the imperishable, and the mortal puts on immortality, then shall come to pass the saying that is written:

"Death is swallowed up in victory."
55 "O death, where is your victory?
O death, where is your sting?"

56 The sting of death is sin, and the power of sin is the law. 57 But thanks be to God, who gives us the victory through our Sovereign [or Lord] Jesus Christ.

58 Therefore, my beloved friends, be steadfast, immovable, always abounding in the work of the Sovereign [or Lord], knowing that in the Sovereign [or Lord], your labor is not in vain.

# Gospel ~ Luke 6:39-49

*Jesus teaches that hearers of the word should be doers also.*

<sup>39</sup> Jesus also told them a parable: "Can one who is blind lead another blind person? Will they not both fall into a pit? <sup>40</sup> A disciple is not above a teacher, but everyone when fully taught will be like the teacher. <sup>41</sup> Why do you see the speck that is in your neighbor's eye, but do not notice the log that is in your own eye? <sup>42</sup> Or how can you say to your neighbor, 'Friend, let me take out the speck that is in your eye,' when you yourself do not see the log that is in your own eye? You hypocrite, first take the log out of your own eye, and then you will see clearly to take out the speck that is in your neighbor's eye.

<sup>43</sup> "For no good tree bears bad fruit, nor again does a bad tree bear good fruit; <sup>44</sup> for each tree is known by its own fruit. For figs are not gathered from thorns, nor are grapes picked from a bramble bush. <sup>45</sup> The good person out of the good treasure of the heart produces good, and the evil person out of evil treasure produces evil; for such a one speaks out of the abundance of the heart.

<sup>46</sup> "Why do you call me 'Sovereign, Sovereign' [[*or* 'Lord, Lord']], and not do what I tell you? <sup>47</sup> All who come to me and hear my words and do them, I will show you what they are like: <sup>48</sup> they are like a person building a house, who dug deep, and laid the foundation upon rock; and when a flood arose, the stream broke against that house, and could not shake it, because it had been well built. <sup>49</sup> But whoever hears and does not do them is like a person who built a house on the ground without a foundation, against which the stream broke, and immediately it fell, and the ruin of that house was great."

# LAST SUNDAY AFTER EPIPHANY

## Lesson 1 ~ Exodus 34:29-35

*When Moses came down from talking with God, his face shone and he covered it with a veil.*

[29] When Moses came down from Mount Sinai, with the two tables of the testimony in his hand as he came down from the mountain, Moses did not know that the skin of his face shone because he had been talking with God. [30] And when Aaron and all the people of Israel saw Moses, the skin of his face shone, and they were afraid to come near him. [31] But Moses called to them; and Aaron and all the leaders of the congregation returned to him, and Moses talked with them. [32] And afterward all the people of Israel came near, and Moses gave them in commandment all that GOD [[*or* the LORD]] had spoken with him in Mount Sinai. [33] And when Moses had finished speaking with them, he put a veil on his face; [34] but whenever Moses went in before GOD [[*or* the LORD]] to speak with God, he took the veil off, until he came out; and when Moses came out, and told the people of Israel what he was commanded, [35] the people of Israel saw the face of Moses, that the skin of Moses' face shone; and Moses would put the veil upon his face again, until he went in to speak with God.

## Psalm 99

[1] GOD [[*or* The LORD]] reigns; let all people tremble!
    God sits enthroned upon the cherubim; let the earth quake!
[2] GOD [[*or* The LORD]] is great in Zion,
    and is exalted over all the nations.
[3] Let them praise your great and terrible name!
    Holy is God!
[4] Mighty Ruler,□ lover of justice,
    you have established equity;
  you have executed justice
    and righteousness in Jacob.
[5] Extol the SOVEREIGN [[*or* LORD]] our God;
    worship at God's footstool!
    Holy is God!
[6] Moses and Aaron were among the priests of God,
    Samuel also was among those who called on God's name.

---

□RSV *King*. See Appendix.

They cried to GOD [[*or* the LORD]] who answered them
<sup></sup>⁷ and spoke to them in the pillar of cloud.

They kept God's testimonies,
and the statutes that God gave them.
⁸ O SOVEREIGN [[*or* LORD]] our God, you answered them;
you were a forgiving God to them,
but an avenger of their wrongdoings.
⁹ Extol the SOVEREIGN [[*or* LORD]] our God,
and worship at God's holy mountain;
for the SOVEREIGN [[*or* LORD]] our God is holy!

## Lesson 2 ~ 2 Corinthians 3:12-13, (14-15), 16–4:2

*We are changed when we look upon the glory of the Sovereign.*

¹² Since we have such a hope, we are very bold, ¹³ not like Moses, who put a veil over his face so that the Israelites might not see the end of the fading splendor. ¹⁴ But their minds were hardened; for to this day, when they read the old covenant, that same veil remains unlifted, because only through Christ is it taken away. ¹⁵ Yes, to this day whenever Moses is read a veil lies over their minds; ¹⁶ but when one turns to the Sovereign [[*or* Lord]] the veil is removed. ¹⁷ Now the Sovereign [[*or* Lord]] is the Spirit, and where the Spirit of the Sovereign [[*or* Lord]] is, there is freedom. ¹⁸ And we all, with unveiled face, beholding the glory of the Sovereign [[*or* Lord]], are being changed into the same likeness from one degree of glory to another; for this comes from the Sovereign [[*or* Lord]] who is the Spirit.

⁴:¹ Therefore, having this ministry by the mercy of God, we do not lose heart. ² We have renounced disgraceful, underhanded ways; we refuse to practice cunning or to tamper with God's word, but by the open statement of the truth we would commend ourselves to everyone's conscience in the sight of God.

# Gospel ~ Luke 9:28-36

*Peter, John, and James witness the transfiguration of Jesus.*

28 Now about eight days after these sayings Jesus took Peter and John and James, and went up on the mountain to pray. 29 And as Jesus was praying, the appearance of his countenance was altered, and his raiment became dazzlingly bright. 30 And two men talked with him, Moses and Elijah, 31 who appeared in glory and spoke of Jesus' departure, which he was to accomplish at Jerusalem. 32 Now Peter and those who were with him were heavy with sleep, and when they wakened they saw Jesus' glory and the two men who stood with him. 33 And as the two were parting from Jesus, Peter said to him, "Teacher,† it is well that we are here; let us make three booths, one for you and one for Moses and one for Elijah"—not knowing what he said. 34 As Peter said this, a cloud came and over-shadowed them; and they were afraid as they entered the cloud. 35 And a voice came out of the cloud, saying, "This is my Child,◇ my Chosen; to this one you shall listen!" 36 And when the voice had spoken, Jesus was found alone. And they kept silence and told no one in those days anything of what they had seen.

---

†RSV *Master.* See Appendix.
◇RSV *Son.* See Appendix.

# ASH WEDNESDAY

## Lesson 1 ~ Joel 2:1-2, 12-17a

*God calls the people to fasting and repentance.*

<sup>1</sup> Blow the trumpet in Zion;
    sound the alarm on my holy mountain!
Let all the inhabitants of the land tremble,
    for the day of GOD [*or* the LORD] is coming, it is near,
<sup>2</sup> a day of shadow and gloom,
    a day of clouds and thick shadow!
Like a blanket there is spread upon the mountains
    a great and powerful people;
their like has never been from of old,
    nor will be again after them
    through the years of all generations.
<sup>12</sup> "Yet even now," says the SOVEREIGN [*or* LORD],
    "return to me with all your heart,
with fasting, with weeping, and with mourning;
<sup>13</sup>    and rend your hearts and not your garments."
Return to the SOVEREIGN [*or* LORD], your God,
    for God is gracious and merciful,
slow to anger, and abounding in steadfast love,
    and repents of evil.
<sup>14</sup> Who knows whether God will not turn and repent,
    and leave a blessing behind,
a cereal offering and a drink offering
    for the SOVEREIGN [*or* LORD], your God?
<sup>15</sup> Blow the trumpet in Zion;
    sanctify a fast;
call a solemn assembly;
<sup>16</sup>    gather the people.
Sanctify the congregation;
    assemble the elders;
gather the children,
    even nursing infants.
Let the bridegroom leave his room,
    and the bride her chamber.
<sup>17</sup> Between the vestibule and the altar
    let the priests, the ministers of GOD [*or* the LORD], weep
and say, "Spare your people, O SOVEREIGN [*or* LORD],
    and make not your heritage a reproach,
    a byword among the nations."

# Psalm 51:1-12

¹ Have mercy on me, O God, according to your steadfast love;
  according to your abundant mercy blot out my transgressions.
² Wash me thoroughly from my iniquity,
  and cleanse me from my sin!
³ For I know my transgressions,
  and my sin is ever before me.
⁴ Against you, you only, have I sinned,
  and done that which is evil in your sight,
 so that you are justified in your sentence
  and blameless in your judgment.
⁵ I was brought forth in iniquity,
  and in sin did my mother conceive me.
⁶ You desire truth in the inward being;
  therefore teach me wisdom in my secret heart.
⁷ Purge me with hyssop, and I shall be clean;
  wash me, and I shall be cleaner than snow.
⁸ Fill me with joy and gladness;
  let the bones which you have broken rejoice.
⁹ Hide your face from my sins,
  and blot out all my iniquities.
¹⁰ Create in me a clean heart, O God,
  and put a new and right spirit within me.
¹¹ Cast me not away from your presence,
  and take not your holy Spirit from me.
¹² Restore to me the joy of your salvation,
  and uphold me with a willing spirit.

## Lesson 2 ~ 2 Corinthians 5:20b–6:2 (3-10 optional)

*Paul writes to the Corinthians of his ministry of reconciliation.*

²⁰ We beseech you on behalf of Christ, be reconciled to God. ²¹ For our sake God made to be sin the one who knew no sin, so that in this very one we might become the righteousness of God.

⁶:¹ Working together with God, then, we entreat you not to accept the grace of God in vain. ² For God says,

"At the acceptable time I have listened to you,
and helped you on the day of salvation."

Now is the acceptable time; now is the day of salvation. ³ We put no obstacle in anyone's way, so that no fault may be found with our ministry,

[4] but as servants of God we commend ourselves in every way: through great endurance, in afflictions, hardships, calamities, [5] beatings, imprisonments, tumults, labors, watching, hunger; [6] by purity, knowledge, forbearance, kindness, the Holy Spirit, genuine love, [7] truthful speech, and the power of God; with the weapons of righteousness for the right hand and for the left; [8] in honor and dishonor, in ill repute and good repute. We are treated as impostors, and yet are true; [9] as unknown, and yet well known; as dying, and yet we live; as punished, and yet not killed; [10] as sorrowful, yet always rejoicing; as poor, yet making many rich; as having nothing, and yet possessing everything.

### Gospel ~ Matthew 6:1-6, 16-21

*Jesus tells the disciples to lay up treasure in heaven.*

[1] Beware of practicing your piety before others in order to be seen by them; for then you will have no reward from [God] your Father [and Mother*] who is in heaven.

[2] Thus, when you give alms, sound no trumpet before you, as the hypocrites do in the synagogues and in the streets, that they may be praised by others. Truly, I say to you, they have received their reward. [3] But when you give alms, do not let your left hand know what your right hand is doing, [4] so that your alms may be in secret; and God⊗ who sees in secret will reward you.

[5] And when you pray, you must not be like the hypocrites; for they love to stand and pray in the synagogues and at the street corners, that they may be seen by others. Truly, I say to you, they have received their reward. [6] But when you pray, go into your room and shut the door and pray to God⊗ who is in secret; and God⊗ who sees in secret will reward you.

[16] And when you fast, do not look dismal, like the hypocrites, for they disfigure their faces that their fasting may be seen by others. Truly, I say to you, they have received their reward. [17] But when you fast, anoint your head and wash your face, [18] that your fasting may not be seen by others but by God⊗ who is in secret; and God⊗ who sees in secret will reward you.

[19] Do not lay up for yourselves treasures on earth, where moth and rust consume and where thieves break in and steal, [20] but lay up for yourselves treasures in heaven, where neither moth nor rust consumes and where thieves do not break in and steal. [21] For where your treasure is, there will your heart be also.

---

*Addition to the text. See "Metaphor" and "God the Father and Mother" in the Appendix.
⊗RSV *your Father*. See Appendix.

# LENT 1

## Lesson 1 ~ Deuteronomy 26:1-11

*Israel confesses God's work in history.*

[1] When you come into the land which the SOVEREIGN [[*or* LORD]] your God gives you for an inheritance, and have taken possession of it, and live in it, [2] you shall take some of the first of all the fruit of the ground, which you harvest from your land that the SOVEREIGN [[*or* LORD]] your God gives you, and you shall put it in a basket, and you shall go to the place which the SOVEREIGN [[*or* LORD]] your God will choose, to make God's name to dwell there. [3] And you shall go to the priest who is in office at that time, and say, "I declare this day to the SOVEREIGN [[*or* LORD]] your God that I have come into the land which GOD [[*or* the LORD]] swore to our ancestors to give us." [4] Then the priest shall take the basket from your hand, and set it down before the altar of the SOVEREIGN [[*or* LORD]] your God.

[5] And you shall make response before the SOVEREIGN [[*or* LORD]] your God, "A wandering Aramean was my father, who went down into Egypt and sojourned there, few in number; and there he became a nation, great, mighty, and populous. [6] And the Egyptians treated us harshly, and afflicted us, and laid upon us hard bondage. [7] Then we cried to the SOVEREIGN [[*or* LORD]] the God of our ancestors, and GOD [[*or* the LORD]] heard our voice, and saw our affliction, our toil, and our oppression; [8] and GOD [[*or* the LORD]] brought us out of Egypt with a mighty hand and an outstretched arm, with great terror, with signs and wonders, [9] and brought us into this place and gave us this land, a land flowing with milk and honey. [10] And now I bring the first of the fruit of the ground, which you, O GOD [[*or* LORD]], have given me." And you shall set it down before the SOVEREIGN [[*or* LORD]] your God, and worship before the SOVEREIGN [[*or* LORD]] your God; [11] and you shall rejoice in all the good which the SOVEREIGN [[*or* LORD]] your God has given to you and to your house, you, and the Levite, and the resident alien who is among you.

## Psalm 91:9-16

9 Because you have made GOD [[or the LORD]] your refuge,
   the Most High your habitation,
10 no evil shall befall you,
   no scourge come near your tent.
11 For God will give the angels charge of you
   to guard you in all your ways.
12 On their hands they will bear you up,
   lest you dash your foot against a stone.
13 You will tread on the lion and the adder,
   the young lion and the serpent you will trample underfoot.
14 Whoever clings to me in love, I will deliver;
   I will protect the one who knows my name.
15 When that one calls to me, I will answer;
   I will be present in trouble,
   I will rescue and honor whoever calls.
16 With long life I will satisfy them,
   and show forth my salvation.

## Lesson 2 ~ Romans 10:8b-13

*Paul teaches that salvation is given to everyone who believes.*

8 The word is near you, on your lips and in your heart (that is, the word of faith which we preach); 9 because, if you confess with your lips that Jesus is Sovereign [[or Lord]] and believe in your heart that God raised Jesus from the dead, you will be saved. 10 For if it is believed with the heart, there is righteousness, and if it is confessed with the mouth there is salvation. 11 The scripture says, "No one who believes in Jesus will be put to shame." 12 For there is no distinction between Jew and Greek; the same Sovereign [[or Lord]] is Sovereign [[or Lord]] of all and bestows riches upon all who call. 13 For, "everyone who calls upon the name of the Sovereign [[or Lord]] will be saved."

# Gospel ~ Luke 4:1-13

*Jesus is tempted by the devil.*

[1] And Jesus, full of the Holy Spirit, returned from the Jordan, and was led by the Spirit [2] for forty days in the wilderness, tempted by the devil. And Jesus ate nothing in those days; and when they were ended, he was hungry. [3] The devil said to Jesus, "If you are the Child◇ of God, command this stone to become bread." [4] And Jesus answered, "It is written, 'One shall not live by bread alone.'" [5] And the devil took Jesus up, and showed him all the kingdoms of the world in a moment of time, [6] and said, "To you I will give all this authority and their glory; for it has been delivered to me, and I give it to whom I will. [7] If you, then, will worship me, it shall all be yours." [8] And Jesus answered, "It is written,

'You shall worship the Sovereign [[*or* Lord]] your God,
    and God only shall you serve.'"

[9] And the devil took Jesus to Jerusalem, and set him on the pinnacle of the temple, and said, "If you are the Child◇ of God, throw yourself down from here; [10] for it is written,

'God will give the angels charge of you, to guard you,'

[11] and

'On their hands they will bear you up,
    lest you strike your foot against a stone.'"

[12] And Jesus replied, "It is said, 'You shall not tempt the Sovereign [[*or* Lord]] your God.'" [13] And the devil, having ended every temptation, departed from Jesus until an opportune time.

---

◇RSV *Son*. See Appendix.

# LENT 2

## Lesson 1 ~ Genesis 15:1-12, 17-18

*God makes a covenant with Abram.*

¹ After these things the word of GOD [[*or* the LORD]] came to Abram in a vision, "Fear not, Abram, I am your shield; your reward shall be very great." ² But Abram said, "O Sovereign [[*or* Lord]] GOD, what will you give me, for I continue childless, and the heir of my house is Eliezer of Damascus?" ³ And Abram said, "You have given me no offspring; and a slave born in my house will be my heir." ⁴ And the word of GOD [[*or* the LORD]] came to Abram, "This one shall not be your heir; your own offspring shall be your heir." ⁵ And God brought Abram outside and said, "Look toward heaven, and number the stars, if you are able to number them." Then God said, "So shall your descendants be." ⁶ And Abram believed GOD [[*or* the LORD]] who reckoned it to him as righteousness.

⁷ And God said to Abram, "I am the SOVEREIGN [[*or* LORD]] who brought you from Ur of the Chaldeans, to give you this land to possess." ⁸ But Abram said, "O Sovereign [[*or* Lord]] GOD, how am I to know that I shall possess it?" ⁹ God replied, "Bring me a heifer three years old, a she-goat three years old, a ram three years old, a turtledove, and a young pigeon." ¹⁰ And Abram brought God all these, cut them in two, and laid each half over against the other, but did not cut the birds in two. ¹¹ And when birds of prey came down upon the carcasses, Abram drove them away.

¹² As the sun was going down, a deep sleep fell on Abram; and a dread and great shadow fell upon him.

¹⁷ When the sun had gone down and it was night, a smoking fire pot and a flaming torch passed between these pieces. ¹⁸ On that day GOD [[*or* the LORD]] made a covenant with Abram, saying, "To your descendants I give this land, from the river of Egypt to the great river, the river Euphrates."

# Psalm 127

¹ Unless GOD [[*or* the LORD]] builds the house,
  those who build it labor in vain.
 Unless GOD [[*or* the LORD]] watches over the city,
  the watcher stays awake in vain.
² It is in vain that you rise up early
  and go late to rest,
 eating the bread of anxious toil;
  for God gives sleep to God's beloved.
³ Children are a heritage from GOD [[*or* the LORD]],
  the fruit of the womb a reward.
⁴ Like arrows in the hand of a warrior
  are the children of one's youth.
⁵ Happy is the one who has
  a quiver full of them!
 That one shall not be put to shame
  when speaking with enemies in the gate.


## Lesson 2 ~ Philippians 3:17–4:1

*Paul urges the Philippians to stand firm while they await the Sovereign Jesus Christ.*

¹⁷ Brothers and sisters, join in imitating me, and mark those who so live as you have an example in us. ¹⁸ For many, of whom I have often told you and now tell you even with tears, live as enemies of the cross of Christ. ¹⁹ Their end is destruction, their god is the belly, and they glory in their shame, with minds set on earthly things. ²⁰ But our commonwealth is in heaven, and from it we await a Savior, the Sovereign [[*or* Lord]] Jesus Christ, ²¹ who will change our lowly body to be like Christ's glorious body, by the power which enables Christ even to subject all things to Christ's self.

⁴:¹ Therefore, my sisters and brothers, whom I love and long for, my joy and crown, stand firm thus in the Sovereign [[*or* Lord]], my beloved.

## Gospel ~ Luke 13:31-35

*Jesus defies the threat from Herod and grieves over Jerusalem.*

[31] At that very hour some Pharisees came, and said to Jesus, "Get away from here, for Herod wants to kill you." [32] And Jesus said to them, "Go and tell that fox, 'I cast out demons and perform cures today and tomorrow, and the third day I finish my course. [33] Nevertheless I must go on my way today and tomorrow and the day following; for it cannot be that a prophet should perish away from Jerusalem.' [34] O Jerusalem, Jerusalem, killing the prophets and stoning those who are sent to you! How often would I have gathered your children together as a hen gathers her brood under her wings, and you would not! [35] And now your house is forsaken. And I tell you, you will not see me until you say, 'Blessed is the one who comes in the name of the Sovereign [[or Lord]]!'"

## Gospel (alternate) ~ Luke 9:28-36

*Peter, John, and James witness the transfiguration of Jesus.*

[28] Now about eight days after these sayings Jesus took Peter and John and James, and went up on the mountain to pray. [29] And as Jesus was praying, the appearance of his countenance was altered, and his raiment became dazzlingly bright. [30] And two men talked about him, Moses and Elijah, [31] who appeared in glory and spoke of Jesus' departure, which he was to accomplish at Jerusalem. [32] Now Peter and those who were with him were heavy with sleep, and when they wakened they saw Jesus' glory and the two men who stood with him. [33] And as the two were parting from Jesus, Peter said to him, "Teacher,[†] it is well that we are here; let us make three booths, one for you and one for Moses and one for Elijah"—not knowing what he said. [34] As Peter said this, a cloud came and overshadowed them; and they were afraid as they entered the cloud. [35] And a voice came out of the cloud, saying, "This is my Child,[◊] my Chosen; to this one you shall listen!" [36] And when the voice had spoken, Jesus was found alone. And they kept silence and told no one in those days anything of what they had seen.

---

†RSV *Master.* See Appendix.
◊RSV *Son.* See Appendix.

22 MAR 92

# LENT 3

## Lesson 1 ~ Exodus 3:1-15

*God reveals God's name to Moses from the burning bush.*

¹ Now Moses was keeping the flock of his father-in-law, Jethro, the priest of Midian, and he led his flock to the west side of the wilderness, and came to Horeb, the mountain of God. ² And the angel of GOD [[*or* the LORD]] appeared to him in a flame of fire out of the midst of a bush; and Moses looked, and the bush was burning, yet it was not consumed. ³ And Moses said, "I will turn aside and see this great sight, why the bush is not burnt." ⁴ When GOD [[*or* the LORD]] saw that Moses turned aside to see, God called to him out of the bush, "Moses, Moses!" And he said, "Here am I." ⁵ Then God said, "Do not come near; put off your shoes from your feet, for the place on which you are standing is holy ground." ⁶ And God said, "I am the God of your ancestor, the God of Abraham [*and Sarah**], the God of Isaac [*and Rebecca**], and the God of Jacob [*and Rachel and Leah**]." And Moses hid his face, for he was afraid to look at God.

⁷ Then GOD [[*or* the LORD]] said, "I have seen the affliction of my people who are in Egypt, and have heard their cry because of their taskmasters; I know their sufferings, ⁸ and I have come down to deliver them out of the hand of the Egyptians, and to bring them up out of that land to a good and broad land, a land flowing with milk and honey, to the place of the Canaanites, the Hittites, the Amorites, the Perizzites, the Hivites, and the Jebusites. ⁹ And now the cry of the people of Israel has come to me, and I have seen the oppression with which the Egyptians oppress them. ¹⁰ Come, I will send you to Pharaoh that you may bring forth my people, the children of Israel, out of Egypt." ¹¹ But Moses said to God, "Who am I that I should go to Pharaoh, and bring the children of Israel out of Egypt?" ¹² God said, "But I will be with you; and this shall be the sign for you, that I have sent you: when you have brought forth the people out of Egypt, you shall serve God upon this mountain."

¹³ Then Moses said to God, "If I come to the people of Israel and say to them, 'The God of your ancestors has sent me to you,' and they ask me, 'What is the name of that God?' what shall I say to them?" ¹⁴ God said to Moses, "I AM WHO I AM." And God said, "Say this to the people of Israel, 'I AM has sent me to you.'" ¹⁵ God also said to Moses, "Say this to the people of Israel, 'The SOVEREIGN [[*or* LORD]], the God of your ancestors, the God of Abraham [*and Sarah**], the God of Isaac [*and Rebecca**], and

---

*Addition to the text. See "Addition of Women's Names to the Text" in the Appendix.

84

the God of Jacob [*and Rachel and Leah**], has sent me to you': this is my name forever, and thus I am to be remembered throughout all generations."

## Psalm 103:1-13

[1] Bless GOD [[*or* the LORD]], O my soul;
  and all that is within me, bless God's holy name!
[2] Bless GOD [[*or* the LORD]], O my soul,
  and forget not all God's benefits,
[3] who forgives all your iniquity,
  who heals all your diseases,
[4] who redeems your life from the Pit,
  who crowns you with steadfast love and mercy,
[5] who satisfies you with good as long as you live
  so that your youth is renewed like the eagle's.
[6] GOD [[*or* The LORD]] works vindication
  and justice for all who are oppressed.
[7] God made known God's ways to Moses,
  God's acts to the people of Israel.
[8] GOD [[*or* The LORD]] is merciful and gracious,
  slow to anger and abounding in steadfast love,
[9] not always chiding,
  and not remaining angry for ever.
[10] God does not deal with us according to our sins,
  nor repay us according to our iniquities.
[11] For as the heavens are high above the earth,
  so great is God's steadfast love toward those who fear God;
[12] as far as the east is from the west,
  so far does God remove our transgressions from us.
[13] As parents pity their children,
  so GOD [[*or* the LORD]] pities those who fear God.

---

*Addition to the text. See "Addition of Women's Names to the Text" in the Appendix.

## Lesson 2 ~ 1 Corinthians 10:1-13

*Paul compares the testing of the Corinthians with the testing of Israel in the wilderness.*

[1] I want you to know, sisters and brothers, that our ancestors were all under the cloud, and all passed through the sea, [2] and all were baptized into Moses in the cloud and in the sea, [3] and all ate the same supernatural food [4] and all drank the same supernatural drink. For they drank from the supernatural Rock which followed them, and the Rock was Christ. [5] Nevertheless with most of them God was not pleased; for they were overthrown in the wilderness.

[6] Now these things are warnings for us, not to desire evil as they did. [7] Do not be idolaters as some of them were; as it is written, "The people sat down to eat and drink and rose up to dance." [8] We must not indulge in immorality as some of them did, and twenty-three thousand fell in a single day. [9] We must not put the Sovereign [[*or* Lord]] to the test, as some of them did and were destroyed by serpents; [10] nor grumble, as some of them did and were destroyed by the Destroyer. [11] Now these things happened to them as a warning, but they were written down for our instruction, upon whom the end of the ages has come. [12] Therefore let any who think that they stand take heed lest they fall. [13] No temptation has overtaken you that is not common to everyone. God is faithful, and will not let you be tempted beyond your strength; but with the temptation God will also provide the way of escape, so that you may be able to endure it.

## Gospel (alternate) ~ Luke 13:10-17 +

*Jesus heals a daughter of the covenant.*

[10] Now Jesus was teaching in one of the synagogues on the sabbath. [11] And there was a woman who had had a spirit of infirmity for eighteen years; she was bent over and could not fully straighten herself. [12] And when Jesus saw her, he called her and said, "Woman, you are freed from your infirmity." [13] And Jesus laid his hands upon her, and immediately she was made straight, and she praised God. [14] But the ruler of the synagogue, indignant because Jesus had healed on the sabbath, said to the people, "There are six days on which work ought to be done; come on those days and be healed, and not on the sabbath day." [15] Then the Sovereign [[or Lord]] answered, "You hypocrites! Does not each of you on the sabbath untie your ox or your donkey from the manger, and lead it away to water it? [16] And ought not this woman, a daughter of Abraham [and Sarah*] whom Satan bound for eighteen years, be loosed from this bond on the sabbath day?" [17] As Jesus said this, all his adversaries were put to shame; and all the people rejoiced at all the glorious things that Jesus did.

## Gospel ~ Luke 13:1-9

*Jesus warns the people to repent.*

[1] There were some present at that very time who told Jesus of the Galileans whose blood Pilate had mingled with their sacrifices. [2] And Jesus answered them, "Do you think that these Galileans were worse sinners than all the other Galileans, because they suffered thus? [3] I tell you, No; but unless you repent you will all likewise perish. [4] Or those eighteen upon whom the tower in Siloam fell and killed them, do you think that they were worse offenders than all the others who dwelt in Jerusalem? [5] I tell you, No; but unless you repent you will all likewise perish."

[6] And Jesus told this parable: "A man who had a fig tree planted in a vineyard came seeking fruit on it, and finding none, [7] said to the vinedresser, 'These three years I have come seeking fruit on this fig tree, and I find none. Cut it down; why should it use up the ground?' [8] And the vinedresser answered, 'Let it alone, sir, this year also, till I dig about it and put on manure. [9] And if it bears fruit next year, well and good; but if not, you can cut it down.'"

---

+Lection added. See Appendix, p. 263.
* Addition to the text. See "Addition of Women's Names to the Text" in the Appendix.

# LENT 4

## Lesson 1 ~ Joshua 5:9-12

*The people of Israel enjoy the first harvest in the land of Canaan.*

⁹ And GOD [[*or* the LORD]] said to Joshua, "This day I have rolled away the reproach of Egypt from you." And so the name of that place is called Gilgal to this day.
¹⁰ While the people of Israel were encamped in Gilgal they kept the passover on the fourteenth day of the month at evening in the plains of Jericho. ¹¹ And on the morrow after the passover, on that very day, they ate of the produce of the land, unleavened cakes and parched grain. ¹² And the manna ceased on the morrow, when they ate of the produce of the land; and the people of Israel had manna no more, but ate of the fruit of the land of Canaan that year.

## Psalm 34:1-8

¹ I will bless GOD [[*or* the LORD]] at all times;
　　God's praise shall continually be in my mouth.
² My soul makes its boast in GOD [[*or* the LORD]];
　　let those who are afflicted hear and be glad.
³ O magnify GOD [[*or* the LORD]] with me,
　　and let us exalt God's name together!
⁴ I sought GOD [[*or* the LORD]], who answered me,
　　and delivered me from all my fears.
⁵ Look to God, and be radiant;
　　so your faces shall never be ashamed.
⁶ This poor one cried, and GOD [[*or* the LORD]] heard me,
　　and saved me out of all my troubles.
⁷ The angel of GOD [[*or* the LORD]] encamps
　　around those who fear God, and delivers them.
⁸ O taste and see that GOD [[*or* the LORD]] is good!
　　Happy is the one who takes refuge in God!

## Lesson 2 ~ 2 Corinthians 5:16-21

*Paul writes that in Christ everything is made new.*

¹⁶ From now on, therefore, we regard no one from a human point of view; even though we once regarded Christ from a human point of view, we regard Christ thus no longer. ¹⁷ Therefore, if anyone is in Christ, there

is a new creation; the old has passed away—the new has come. [18] All this is from God, who through Christ reconciled us to God's self and gave us the ministry of reconciliation; [19] that is, God was in Christ reconciling the world to God's self, not counting their trespasses against them, and entrusting to us the message of reconciliation. [20] So we are ambassadors for Christ, God making God's appeal through us. We beseech you on behalf of Christ, be reconciled to God. [21] For our sake God made to be sin the one who knew no sin, so that in this very one we might become the righteousness of God.

### Gospel ~ Luke 15:1-3, 11-32

*Jesus tells a parable about forgiveness and reconciliation.*

[1] Now the tax collectors and sinners were all drawing near to hear Jesus. [2] And the Pharisees and the scribes murmured, saying, "This man receives sinners and eats with them."

[3] So Jesus told them this parable:

[11] "There was a man who had two sons; [12] and the younger of them said to his father, 'Father, give me the share of property that falls to me.' And he divided his living between them. [13] Not many days later, the younger son gathered all he had and took his journey into a far country, and there squandered his property in loose living. [14] And when he had spent everything, a great famine arose in that country, and he began to be in want. [15] So he went and joined himself to one of the citizens of that country, who sent him into his fields to feed swine. [16] And he would gladly have fed on the pods that the swine ate; and no one gave him anything. [17] But when he came to himself he said, 'How many of my father's hired servants have bread enough and to spare, but I perish here with hunger! [18] I will arise and go to my father, and I will say to him, "Father, I have sinned against heaven and before you; [19] I am no longer worthy to be called your son; treat me as one of your hired servants."' [20] And he arose and came to his father. But while he was yet at a distance, his father saw him and had compassion, and ran and embraced him and kissed him. [21] And the son said to him, 'Father, I have sinned against heaven and before you; I am no longer worthy to be called your son.' [22] But the father said to the servants, 'Bring quickly the best robe, and put it on him; and put a ring on his hand, and shoes on his feet; [23] and bring the fatted calf and kill it, and let us eat and make merry; [24] for this my son was dead and is alive again, was lost and is found.' And they began to make merry.

[25] "Now his elder son was in the field; and as he came and drew near to the house, he heard music and dancing. [26] And he called one of the servants and asked what this meant. [27] And the servant said to him, 'Your

brother has come, and your father has killed the fatted calf, because he has received him safe and sound.' [28] But the elder son was angry and refused to go in. His father came out and entreated him, [29] but he answered his father, 'These many years I have served you, and I never disobeyed your command; yet you never gave me a kid, that I might make merry with my friends. [30] But when this son of yours came, who has devoured your living with harlots, you killed for him the fatted calf!' [31] And he said to him, 'Son, you are always with me, and all that is mine is yours. [32] It was fitting to make merry and be glad, for this your brother was dead, and is alive; he was lost, and is found.' "

# LENT 5

## Lesson 1 ~ Isaiah 43:16-21

*Isaiah announces God's promise of a new creation.*

<sup>16</sup> Thus says the SOVEREIGN [[*or* LORD]],
    who makes a way in the sea,
    a path in the mighty waters,
<sup>17</sup> who brings forth chariot and horse,
    army and warrior;
  they lie down, they cannot rise,
    they are extinguished, quenched like a wick:
<sup>18</sup> "Remember not the former things,
    nor consider the things of old.
<sup>19</sup> Behold, I am doing a new thing;
    now it springs forth, do you not perceive it?
  I will make a way in the wilderness
    and rivers in the desert.
<sup>20</sup> The wild beasts will honor me,
    the jackals and the ostriches;
  for I give water in the wilderness,
    rivers in the desert,
  to give drink to my chosen people,
<sup>21</sup>   the people whom I formed for myself
  that they might declare my praise."

# Psalm 126

¹ When GOD [or the LORD] restored the fortunes of Zion,
   we were like those who dream.
² Then our mouth was filled with laughter,
   and our tongue with shouts of joy;
  then they said among the nations,
    "GOD [or The LORD] has done great things for them."
³ GOD [or The LORD] has done great things for us;
   we are glad.
⁴ Restore our fortunes, O GOD [or LORD],
   like the watercourses in the Negeb!
⁵ May those who sow in tears
   reap with shouts of joy!
⁶ Those who go forth weeping,
   bearing the seed for sowing,
  shall come home with shouts of joy,
    bringing their sheaves of grain.


## Lesson 2 ~ Philippians 3:8-14

*Paul describes his life in Christ.*

⁸ Indeed I count everything as loss because of the surpassing worth of knowing Christ Jesus my Sovereign [or Lord], for whose sake I have suffered the loss of all things, and count them as refuse, in order that I may gain Christ ⁹ and be found in Christ, not having a righteousness of my own, based on law, but that which is through faith in Christ, the righteousness from God that depends on faith; ¹⁰ that I may know Christ and the power of Christ's resurrection, and may share Christ's sufferings, taking the same form that Christ took in death, ¹¹ that if possible I may attain the resurrection from the dead.

¹² Not that I have already obtained the goal or am already perfect; but I press on to make it my own, because I have been taken hold of by Christ Jesus. ¹³ Sisters and brothers, I do not consider that I have made it my own; but one thing I do, forgetting what lies behind and straining forward to what lies ahead, ¹⁴ I press on toward the goal for the prize of the upward call of God in Christ Jesus.

## Gospel ~ John 12:1-8

*Mary of Bethany anoints the feet of Jesus.*

¹ Six days before the Passover, Jesus came to Bethany, where Lazarus was, whom Jesus had raised from the dead. ² There they made Jesus a supper; Martha served, and Lazarus was one of those at the table. ³ Mary took a pound of costly ointment of pure nard and anointed the feet of Jesus and wiped them with her hair; and the house was filled with the fragrance of the ointment. ⁴ But Judas Iscariot, one of the disciples (the one who was to betray Jesus), said, ⁵ "Why was this ointment not sold for three hundred denarii and given to the poor?" ⁶ This Judas said, not that he cared for the poor but because he was a thief, and having the money box, he used to take what was put into it. ⁷ Jesus said, "Let her alone, let her keep it for the day of my burial. ⁸ The poor you always have with you, but you do not always have me."

# LENT 6, PASSION SUNDAY

## Lesson 1 ~ Isaiah 50:4-9a

*The prophet Isaiah tells of the suffering of the one who obeys God.*

⁴ The Sovereign [[or Lord]] GOD has given me
  the tongue of those who are taught,
that I may know how to sustain with a word
  one who is weary.
Morning by morning God wakens,
  God wakens my ear
to hear as those who are taught.
⁵ The Sovereign [[or Lord]] GOD has opened my ear,
  and I was not rebellious,
  I turned not backward.
⁶ I gave my back to the smiters,
  and my cheeks to those who pulled out my beard;
I hid not my face
  from shame and spitting.
⁷ For the Sovereign [[or Lord]] GOD helps me;
  therefore I have not been confounded;
therefore I have set my face like a flint,
  and I know that I shall not be put to shame;
⁸   the one who vindicates me is near.
Who will contend with me?
  Let us stand together.
Who are my adversaries?
  Let them come near to me.
⁹ The Sovereign [[or Lord]] GOD helps me;
  who will declare me guilty?

## Psalm 31:9-16

⁹ Be gracious to me, O GOD [[or LORD]], for I am in distress;
  my eye is wasted from grief,
  my soul and my body also.
¹⁰ For my life is spent with sorrow,
  and my years with sighing;
my strength fails because of my misery,
  and my bones waste away.

<sup>11</sup> I am the scorn of all my adversaries,
    a horror to my neighbors,
  an object of dread to my acquaintances;
    those who see me in the street flee from me.
<sup>12</sup> I have passed out of mind like one who is dead;
    I have become like a broken vessel.
<sup>13</sup> For I hear the whispering of many—
    terror on every side!—
  as they scheme together against me,
    as they plot to take my life.
<sup>14</sup> But I trust in you, O GOD [[or LORD]],
    I say, "You are my God."
<sup>15</sup> My times are in your hand;
    deliver me from the hand of my enemies and persecutors!
<sup>16</sup> Let your face shine on your servant;
    save me in your steadfast love!

### Lesson 2 ~ Philippians 2:5-11

*Paul speaks about the Sovereign Jesus Christ.*

<sup>5</sup> Have this mind among yourselves, which is yours in Christ Jesus, <sup>6</sup>who, though being in the form of God, did not count equality with God a thing to be grasped, <sup>7</sup>but emptied Christ's self, taking the form of a servant, being born in the likeness of human beings. <sup>8</sup>And being found in human form, Christ humbled Christ's self and became obedient unto death, even death on a cross. <sup>9</sup>Therefore God has highly exalted Jesus and bestowed on Jesus the name which is above every name, <sup>10</sup>that at the name of Jesus every knee should bow, in heaven and on earth and under the earth, <sup>11</sup>and every tongue confess that Jesus Christ is Sovereign [[or Lord]], to the glory of God the Father [*and Mother**].

### Gospel ~ Luke 22:14–23:56

*Luke recounts Jesus' last supper, trial, and death.*

<sup>14</sup> And when the hour came, Jesus sat at table, and the apostles with him. <sup>15</sup>And Jesus said to them, "I have earnestly desired to eat this passover with you before I suffer; <sup>16</sup>for I tell you I shall not eat it until it is fulfilled in the realm☆ of God." <sup>17</sup>And Jesus took a cup, and, having given

---

*Addition to the text. See "Metaphor" and "God the Father and Mother" in the Appendix.
☆ RSV *kingdom*. See Appendix.

thanks, said, "Take this, and divide it among yourselves; [18] for I tell you that from now on I shall not drink of the fruit of the vine until the realm☆ of God comes." [19] And Jesus took bread, and, having given thanks, broke it and gave it to them, saying, "This is my body which is given for you. Do this in remembrance of me." [20] And likewise the cup after supper, saying, "This cup which is poured out for you is the new covenant in my blood. [21] But the hand of the one who betrays me is with me on the table. [22] For the Human One○ goes as it has been determined; but woe to that person by whom the Human One is betrayed!" [23] And they began to question one another, which of them it was that would do this.

[24] A dispute also arose among them, which of them was to be regarded as the greatest. [25] And Jesus said to them, "The rulers□ of the Gentiles lord it over them; and those in authority over them are called benefactors. [26] But not so with you; rather let the greatest among you become as the youngest, and the leader as one who serves. [27] For which is the greater, one who sits at table, or one who serves? Is it not the one who sits at table? But I am among you as one who serves.

[28] "You are those who have continued with me in my trials; [29] and I assign a dominion☆ to you, as [God] my Father [and Mother*] assigned one to me, [30] that you may eat and drink at my table in my dominion,☆ and sit on thrones judging the twelve tribes of Israel.

[31] "Simon, Simon: Satan demanded to have you, in order to sift you like wheat, [32] but I have prayed for you that your faith may not fail; and when you have turned again, strengthen your brothers and sisters." [33] And Simon said to Jesus, "Sovereign [[or Lord]], I am ready to go with you to prison and to death." [34] Jesus said, "I tell you, Peter, the cock will not crow this day, until you deny three times that you know me."

[35] And Jesus said to them, "When I sent you out with no purse or bag or sandals, did you lack anything?" They said, "Nothing." [36] He said to them, "But now, whoever has a purse, take it, and likewise a bag. And whoever has no sword, sell your mantle and buy one. [37] For I tell you that this scripture must be fulfilled in me, 'And he was reckoned with transgressors'; for what is written about me has its fulfillment." [38] And they said, "Look, Sovereign [[or Lord]], here are two swords." And Jesus said to them, "It is enough."

[39] And Jesus came out, and went, as was his custom, to the Mount of Olives; and the disciples followed him. [40] And having come to the place, he said to them, "Pray that you may not enter into temptation." [41] And Jesus withdrew from them about a stone's throw, and knelt down and

---

☆RSV *kingdom*. See Appendix.
○RSV *Son of man*. See Appendix.
□RSV *kings*. See Appendix.
*Addition to the text. See "Metaphor" and "God the Father and Mother" in the Appendix.

prayed, ⁴²"[God, my] Father [and Mother*], if you are willing, remove this cup from me; nevertheless not my will, but yours, be done." ⁴⁵And when Jesus rose from prayer, he came to the disciples and found them sleeping from sorrow, ⁴⁶and said to them, "Why do you sleep? Rise and pray that you may not enter into temptation."

⁴⁷While Jesus was still speaking, there came a crowd, and the man called Judas, one of the twelve, was leading them. Judas drew near to Jesus to kiss him; ⁴⁸but Jesus said, "Judas, would you betray the Human One○ with a kiss?" ⁴⁹And when those who were standing nearby saw what would follow, they said, "Sovereign [or Lord], shall we strike with the sword?" ⁵⁰And one of them struck the slave of the high priest and cut off his right ear. ⁵¹But Jesus said, "No more of this!" And Jesus touched the ear of the slave and healed him. ⁵²Then Jesus said to the chief priests and officers of the temple and elders, who had come out against him, "Have you come out as against a robber, with swords and clubs? ⁵³When I was with you day after day in the temple, you did not lay hands on me. But this is your hour, and the power of evil."

⁵⁴Then they seized Jesus and led him away, bringing him into the high priest's house. Peter followed at a distance; ⁵⁵and when they had kindled a fire in the middle of the courtyard and sat down together, Peter sat among them. ⁵⁶Then a womanservant, seeing him as he sat in the light and gazing at him, said, "This man also was with him." ⁵⁷But Peter denied it, saying, "Woman, I do not know him." ⁵⁸And a little later someone else saw Peter, and said, "You also are one of them." But Peter said, "Man, I am not." ⁵⁹And after an interval of about an hour still another insisted, saying, "Certainly this man also was with him; for he is a Galilean." ⁶⁰But Peter said, "Man, I do not know what you are saying." And immediately, while Peter was still speaking, the cock crowed. ⁶¹And the Sovereign [or Lord] turned and looked at Peter. And Peter remembered the word which the Sovereign [or Lord] had said to him, "Before the cock crows today, you will deny me three times." ⁶²And Peter went out and wept bitterly.

⁶³Now the men who were holding Jesus mocked him and beat him; ⁶⁴they also blindfolded him and asked, "Prophesy! Who is it that struck you?" ⁶⁵And they spoke many other words against Jesus, reviling him.

⁶⁶When day came, the assembly of the elders of the people gathered together, both chief priests and scribes; and they led him away to their council, and they said, ⁶⁷"If you are the Christ, tell us." But Jesus said to them, "If I tell you, you will not believe; ⁶⁸and if I ask you, you will not answer. ⁶⁹But from now on the Human One○ shall be seated at the right hand of the power of God." ⁷⁰And they all said, "Are you the Child◇ of

---

*Addition to the text. See "Metaphor" and "God the Father and Mother" in the Appendix.
○RSV Son of man. See Appendix.
◇RSV Son. See Appendix.

God, then?" And Jesus said to them, "You say that I am." ⁷¹ And they said, "What further testimony do we need? We have heard it ourselves from his own lips."

²³:¹ Then the whole company of them arose, and brought Jesus before Pilate. ² And they began to accuse him, saying, "We found this man perverting our nation, and forbidding us to give tribute to Caesar, and saying that he himself is Christ a king." ³ And Pilate asked Jesus, "Are you the King of the Jews?" And Jesus answered Pilate, "You have said so." ⁴ And Pilate said to the chief priests and the multitudes, "I find no crime in this man." ⁵ But they were urgent, saying, "He stirs up the people, teaching throughout all Judea, from Galilee even to this place."

⁶ When Pilate heard this, he asked whether the man was a Galilean. ⁷ And when he learned that Jesus belonged to Herod's jurisdiction, Pilate sent Jesus over to Herod, who was himself in Jerusalem at that time. ⁸ When Herod saw Jesus, he was very glad, for he had long desired to see him, because he had heard about Jesus, and was hoping to see some sign done by him. ⁹ So Herod questioned Jesus at some length; but he made no answer. ¹⁰ The chief priests and the scribes stood by, vehemently accusing him. ¹¹ And Herod with his soldiers treated Jesus with contempt and mocked him; then, arraying Jesus in gorgeous apparel, Herod sent him back to Pilate. ¹² And Herod and Pilate became friends with each other that very day, for before this they had been at enmity with each other.

¹³ Pilate then called together the chief priests and the rulers and the people, ¹⁴ and said to them, "You brought me this man as one who was perverting the people; and after examining him before you, I did not find this man guilty of any of your charges; ¹⁵ neither did Herod, for he sent him back to us. Nothing deserving death has been done by him; ¹⁶ I will therefore chastise and release him."

¹⁸ But they all cried out together, "Away with this man, and release to us Barabbas," ¹⁹ who had been thrown into prison for an insurrection started in the city, and for murder. ²⁰ Pilate addressed them once more, desiring to release Jesus; ²¹ but they shouted out, "Crucify, crucify him!" ²² A third time Pilate said to them, "Why, what evil has he done? I have found in him no crime deserving death; I will therefore chastise and release him." ²³ But they were urgent, demanding with loud cries that Jesus should be crucified. And their voices prevailed. ²⁴ So Pilate gave sentence that their demand should be granted. ²⁵ He released the one who had been thrown into prison for insurrection and murder, whom they asked for; but Jesus he delivered up to their will.

²⁶ And as they led Jesus away, they seized some one named Simon of Cyrene, who was coming in from the country, and laid on him the cross, to carry it behind Jesus. ²⁷ And there followed him a great multitude of the people, and of women who bewailed and lamented him. ²⁸ But Jesus turning to them said, "Daughters of Jerusalem, do not weep for me, but weep for yourselves and for your children. ²⁹ For the days are coming when they

will say, 'Blessed are the barren, and the wombs that never bore, and the breasts that never gave milk!' [30] Then they will begin to say to the mountains, 'Fall on us'; and to the hills, 'Cover us.' [31] For if they do this when the wood is green, what will happen when it is dry?"

[32] Two others also, who were criminals, were led away to be put to death with Jesus. [33] And when they came to the place which is called The Skull, there they crucified Jesus, and the criminals, one on the right and one on the left. [34] And Jesus said, "Gracious God,⊗ forgive them; for they know not what they do." And they cast lots to divide his garments. [35] And the people stood by, watching; but the rulers scoffed at Jesus, saying, "He saved others; let him save himself, if he is the Christ of God, the Chosen One!" [36] The soldiers also mocked Jesus, coming up and offering him vinegar, [37] and saying, "If you are the King of the Jews, save yourself!" [38] There was also an inscription over him, "This is the King of the Jews."

[39] One of the criminals who were hanged railed at Jesus, saying, "Are you not the Christ? Save yourself and us!" [40] But the other rebuked him, saying, "Do you not fear God, since you are under the same sentence of condemnation? [41] And we indeed justly; for we are receiving the due reward of our deeds; but this one has done nothing wrong." [42] And he said, "Jesus, remember me when you come into your realm.☆" [43] And Jesus said, "Truly, I say to you, today you will be with me in Paradise."

[44] It was now about the sixth hour, and there was darkness over the whole land until the ninth hour, [45] while the sun's light failed; and the curtain of the temple was torn in two. [46] Then Jesus, crying with a loud voice, said, "[God, my] Father [and Mother*], into your hands I commit my spirit!" And having said this, Jesus died. [47] Now when the centurion saw what had taken place, he praised God, and said, "Certainly this man was innocent!" [48] And all the multitudes who assembled to see the sight, when they saw what had taken place, returned home beating their breasts. [49] And all Jesus' acquaintances and the women who had followed him from Galilee stood at a distance and saw these things.

[50] Now there was a man named Joseph from the Jewish town of Arimathea. He was a member of the council, a good and righteous person, [51] who had not consented to their purpose and deed, and he was looking for the realm☆ of God. [52] This man went to Pilate and asked for the body of Jesus. [53] Then Joseph took the body down and wrapped it in a linen shroud, and laid the body in a rock-hewn tomb, where no one had ever yet been laid. [54] It was the day of Preparation, and the sabbath was beginning. [55] The women who had come with Jesus from Galilee followed, and saw the tomb, and how the body was laid; [56] then they returned, and prepared spices and ointments.

On the sabbath they rested according to the commandment.

---

⊗RSV *Father*. See Appendix.
☆RSV *kingdom*. See Appendix.
*Addition to the text. See "Metaphor" and "God the Father and Mother" in the Appendix.

# LENT 6, PALM SUNDAY

## Lesson 1 ~ Isaiah 50:4-9a

*The prophet Isaiah tells of the suffering of the one who obeys God.*

<sup>4</sup> The Sovereign [[*or* Lord]] GOD has given me
    the tongue of those who are taught,
that I may know how to sustain with a word
    one who is weary.
Morning by morning God wakens,
    God wakens my ear
to hear as those who are taught.
<sup>5</sup> The Sovereign [[*or* Lord]] GOD has opened my ear,
    and I was not rebellious,
    I turned not backward.
<sup>6</sup> I gave my back to the smiters,
    and my cheeks to those who pulled out my beard;
    I hid not my face
    from shame and spitting.
<sup>7</sup> For the Sovereign [[*or* Lord]] GOD helps me;
    therefore I have not been confounded;
therefore I have set my face like a flint,
    and I know that I shall not be put to shame;
<sup>8</sup>    the one who vindicates me is near.
Who will contend with me?
    Let us stand together.
Who are my adversaries?
    Let them come near to me.
<sup>9</sup> The Sovereign [[*or* Lord]] GOD helps me;
    who will declare me guilty?

## Psalm 118:19-29

<sup>19</sup> Open to me the gates of righteousness,
    that I may enter through them
    and give thanks to GOD [[*or* the LORD]].
<sup>20</sup> This is the gate of GOD [[*or* the LORD]];
    the righteous shall enter through it.
<sup>21</sup> I thank you that you have answered me
    and have become my salvation.
<sup>22</sup> The stone which the builders rejected
    has become the head of the corner.

²³ This is GOD's [[*or* the LORD's]] doing;
　　it is marvelous in our eyes.
²⁴ This is the day which GOD [[*or* the LORD]] has made;
　　let us rejoice and be glad in it.
²⁵ Save us, we beseech you, O GOD [[*or* LORD]]!
　　O GOD [[*or* LORD]], we beseech you, give us success!
²⁶ Blessed be the one who enters in the name of GOD [[*or* the LORD]]!
　　We bless you from the house of GOD [[*or* the LORD]].
²⁷ The SOVEREIGN [[*or* LORD]] is God,
　　who has caused light to shine upon us.
　Bind the festal procession with branches,
　　up to the horns of the altar!
²⁸ You are my God, and I will give thanks to you;
　　you are my God, I will extol you.
²⁹ O give thanks to GOD [[*or* the LORD]], for God is good;
　　for God's steadfast love endures for ever!

## Lesson 2 ~ Philippians 2:5-11

*Paul speaks about the Sovereign Jesus Christ.*

⁵ Have this mind among yourselves, which is yours in Christ Jesus, ⁶ who, though being in the form of God, did not count equality with God a thing to be grasped, ⁷ but emptied Christ's self, taking the form of a servant, being born in the likeness of human beings. ⁸ And being found in human form, Christ humbled Christ's self and became obedient unto death, even death on a cross. ⁹ Therefore God has highly exalted Jesus and bestowed on Jesus the name which is above every name, ¹⁰ that at the name of Jesus every knee should bow, in heaven and on earth and under the earth, ¹¹ and every tongue confess that Jesus Christ is Sovereign [[*or* Lord]], to the glory of God the Father [*and Mother**]].

---

*Addition to the text. See "Metaphor" and "God the Father and Mother" in the Appendix.

101

# Gospel ~ Luke 19:28-40

*Luke recounts Jesus' triumphal entry into Jerusalem.*

<sup>28</sup> And having said this, Jesus went on ahead, going up to Jerusalem. <sup>29</sup> When he drew near to Bethphage and Bethany, at the mount that is called Olivet, he sent two of the disciples, <sup>30</sup> saying, "Go into the village opposite, where on entering you will find a colt tied, on which no one has ever yet sat; untie it and bring it here. <sup>31</sup> If anyone asks you, 'Why are you untying it?' you shall say this, 'The Sovereign [[*or* Lord]] has need of it.' " <sup>32</sup> So those who were sent went away and found it as Jesus had told them. <sup>33</sup> And as they were untying the colt, its owners said to them, "Why are you untying the colt?" <sup>34</sup> And they said, "The Sovereign [[*or* Lord]] has need of it." <sup>35</sup> And they brought it to Jesus, and throwing their garments on the colt they set him upon it. <sup>36</sup> And as Jesus rode along, they spread their garments on the road. <sup>37</sup> As he was now drawing near, at the descent of the Mount of Olives, the whole multitude of the disciples began to rejoice and praise God with a loud voice for all the mighty works that they had seen, <sup>38</sup> saying, "Blessed is the King who comes in the name of the Sovereign [[*or* Lord]]! Peace in heaven and glory in the highest!" <sup>39</sup> And some of the Pharisees in the multitude said to Jesus, "Teacher, rebuke your disciples." <sup>40</sup> He answered, "I tell you, if these were silent, the very stones would cry out."

# MONDAY OF HOLY WEEK

## Lesson 1 ~ Isaiah 42:1-9

*God speaks through the prophet Isaiah about God's servant.*

¹ Here is my servant, whom I uphold,
    my chosen, in whom my soul delights;
I have put my Spirit upon my servant,
    who will bring forth justice to the nations.
² My servant will not cry or speak out,
    nor be heard in the street;
³ My servant will not break a bruised reed,
    nor quench a dimly burning wick,
    but will faithfully bring forth justice.
⁴ My servant will not fail or be discouraged
    till justice has been established in the earth;
    and the coastlands wait for the servant's law.
⁵ Thus says God, the SOVEREIGN [[or LORD]],
    who created the heavens and stretched them out,
    who spread forth the earth and what comes from it,
who gives breath to the people upon it
    and spirit to those who walk in it:
⁶ "I am the SOVEREIGN [[or LORD]], I have called you in righteousness,
    I have taken you by the hand and kept you;
I have given you as a covenant to the people,
    a light to the nations,
⁷    to open the eyes that are blind,
to bring out the prisoners from the dungeon,
    from the prison those who sit with no light.
⁸ I am the SOVEREIGN [[or LORD]], that is my name;
    my glory I give to no other,
    nor my praise to graven images.
⁹ Now the former things have come to pass,
    and new things I declare;
before they spring forth
    I tell you of them."

## Psalm 36:5-10

[5] Your steadfast love, O GOD [[or LORD]], extends to the heavens,
  your faithfulness to the clouds.
[6] Your righteousness is like the mountains of God,
  your judgments are like the great deep;
  all living things you save, O GOD [[or LORD]].
[7] How precious is your steadfast love, O God!
  All people may take refuge in the shadow of your wings.
[8] They feast on the abundance of your house,
  and you give them drink from the river of your delights.
[9] For with you is the fountain of life;
  in your light do we see light.
[10] O continue your steadfast love to those who know you,
  and your salvation to the upright of heart!


## Lesson 2 ~ Hebrews 9:11-15

*Christ is the mediator of a new covenant.*

[11] But when Christ appeared as a high priest of the good things that have come, then through the greater and more perfect tent (not made with hands, that is, not of this creation) [12] Christ entered once for all into the Holy Place, taking not the blood of goats and calves but Christ's own blood, thus securing an eternal redemption. [13] For if the sprinkling of defiled persons with the blood of goats and bulls and with the ashes of a heifer sanctifies for the purification of the flesh, [14] how much more shall the blood of Christ—who through the eternal Spirit offered Christ's self as an unblemished sacrifice to God—purify your conscience from dead works to serve the living God.

[15] Therefore Christ is the mediator of a new covenant, so that those who are called may receive the promised eternal inheritance, since a death has occurred which redeems them from the transgressions under the first covenant.

# Gospel ~ John 12:1-11

*Mary of Bethany anoints the feet of Jesus.*

[1] Six days before the Passover, Jesus came to Bethany, where Lazarus was, whom Jesus had raised from the dead. [2] There they made Jesus a supper; Martha served, and Lazarus was one of those at the table. [3] Mary took a pound of costly ointment of pure nard and anointed the feet of Jesus and wiped them with her hair; and the house was filled with the fragrance of the ointment. [4] But Judas Iscariot, one of the disciples (the one who was to betray Jesus), said, [5] "Why was this ointment not sold for three hundred denarii and given to the poor?" [6] This Judas said, not that he cared for the poor but because he was a thief, and having the money box, he used to take what was put into it. [7] Jesus said, "Let her alone, let her keep it for the day of my burial. [8] The poor you always have with you, but you do not always have me."

[9] When the great crowd of the Jews learned that Jesus was there, they came, not only on account of Jesus but also to see Lazarus, whom Jesus had raised from the dead. [10] So the chief priests planned to put Lazarus also to death, [11] because on account of him many of the Jews were going away and believing in Jesus.

# TUESDAY OF HOLY WEEK

## Lesson 1 ~ Isaiah 49:1-7

*The servant of God speaks through the prophet Isaiah.*

<sup>1</sup> Listen to me, O coastlands,
    and hearken, you nations from afar.
GOD [*or* The LORD] called me from the womb,
    and from the body of my mother God named my name.
<sup>2</sup> God made my mouth like a sharp sword,
    in the shadow of God's hand I was hidden;
God made me a polished arrow,
    in the quiver I was hidden away.
<sup>3</sup> And God said to me, "You are my servant,
    Israel, in whom I will be glorified."
<sup>4</sup> But I said, "I have labored in vain,
    I have spent my strength for nothing and vanity;
yet surely my right is with the SOVEREIGN [*or* LORD],
    and my recompense with my God."
<sup>5</sup> And now GOD [*or* the LORD] says,
    who formed me from the womb to be God's servant,
to bring Jacob back to God,
    and that Israel might be gathered to God,
for I am honored in the eyes of the SOVEREIGN [*or* LORD],
    and my God has become my strength—
<sup>6</sup> God says:
"It is too light a thing that you should be my servant
    to raise up the tribes of Jacob
    and to restore the preserved of Israel;
 I will give you as a light to the nations,
    that my salvation may reach to the end of the earth."
<sup>7</sup> Thus says the SOVEREIGN [*or* LORD],
    the Redeemer of Israel and Israel's Holy One,
to one deeply despised, abhorred by the nations,
    the servant of rulers:
"Monarchs[□] shall see and arise;
    rulers, and they shall prostrate themselves;
because of the SOVEREIGN [*or* LORD], who is faithful,
    the Holy One of Israel, who has chosen you."

---

□RSV *Kings*. See Appendix.

# Psalm 71:1-12

[1] In you, O GOD [[*or* LORD]], do I take refuge;
   let me never be put to shame!
[2] In your righteousness deliver me and rescue me;
   incline your ear to me, and save me!
[3] Be to me a rock of refuge,
   a strong fortress, to save me,
   for you are my rock and my fortress.
[4] Rescue me, O my God, from the hand of the wicked,
   from the grasp of the unjust and the cruel.
[5] For you, O God [[*or* Lord]], are my hope,
   my trust, O GOD [[*or* LORD]], from my youth.
[6] Upon you I have leaned from my birth;
   you are the one who took me from my mother's womb.
My praise is continually of you.
[7] I have been as a portent to many;
   but you are my strong refuge.
[8] My mouth is filled with your praise,
   and with your glory all the day.
[9] Do not cast me off in the time of old age;
   forsake me not when my strength is spent.
[10] For my enemies speak concerning me,
   those who watch for my life consult together,
[11] and say, "God has forsaken the one who trusted;
   pursue and seize the forsaken one,
   for there is no one to give deliverance."
[12] O God, be not far from me;
   O my God, make haste to help me!

## Lesson 2 ~ 1 Corinthians 1:18-31

*Paul writes to the Christians at Corinth about the wisdom of God.*

¹⁸ For the word of the cross is folly to those who are perishing, but to us who are being saved it is the power of God. ¹⁹ For it is written,

> "I will destroy the wisdom of the wise,
> and the cleverness of the clever I will thwart."

²⁰ Where is the wise one? Where is the scribe? Where is the debater of this age? Has not God made foolish the wisdom of the world? ²¹ For since, in the wisdom of God, the world did not know God through wisdom, it pleased God through the folly of what we preach to save those who believe. ²² For Jews demand signs and Greeks seek wisdom, ²³ but we preach Christ crucified, a stumbling block to Jews and folly to Gentiles, ²⁴ but to those who are called, both Jews and Greeks, Christ the power of God and the wisdom of God. ²⁵ For the foolishness of God is wiser than human wisdom, and the weakness of God is stronger than human strength.

²⁶ For consider your call, my friends; not many of you were wise according to worldly standards, not many were powerful, not many were of noble birth; ²⁷ but God chose what is foolish in the world to shame the wise, God chose what is weak in the world to shame the strong, ²⁸ God chose what is low and despised in the world, even things that are not, to bring to nothing things that are, ²⁹ so that no human being might boast in the presence of God. ³⁰ God is the source of your life in Christ Jesus, whom God made our wisdom, our righteousness and sanctification and redemption; ³¹ therefore, as it is written, "Let the one who boasts, boast of the Sovereign [[or Lord]]."

# Gospel ~ John 12:20-36

*Jesus speaks of the glorification of the Human One.*

<sup>20</sup> Now among those who went up to worship at the feast were some Greeks. <sup>21</sup> So these came to Philip, who was from Bethsaida in Galilee, and said, "Sir, we wish to see Jesus." <sup>22</sup> Philip went and told Andrew; Andrew went with Philip and they told Jesus. <sup>23</sup> And Jesus answered them, "The hour has come for the Human One○ to be glorified. <sup>24</sup> Truly, truly, I say to you, unless a grain of wheat falls into the earth and dies, it remains alone; but if it dies, it bears much fruit. <sup>25</sup> Whoever loves their life loses it, and whoever hates their life in this world will keep it for eternal life. <sup>26</sup> Anyone who serves me must follow me; and where I am, there shall my servant be also; anyone who serves me will be honored by [*God*] the Father [*and Mother\**].

<sup>27</sup> "Now is my soul troubled. And what shall I say? 'God,⊗ save me from this hour'? No, for this purpose I have come to this hour. <sup>28</sup> God,⊗ glorify your name." Then a voice came from heaven, "I have glorified it, and I will glorify it again." <sup>29</sup> The crowd standing by heard it and said that it had thundered. Others said, "An Angel has spoken to him." <sup>30</sup> Jesus answered, "This voice has come for your sake, not for mine. <sup>31</sup> Now is the judgment of this world, now shall the ruler of this world be cast out; <sup>32</sup> and I, when I am lifted up from the earth, will draw all people to myself." <sup>33</sup> Jesus said this to show by what death he was to die. <sup>34</sup> The crowd answered, "We have heard from the law that the Christ remains for ever. How can you say that the Human One○ must be lifted up? Who is this Human One○?" <sup>35</sup> Jesus said to them, "The light is with you for a little longer. Walk while you have the light, lest the night overtake you; those who walk in the night do not know where they are going. <sup>36</sup> While you have the light, believe in the light, that you may become children of light."

Having said this, Jesus departed and hid from them.

---

○ RSV *Son of man*. See Appendix.
\* Addition to the text. See "Metaphor" and "God the Father and Mother" in the Appendix.
⊗ *Father*. See Appendix.

15APR92

# WEDNESDAY OF HOLY WEEK

## Lesson 1 ~ Isaiah 50:4-9a

*The prophet Isaiah tells of the suffering of the one who obeys God.*

⁴ The Sovereign [*or* Lord] GOD has given me
    the tongue of those who are taught,
  that I may know how to sustain with a word
    one who is weary.
  Morning by morning God wakens,
    God wakens my ear
    to hear as those who are taught.
⁵ The Sovereign [*or* Lord] GOD has opened my ear,
    and I was not rebellious,
    I turned not backward.
⁶ I gave my back to the smiters,
    and my cheeks to those who pulled out my beard;
  I hid not my face
    from shame and spitting.
⁷ For the Sovereign [*or* Lord] GOD helps me;
    therefore I have not been confounded;
  therefore I have set my face like a flint,
    and I know that I shall not be put to shame;
⁸    the one who vindicates me is near.
  Who will contend with me?
    Let us stand together.
  Who are my adversaries?
    Let them come near to me.
⁹ The Sovereign [*or* Lord] GOD helps me;
    who will declare me guilty?

# Psalm 70

1 Be pleased, O God, to deliver me!
  O GOD [[or LORD]], make haste to help me!
2 Let them be put to shame and confusion
    who seek my life!
  Let them be turned back and brought to dishonor
    who desire my hurt!
3 Let them be appalled because of their shame
    who say, "Aha, Aha!"
4 May all who seek you
    rejoice and be glad in you!
  May those who love your salvation
    say evermore, "God is great!"
5 But I am poor and needy;
    hasten to me, O God!
  You are my help and my deliverer;
    O GOD [[or LORD]], do not tarry!


## Lesson 2 ~ Hebrews 12:1-3

*Jesus is the pioneer and perfecter of our faith.*

1 Therefore, since we are surrounded by so great a cloud of witnesses, let us also lay aside every weight, and sin which clings so closely, and let us run with perseverance the race that is set before us, 2 looking to Jesus the pioneer and perfecter of our faith, who for the joy that was set before him endured the cross, despising the shame, and is seated at the right hand of the throne of God.

3 Consider the one who endured from sinners such hostility against himself, so that you may not grow weary or fainthearted.

## Gospel ~ John 13:21-30

*Judas is identified as the one who will betray Jesus.*

[21] Having spoken thus, Jesus was troubled in spirit, and testified, "Truly, truly, I say to you, one of you will betray me." [22] The disciples looked at one another, uncertain of whom he spoke. [23] One of the disciples, whom Jesus loved, was lying close to his breast; [24] so Simon Peter beckoned to that disciple and said, "Tell us who it is of whom he speaks." [25] So lying thus, close to the breast of Jesus, the one whom Jesus loved said to him, "Sovereign, [[or Lord]], who is it?" [26] Jesus answered, "It is the one to whom I shall give this morsel when I have dipped it." Having dipped the morsel, he gave it to Judas, the son of Simon Iscariot. [27] Then after the morsel, Satan entered into Judas. Jesus said to him, "What you are going to do, do quickly." [28] Now no one at the table knew why Jesus said to him, "Sovereign [[or Lord]], who is it?" [26] Jesus answered, "It is the box, Jesus was telling him, "Buy what we need for the feast," or that Judas should give something to the poor. [30] So, after receiving the morsel, Judas immediately went out; and it was night.

# MAUNDY THURSDAY

*(For those who want the foot washing emphasis every year, the Year A readings are used each year.)*

## Lesson 1 ~ Jeremiah 31:31-34

*God promises a new covenant with the houses of Israel and Judah.*

³¹ The days are coming, says the SOVEREIGN [[*or* LORD]], when I will make a new covenant with the house of Israel and the house of Judah, ³² not like the covenant which I made with their ancestors when I took them by the hand to bring them out of the land of Egypt, my covenant which they broke, though I was married to them, says the SOVEREIGN [[*or* LORD]]. ³³ But this is the covenant which I will make with the house of Israel after those days, says the SOVEREIGN [[*or* LORD]]: I will put my law within them, and I will write it upon their hearts; and I will be their God, and they shall be my people. ³⁴ And no longer shall each one teach a neighbor and each a brother or sister, saying, "Know GOD [[*or* the LORD]]," for they shall all know me, from the least of them to the greatest, says the SOVEREIGN [[*or* LORD]]; for I will forgive their iniquity, and I will remember their sin no more.

## Psalm 116:12-19

*(Psalm 116:12-19 is used at the Eucharist on Maundy [Holy] Thursday. Psalm 89:20-21, 24, 26, below, is used at the Chrism service.)*

¹² What shall I render to GOD [[*or* the LORD]]
  for all God's bounty to me?
¹³ I will lift up the cup of salvation
  and call on the name of GOD [[*or* the LORD]],
¹⁴ I will pay my vows to GOD [[*or* the LORD]]
  in the presence of all God's people.
¹⁵ Precious in the sight of GOD [[*or* the LORD]]
  is the death of the saints.
¹⁶ O GOD [[*or* LORD]], I am your servant;
  I am your servant, the child of your womanservant.
  You have loosed my bonds.
¹⁷ I will offer to you the sacrifice of thanksgiving
  and call on the name of GOD [[*or* the LORD]].

<sup>18</sup> I will pay my vows to GOD [[*or* the LORD]]
in the presence of all God's people,
<sup>19</sup> in the courts of the house of GOD [[*or* the LORD]],
in your midst, O Jerusalem.
Praise GOD [[*or* the LORD]]!


### Psalm 89:20-21, 24, 26

<sup>20</sup> I have found David, my servant;
with my holy oil I have anointed him;
<sup>21</sup> so that my hand shall ever abide with David,
my arm also shall strengthen him.
<sup>24</sup> My faithfulness and my steadfast love shall be with him,
and in my name shall David's horn be exalted.
<sup>26</sup> He shall cry to me, "You are my Parent,
my God, and the Rock of my salvation."


### Lesson 2 ~ Hebrews 10:16-25

*The author of the letter to the Hebrews urges confidence and steadfastness in the faith.*

<sup>16</sup> "This is the covenant that I will make with them
after those days, says the Sovereign [[*or* Lord]]:
I will put my laws on their hearts, and write them on their minds,"
<sup>17</sup> then it is added,
"I will remember their sins and their misdeeds no more."
<sup>18</sup> Where there is forgiveness of these, there is no longer any offering for sin.

<sup>19</sup> Therefore, brothers and sisters, since we have confidence to enter the sanctuary by the blood of Jesus, <sup>20</sup> by the new and living way which Jesus opened for us through the curtain, that is, through Jesus' flesh, <sup>21</sup> and since we have a great priest over the house of God, <sup>22</sup> let us draw near with a true heart in full assurance of faith, with our hearts sprinkled clean from an evil conscience and our bodies washed with pure water. <sup>23</sup> Let us hold fast the confession of our hope without wavering, for the one who promised is faithful; <sup>24</sup> and let us consider how to stir up one another to love and good works, <sup>25</sup> not neglecting to meet together, as is the habit of some, but encouraging one another, and all the more as you see the Day drawing near.

# Gospel ~ Luke 22:7-20

*Jesus eats the passover meal with the disciples.*

[7] Then came the day of Unleavened Bread, on which the passover lamb had to be sacrificed. [8] So Jesus sent Peter and John, saying, "Go and prepare the passover for us, that we may eat it." [9] They said to him, "Where will you have us prepare it?" [10] Jesus said to them, "When you have entered the city, a man carrying a jar of water will meet you; follow him into the house which he enters, [11] and tell the householder, 'The Teacher says to you, Where is the guest room, where I am to eat the passover with my disciples?' [12] And the householder will show you a large upper room furnished; there make ready." [13] And they went, and found it as Jesus had told them; and they prepared the passover.

[14] And when the hour came, Jesus sat at table, and the apostles with him. [15] And Jesus said to them, "I have earnestly desired to eat this passover with you before I suffer; [16] for I tell you I shall not eat it until it is fulfilled in the realm☆ of God." [17] And Jesus took a cup, and, having given thanks, said, "Take this, and divide it among yourselves; [18] for I tell you that from now on I shall not drink of the fruit of the vine until the realm☆ of God comes." [19] And Jesus took bread, and, having given thanks, broke it and gave it to them, saying, "This is my body which is given for you. Do this in remembrance of me." [20] And likewise the cup after supper, saying, "This cup which is poured out for you is the new covenant in my blood."

---

☆RSV *kingdom*. See Appendix.

# GOOD FRIDAY

## Lesson 1 ~ Isaiah 52:13–53:12

*Isaiah writes of the Suffering Servant.*

13 My servant shall prosper,
    shall be exalted and lifted up,
    and shall be very high.
14 As many were astonished at the one
    whose appearance was so marred, beyond human semblance,
    and whose form beyond that of human beings,
15 so many nations will be startled;
    rulers□ shall shut their mouths because of my servant;
  for that which has not been told them they shall see,
    and that which they have not heard they shall understand.
53:1 Who has believed what we have heard?
    And to whom has the arm of GOD [[*or* the LORD]] been revealed?
2 For the servant grew up before God like a young plant,
    and like a root out of dry ground,
  with no form or comeliness that we should admire,
    and no beauty that we should desire.
3 The servant was despised and rejected by everyone,
    was full of sorrows, and acquainted with grief,
  and as one from whom people hide their faces,
    was despised and not esteemed by us.
4 Surely this one has borne our griefs
    and carried our sorrows;
  yet we esteemed the servant stricken,
    smitten by God, and afflicted.
5 But this servant was wounded for our transgressions,
    was bruised for our iniquities,
  bore the chastisement that made us whole
    and the stripes by which we are healed.
6 All we like sheep have gone astray;
    we have turned everyone to our own way;
  and GOD [[*or* the LORD]] has laid on this one
    the iniquity of us all.
7 The servant was oppressed, and was afflicted,
    yet did not say a word;
  like a lamb that is led to the slaughter,
    and like a ewe that before her shearers is dumb,
    the servant did not say a word.

---

□RSV *kings*. See Appendix.

116

<sup>8</sup> By oppression and judgment the servant was taken away;
    and as for that one's generation, who considered
  that the servant was cut off out of the land of the living,
    stricken for the transgression of my people?
<sup>9</sup> Although the servant had done no violence
    and had spoken no deceit,
  the servant was buried with the wicked,
    and with the rich in death.
<sup>10</sup> Yet it was the will of GOD [[*or* the LORD]] to bruise
    and put to grief this one,
  who, after choosing to become an offering for sin,
    shall see offspring, and enjoy long life;
  the will of GOD [[*or* the LORD]] shall prosper in the servant's hand;
<sup>11</sup>   my servant shall see the fruit of the soul's travail and be satisfied;
  by knowledge shall the righteous one, my servant,
    make many to be accounted righteous,
    and shall bear their iniquities.
<sup>12</sup> Therefore I will divide for this one a portion with the great,
    and my servant shall divide the spoil with the strong,
  because my servant poured out life and died,
    and was numbered with the transgressors,
  yet bore the sin of many,
    and made intercession for the transgressors.

### Psalm 22:1-18

<sup>1</sup> My God, my God, why have you forsaken me?
    Why are you so far from helping me, from the words of my groan-
      ing?
<sup>2</sup> O my God, I cry by day, but you do not answer;
    and by night, but find no rest.
<sup>3</sup> Yet you are holy,
    enthroned on the praises of Israel.
<sup>4</sup> In you our ancestors trusted;
    they trusted, and you delivered them.
<sup>5</sup> To you they cried, and were saved;
    in you they trusted, and were not disappointed.
<sup>6</sup> But I am a worm, not human at all;
    scorned by everyone, and despised by the people.

7 All who see me mock at me,
  they make mouths at me, they wag their heads and say,
8 "You trusted in GOD [[*or* the LORD]]; let God deliver you,
  let God rescue you, for God delights in you!"
9 Yet you, O God, are the one who took me from the womb;
  you kept me safe upon my mother's breasts.
10 Upon you I was cast from my birth,
  and since my mother bore me you have been my God.
11 Be not far from me,
  for trouble is near
  and there is none to help.
12 Many bulls encompass me,
  strong bulls of Bashan surround me;
13 they open wide their mouths at me,
  like a ravening and roaring lion.
14 I am poured out like water,
  and all my bones are out of joint;
 my heart is like wax,
  it is melted within my breast;
15 my strength is dried up like a potsherd,
  and my tongue cleaves to my jaws;
  you lay me in the dust of death.
16 Even dogs are round about me;
  a company of evildoers encircle me;
  they have pierced my hands and feet—
17 I can count all my bones—
  they stare and gloat over me;
18 they divide my garments among them,
  and for my raiment they cast lots.

## Lesson 2 ~ Hebrews 4:14-16; 5:7-9

*Jesus the high priest learns obedience through suffering.*

14 Since then we have a great high priest who has passed through the heavens, Jesus, the Child◇ of God, let us hold fast our confession. 15 For we have not a high priest who is unable to sympathize with our weaknesses, but one who in every respect has been tempted as we are, yet without sin. 16 Let us then with confidence draw near to the throne of grace, that we may receive mercy and find grace to help in time of need.

5:7 While in the flesh, Jesus offered up prayers and supplications, with loud cries and tears, to the one who was able to save him from death, and was heard for his godly fear. 8 Although a Child◇ [*of God**], Jesus learned obedience through suffering, 9 and being made perfect, became the source of eternal salvation to all who obey Jesus.


## Gospel ~ John 18–19 (or 19:17-30)

*John tells of the arrest and crucifixion of Jesus.*

1 After praying for the disciples, Jesus went forth with them across the Kidron valley, where there was a garden, which they entered. 2 Now Judas, who betrayed him, also knew the place; for Jesus often met there with the disciples. 3 So Judas, procuring a band of soldiers and some officers from the chief priests and the Pharisees, went there with lanterns and torches and weapons. 4 Then Jesus, knowing all that was to befall him, came forward and said to them, "Whom do you seek?" 5 They answered, "Jesus of Nazareth." Jesus said to them, "I am the one." Judas, the betrayer, was standing with them. 6 When Jesus said to them, "I am the one," they drew back and fell to the ground. 7 Again Jesus asked them, "Whom do you seek?" And they said, "Jesus of Nazareth." 8 He answered, "I told you that I am the one; so, if you seek me, let these others go." 9 This was to fulfill the word which he had spoken, "Of those whom you gave me I lost not one." 10 Then Simon Peter, having a sword, drew it and struck the high priest's slave and cut off his right ear. The slave's name was Malchus. 11 Jesus said to Peter, "Put your sword into its sheath; shall I not drink the cup which [*God*] the Father [*and Mother***] has given me?"

12 So the band of soldiers and their captain and the officers of the religious authorities▽ seized and bound Jesus. 13 First they led him to

---

◇RSV 4:14 *Son;* 5:8 *Although he was a Son.* See Appendix.
*Addition to the text.
**Addition to the text. See "Metaphor" and "God the Father and Mother" in the Appendix.
▽RSV *the Jews.* See Appendix.

Annas, who was the father-in-law of Caiaphas, the high priest that year. [14] It was Caiaphas who had given counsel to the religious authorities[∇] that it was expedient that one person should die for the people.

[15] Simon Peter followed Jesus, and so did another disciple, who was known to the high priest, and who entered the court of the high priest along with Jesus, [16] while Peter stood outside at the door. So the other disciple, who was known to the high priest, went out and spoke to the maid who kept the door, and brought Peter in. [17] The maid who kept the door said to Peter, "Are not you also one of this man's disciples?" Peter said, "I am not." [18] Now the servants and officers had made a charcoal fire, because it was cold, and they were standing and warming themselves; Peter also was with them, standing and warming himself.

[19] The high priest then questioned Jesus about his disciples and teaching. [20] Jesus answered the high priest, "I have spoken openly to the world; I have always taught in synagogues and in the temple, where all Jews come together; I have said nothing secretly. [21] Why do you ask me? Ask those who have heard me, what I said to them; they know what I said." [22] When Jesus had said this, one of the officers standing by struck him with his hand, saying, "Is that how you answer the high priest?" [23] Jesus answered the officer, "If I have spoken wrongly, bear witness to the wrong; but if I have spoken rightly, why do you strike me?" [24] Annas then sent Jesus bound to Caiaphas the high priest.

[25] Now Simon Peter was standing and warming himself. They said to him, "Are not you also one of his disciples?" He denied it and said, "I am not." [26] One of the servants of the high priest, a relative of the slave whose ear Peter had cut off, asked, "Did I not see you in the garden with him?" [27] Peter again denied it; and at once the cock crowed.

[28] Then they led Jesus from the house of Caiaphas to the praetorium. It was early. They themselves did not enter the praetorium, so that they might not be defiled, but might eat the passover. [29] So Pilate went out to them and said, "What accusation do you bring against this person?" [30] They answered Pilate, "If this one were not an evildoer, we would not have handed him over." [31] Pilate said to them, "Take him yourselves and make judgment by your own law." The religious authorities[∇] said to Pilate, "It is not lawful for us to put anyone to death." [32] This was to fulfill the word which Jesus had spoken to show by what death he was to die.

[33] Pilate entered the praetorium again and called Jesus, and said, "Are you the King of the Jews?" [34] Jesus answered, "Do you say this of your own accord, or did others say it to you about me?" [35] Pilate answered, "Am I one of you?[⊕] Your own nation and the chief priests have handed you over

---

[∇] RSV the Jews. See Appendix.
[⊕] RSV "Am I a Jew?"

to me; what have you done?" ³⁶ Jesus answered, "My dominion✫ is not of this world; if my dominion✫ were of this world, my servants would fight, that I might not be handed over to the religious authorities;▽ but my dominion✫ is not from the world." ³⁷ Pilate said to Jesus, "So you are a king?" Jesus answered, "You say that I am a king. For this I was born, and for this I have come into the world, to bear witness to the truth. Everyone who is of the truth hears my voice." ³⁸ Pilate said to Jesus, "What is truth?"

And having said this, Pilate went out to the religious authorities▽ again, and told them, "I find no crime in this person. ³⁹ But you have a custom that I should release someone for you at the Passover; will you have me release for you the King of the Jews?" ⁴⁰ They cried out again, "Not Jesus, but Barabbas!" Now Barabbas was a robber.

¹⁹:¹ Then Pilate had Jesus scourged. ² And the soldiers plaited a crown of thorns, and put it on Jesus' head, and arrayed him in a purple robe; ³ they came up, saying, "Hail, King of the Jews!" and struck him with their hands. ⁴ Pilate went out again, and said to them, "See, I am bringing him out to you, that you may know that I find no crime in him." ⁵ So Jesus came out, wearing the crown of thorns and the purple robe. Pilate said to them, "Here he is!" ⁶ When the chief priests and the officers saw Jesus, they cried out, "Crucify, crucify!" Pilate said to them, "Take him your-selves and crucify him, for I find no crime in him." ⁷ The religious authorities▽ answered Pilate, "We have a law, and by that law Jesus ought to die, because he has made himself the Child◇ of God." ⁸ Hearing these words, Pilate was the more afraid. ⁹ Pilate entered the praetorium again and said to Jesus, "Where are you from?" But Jesus gave no answer. ¹⁰ Pilate therefore said to him, "You will not speak to me? Do you not know that I have power to release you, and power to crucify you?" ¹¹ Jesus replied, "You would have no power over me unless it had been given you from above; therefore the one who delivered me to you has the greater sin."

¹² Upon this Pilate sought to release Jesus, but the religious au-thorities▽ cried out, "If you release this person, you are not Caesar's friend; everyone who claims to be a king opposes Caesar." ¹³ Hearing these words, Pilate brought Jesus out and sat down on the judgment seat at a place called The Pavement, and in Hebrew, Gabbatha. ¹⁴ Now it was the day of Preparation of the Passover; it was about the sixth hour. Pilate said to the Jews, "Behold your King!" ¹⁵ They cried out, "Away, away with him, crucify him!" Pilate said to them, "Shall I crucify your King?" The chief priests answered, "We have no king but Caesar." ¹⁶ Then Pilate handed him over to them to be crucified.

---

✫ RSV *kingship*. See Appendix.
▽ RSV 18:38; 19:12 *the Jews;* 19:7 *The Jews.* See Appendix.
◇ RSV *Son.*

¹⁷ So they took Jesus, who went out bearing his own cross, to the place called the place of a skull, which is called in Hebrew Golgotha. ¹⁸ There they crucified him, along with two others, one on either side, and Jesus between them. ¹⁹ Pilate also wrote a title and put it on the cross; it read, "Jesus of Nazareth, the King of the Jews." ²⁰ Many of the Jews read this title, for the place where Jesus was crucified was near the city; and it was written in Hebrew, in Latin, and in Greek. ²¹ The chief priests of the Jews then said to Pilate, "Do not write, 'The King of the Jews,' but, 'This one said, I am King of the Jews.'" ²² Pilate answered, "What I have written I have written."

²³ When the soldiers had crucified Jesus they took his garments and made four parts, one for each soldier; also his tunic. But the tunic was without seam, woven from top to bottom; ²⁴ so they said to one another, "Let us not tear it, but cast lots for it to see whose it shall be." This was to fulfill the scripture,

"They parted my garments among them,
and for my clothing they cast lots."

²⁵ So the soldiers did this. But standing by the cross of Jesus were his mother, and his mother's sister, Mary the wife of Clopas, and Mary Magdalene. ²⁶ When Jesus saw his mother, and the disciple whom he loved standing near, he said to his mother, "Woman, behold, your child!" ²⁷ Then Jesus said to the disciple, "Behold, your mother!" And from that hour the disciple took her home.

²⁸ After this, Jesus, knowing that all was now finished, said (to fulfill the scripture), "I thirst." ²⁹ A bowl full of vinegar stood there; so they put a sponge full of the vinegar on hyssop and held it to his mouth. ³⁰ After receiving the vinegar, Jesus said, "It is finished," and bowed his head and gave up the spirit.

³¹ Since it was the day of Preparation, in order to prevent the bodies from remaining on the cross on the sabbath (for that sabbath was a high day), the religious authorities▽ asked Pilate that their legs might be broken, and that they might be taken away. ³² So the soldiers came and broke the legs of the first, and of the other who had been crucified with Jesus; ³³ but when they came to Jesus and saw that he was already dead, they did not break his legs. ³⁴ But one of the soldiers pierced Jesus' side with a spear, and at once there came out blood and water. ³⁵ The one who saw it has borne witness—this testimony is true, and the witness knows that it is the truth—that you also may believe. ³⁶ For these things took place that the scripture might be fulfilled, "Not a bone of him shall be broken." ³⁷ And again another scripture says, "They shall look on the one whom they have pierced."

---

▽ RSV *the Jews*. See Appendix.

$^{38}$ After this Joseph of Arimathea, who was a disciple of Jesus, but secretly, for fear of the religious authorities,$^{\triangledown}$ asked Pilate for permission to take away the body of Jesus, and Pilate granted it. So Joseph came and took away Jesus' body. $^{39}$ Nicodemus also, who had at first come to Jesus by night, came bringing a mixture of myrrh and aloes, about a hundred pounds' weight. $^{40}$ They took the body of Jesus, and bound it in linen cloths with the spices, as is the burial custom of the Jews. $^{41}$ Now in the place where Jesus was crucified there was a garden, and in the garden a new tomb where no one had ever been laid. $^{42}$ So because of the Jewish day of Preparation, as the tomb was close at hand, they laid Jesus there.

---

$\triangledown$ RSV *the Jews*. See Appendix.

# EASTER

*(If the first lesson is read from the Old Testament, the lection from Acts should be read as Lesson 2.)*

## Lesson 1 ~ Acts 10:34-43

*Peter preaches about Jesus' life, death, and resurrection.*

34 Peter proclaimed, "Truly I perceive that God shows no partiality, 35 but in every nation anyone who fears God and does what is right is acceptable to God. 36 You know the word which God sent to Israel, preaching good news of peace by Jesus Christ (Christ is Sovereign [or Lord] of all), 37 the word which was proclaimed throughout all Judea, beginning from Galilee after the baptism which John preached: 38 how God anointed Jesus of Nazareth with the Holy Spirit and with power; how Jesus went about doing good and healing all that were oppressed by the devil, for God was with him. 39 And we are witnesses to all that Jesus did both in Judea and in Jerusalem. They put Jesus to death by hanging him on a tree; 40 but God raised Jesus on the third day and made Jesus manifest; 41 not to all the people but to us who were chosen by God as witnesses, who ate and drank with Jesus after the resurrection from the dead. 42 And Jesus commanded us to preach to the people, and to testify that Jesus is the one ordained by God to be judge of the living and the dead. 43 To this one all the prophets bear witness that everyone who believes in Jesus Christ receives forgiveness of sins through Jesus' name."

## Lesson 1 (alternate) ~ Isaiah 65:17-25

*The prophet proclaims God's promise of new heavens and a new earth.*

17 For I create new heavens and a new earth;
    and the former things shall not be remembered
    or come into mind.
18 But be glad and rejoice forever
    in that which I create;
  for I create Jerusalem a rejoicing,
    and its people a joy.
19 I will rejoice in Jerusalem,
    and be glad in my people;
  no more shall be heard in it the sound of weeping
    and the cry of distress.
20 No more shall there be in it
    an infant that lives but a few days,

124

or an old person who does not fill out a lifetime,
for the child shall die a hundred years old,
and the sinner a hundred years old shall be accursed.
21 They shall build houses and inhabit them;
they shall plant vineyards and eat their fruit.
22 They shall not build and another inhabit;
they shall not plant and another eat;
for like the days of a tree shall the days of my people be,
and my chosen shall long enjoy the work of their hands.
23 They shall not labor in vain,
or bear children for calamity;
for they shall be the offspring of the blessed of GOD [[or the LORD]],
and their children with them.
24 Before they call I will answer,
while they are yet speaking I will hear.
25 The wolf and the lamb shall feed together,
the lion shall eat straw like the ox;
and dust shall be the serpent's food.
They shall not hurt or destroy
in all my holy mountain,

says the SOVEREIGN [[or LORD]].


### Psalm 118:14-24

14 GOD [[or The LORD]] is my strength and my song,
and has become my salvation.
15 Hark, glad songs of victory
in the tents of the righteous:
"The right hand of GOD [[or the LORD]] does valiantly,
16     the right hand of GOD [[or the LORD]] is exalted,
the right hand of GOD [[or the LORD]] does valiantly!"
17 I shall not die, but I shall live,
and recount the deeds of GOD [[or the LORD]].
18 GOD [[or The LORD]] has chastened me sorely,
but has not given me over to death.
19 Open to me the gates of righteousness,
that I may enter through them
and give thanks to GOD [[or the LORD]].
20 This is the gate of GOD [[or the LORD]];
the righteous shall enter through it.
21 I thank you that you have answered me
and have become my salvation.

22 The stone which the builders rejected
  has become the head of the corner.
23 This is GOD'S 〚*or* the LORD'S〛 doing;
  it is marvelous in our eyes.
24 This is the day which GOD 〚*or* the LORD〛 has made;
  let us rejoice and be glad in it.


## Lesson 2 ~ 1 Corinthians 15:19-26

*(If Isaiah 65:17-25 is read as the first lesson, Acts 10:34-43 should be read as Lesson 2.)*

*Paul writes about the resurrection of Christ.*

19 If for only this life we have hoped in Christ, we are of all people most to be pitied.

20 But in fact Christ has been raised from the dead, the firstfruits of those who have fallen asleep. 21 For as by a human being came death, by a human being has come also the resurrection of the dead. 22 For as in Adam all die, so also in Christ shall all be made alive. 23 But each in the proper order: Christ the first fruits, then at Christ's coming those who belong to Christ. 24 Then comes the end, when Christ delivers the sovereignty☆ to God the Father [*and Mother**], after destroying every rule and every authority and power. 25 For Christ must reign until all enemies are put under Christ's feet. 26 The last enemy to be destroyed is death.

---

☆RSV *kingdom*. See Appendix.
*Addition to the text. See "Metaphor" and "God the Father and Mother" in the Appendix.

# Gospel ~ John 20:1-18

*The risen Christ appears to Mary Magdalene.*

¹ Now on the first day of the week Mary Magdalene came to the tomb early, while it was still dark, and saw that the stone had been taken away from the tomb. ² So she ran, and went to Simon Peter and the other disciple, the one whom Jesus loved, and said to them, "They have taken the Sovereign [[*or* Lord]] out of the tomb, and we do not know where they have laid him." ³ Peter then came out with the other disciple, and they went toward the tomb. ⁴ They both ran, but the other disciple outran Peter, reached the tomb first, ⁵ and stooping to look in, saw the linen cloths lying there, but did not go in. ⁶ Then Simon Peter came, following after, and went into the tomb; Peter saw the linen cloths lying, ⁷ and the napkin, which had been on Jesus' head, not lying with the linen cloths but rolled up in a place by itself. ⁸ Then the other disciple, who reached the tomb first, also went in, and saw and believed; ⁹ for as yet they did not know the scripture, that Jesus must rise from the dead. ¹⁰ Then the disciples went back to their homes.

¹¹ But Mary stood weeping outside the tomb, and as she wept she stooped to look into the tomb; ¹² and she saw two angels in white, sitting where the body of Jesus had lain, one at the head and one at the feet. ¹³ They said to her, "Woman, why are you weeping?" She said to them, "Because they have taken away my Sovereign [[*or* Lord]], and I do not know where they have laid him." ¹⁴ Saying this, she turned round and saw Jesus standing, but she did not know that it was Jesus. ¹⁵ Jesus said to her, "Woman, why are you weeping? Whom do you seek?" Supposing Jesus to be the gardener, she answered, "Sir, if you have carried Jesus away, tell me where you have laid him, and I will take him away." ¹⁶ Jesus said to her, "Mary." She turned and responded in Hebrew, "Rabboni!" (which means Teacher). ¹⁷ Jesus said to her, "Do not hold me, for I have not yet ascended to God; but go to my friends and say to them, I am ascending to [*God*] my Father [*and Mother**] and your Father [*and Mother**], to my God and your God." ¹⁸ Mary Magdalene went and said to the disciples, "I have seen the Sovereign [[*or* Lord]]"; and she told them that Jesus had said these things to her.

---

*Addition to the text. See "Metaphor" and "God the Father and Mother" in the Appendix.

## Gospel (alternate) ~ Luke 24:1-12 [+]

*Mary Magdalene, Joanna, Mary the mother of James, and other women discover the tomb to be empty.*

[1] On the first day of the week, at early dawn, the women went to the tomb, taking the spices which they had prepared. [2] And they found the stone rolled away from the tomb, [3] but when they went in they did not find the body. [4] While they were perplexed about this, two men stood by them in dazzling apparel; [5] and as the women were frightened and bowed their faces to the ground, the two said to them, "Why do you seek the living among the dead? [6] Remember how Jesus told you, while still in Galilee, [7] that the Human One[O] must be delivered into the hands of sinners, and be crucified, and on the third day rise." [8] And the women remembered these words, [9] and returning from the tomb they told all this to the eleven and to all the rest. [10] Now it was Mary Magdalene and Joanna and Mary the mother of James and the other women with them who told this to the apostles; [11] but these words seemed to the apostles an idle tale, and they did not believe the women. [12] But Peter rose and ran to the tomb; stooping and looking in, he saw the linen cloths by themselves; and he went home wondering at what had happened.

---

[+] RSV puts v. 12 in a footnote.
[O] RSV *Son of man*. See Appendix.

# EASTER EVENING

*(If the first lesson is read from the Old Testament, the lection from Acts should be read as Lesson 2.)*

## Lesson 1 ~ Acts 5:29-32

*Peter and the apostles bear witness to the risen Christ.*

29 But Peter and the apostles answered, "We must obey God rather than human beings. 30 The God of our ancestors raised Jesus, whom you killed by hanging on a tree. 31 God exalted this Jesus at God's right hand as Leader and Savior, to give repentance to Israel and forgiveness of sins. 32 And we are witnesses to these things, and so is the Holy Spirit whom God has given to those who obey God."

## Lesson 1 (alternate) ~ Daniel 12:1-3

*Daniel prophesies the events of the end time.*

1 At that time shall arise Michael, the great prince who has charge of your people. And there shall be a time of trouble, such as never has been since there was a nation till that time; but at that time your people shall be delivered, everyone whose name shall be found written in the book. 2 And many of those who sleep in the dust of the earth shall awake, some to everlasting life, and some to shame and everlasting contempt. 3 And those who are wise shall shine like the brightness of the firmament; and those who turn many to righteousness, like the stars forever and ever.

## Psalm 150

1 Praise GOD [[or the LORD]]!
 Praise God in the sanctuary;
  praise God in the mighty firmament!
2 Praise God for mighty deeds;
  praise God according to God's exceeding greatness!
3 Praise God with trumpet sound;
  praise God with lute and harp!
4 Praise God with timbrel and dance;
  praise God with strings and pipe!
5 Praise God with sounding cymbals;
  praise God with loud clashing cymbals!
6 Let everything that breathes praise GOD [[or the LORD]]!
 Praise GOD [[or the LORD]]!

## Lesson 2 ~ 1 Corinthians 5:6-8

*(If Daniel 12:1-3 is read as the first lesson, Acts 5:29-32 should be read as Lesson 2.)*

*Paul writes about the bread of the new passover.*

⁶ Your boasting is not good. Do you not know that a little leaven leavens the whole lump? ⁷ Cleanse out the old leaven that you may be a new lump, as you really are unleavened. For Christ, our paschal lamb, has been sacrificed. ⁸ Let us, therefore, celebrate the festival, not with the old leaven, the leaven of malice and evil, but with the unleavened bread of sincerity and truth.

## Gospel ~ Luke 24:13-49

*Jesus meets two disciples on the road to Emmaus.*

¹³ That very day two of the disciples were going to a village named Emmaus, about seven miles from Jerusalem, ¹⁴ and talking with each other about all these things that had happened. ¹⁵ While they were talking and discussing together, Jesus drew near and went with them. ¹⁶ But their eyes were kept from recognizing Jesus. ¹⁷ And Jesus said to them, "What is this conversation which you are holding with each other as you walk?" And they stood still, looking sad. ¹⁸ Then one of them, named Cleopas, answered, "Are you the only visitor to Jerusalem who does not know the things that have happened there in these days?" ¹⁹ And Jesus said to them, "What things?" And they said, "Concerning Jesus of Nazareth, who was a prophet mighty in deed and word before God and all the people, ²⁰ and how our chief priests and rulers delivered up this Jesus to be condemned to death, and crucified him. ²¹ But we had hoped that Jesus was the one to redeem Israel. Yes, and besides all this, it is now the third day since this happened. ²² Moreover, some women of our company amazed us. They were at the tomb early in the morning ²³ and did not find Jesus' body; and they came back saying that they had even seen a vision of angels, who said that Jesus was alive. ²⁴ Some of those who were with us went to the tomb, and found it just as the women had said; but Jesus they did not see." ²⁵ And Jesus said to them, "O foolish ones, and slow of heart to believe all that the prophets have spoken! ²⁶ Was it not necessary that the Christ should suffer these things and be glorified?" ²⁷ And beginning with Moses and all the prophets, Jesus interpreted to them in all the scriptures the things concerning the Christ.

²⁸ So they drew near to the village to which they were going. Jesus appeared to be going further, ²⁹ but they urged against it, saying, "Stay with us, for it is toward evening and the day is now far spent." So Jesus

went in to stay with them. ³⁰While at table with them, Jesus took the bread and blessed, and broke it, and gave it to them. ³¹And their eyes were opened and they recognized Jesus, who then vanished out of their sight. ³²They said to each other, "Did not our hearts burn within us while Jesus talked to us on the road, and opened to us the scriptures?" ³³And they rose that same hour and returned to Jerusalem; and they found the eleven gathered together and those who were with them, ³⁴who said, "The Sovereign [or Lord] has risen indeed, and has appeared to Simon!" ³⁵Then they told what had happened on the road, and how Jesus was known to them in the breaking of the bread.

³⁶As they were saying this, that very Jesus stood among them. ³⁷But they were startled and frightened, and supposed that they saw a spirit. ³⁸And Jesus said to them, "Why are you troubled, and why do questionings rise in your hearts? ³⁹See my hands and my feet, that it is I myself; handle me, and see; for a spirit has not flesh and bones as you see that I have." ⁴¹And while they still disbelieved for joy, and wondered, Jesus said to them, "Have you anything here to eat?" ⁴²They gave Jesus a piece of broiled fish, ⁴³and Jesus took it and ate before them.

⁴⁴Then Jesus said to them, "These are my words which I spoke to you, while I was still with you, that everything written about me in the law of Moses and the prophets and the psalms must be fulfilled." ⁴⁵Then Jesus opened their minds to understand the scriptures, ⁴⁶and said to them, "Thus it is written, that the Christ should suffer and on the third day rise from the dead, ⁴⁷and that repentance and forgiveness of sins should be preached in Christ's name to all nations, beginning from Jerusalem. ⁴⁸You are witnesses of these things. ⁴⁹And I am sending the promise of [God] my Father [and Mother*] upon you; but stay in the city until you are clothed with power from on high."

---

*Addition to the text. See "Metaphor" and "God the Father and Mother" in the Appendix.

# EASTER 2

## Lesson 1 ~ Acts 5:27-32

*Peter and the apostles bear witness to the risen Christ.*

27 When the officers had brought the apostles, they set them before the council. And the high priest questioned them, 28 saying, "We strictly charged you not to teach in the name of Jesus, yet here you have filled Jerusalem with your teaching and you intend to bring the blood of this person upon us." 29 But Peter and the apostles answered, "We must obey God rather than human beings. 30 The God of our ancestors raised Jesus, whom you killed by hanging on a tree. 31 God exalted this Jesus at God's right hand as Leader and Savior, to give repentance to Israel and forgiveness of sins. 32 And we are witnesses to these things, and so is the Holy Spirit whom God has given to those who obey God."

## Psalm 2

1 Why do the nations conspire,
    and the peoples plot in vain?
2 The kings of the earth set themselves,
    and the rulers take counsel together,
    against GOD [[or the LORD]] and God's anointed, saying,
3 "Let us burst their bonds asunder,
    and cast their cords from us."
4 The One who sits in the heavens laughs,
    and has them in derision.
5 Then God will speak to them in anger,
    and terrify them in fury, saying,
6 "I have set my ruler⬚
    on Zion, my holy hill."
7 I will tell of the decree of GOD [[or the LORD]]:
  God said to me, "You are my child,
    today I have begotten you.
8 Ask of me, and I will make the nations your heritage,
    and the ends of the earth your possession.
9 You shall break them with a rod of iron,
    and dash them in pieces like a potter's vessel."

---

⬚RSV *king*. See Appendix.

¹⁰ Now therefore, O kings, be wise;
  be warned, O rulers of the earth.
¹¹ Serve GOD [or the LORD] with fear,
  with trembling ¹²kiss God's feet,
  lest God be angry, and you perish in the way;
  for God's wrath is quickly kindled.
  Blessed are all who take refuge in God.

## Lesson 2 ~ Revelation 1:4b-8

*John addresses the seven churches in the province of Asia.*

⁴ Grace to you and peace from the one who is and who was and who is to come, and from the seven spirits who are before the throne, ⁵and from Jesus Christ the faithful witness, the firstborn of the dead, and the ruler of kings on earth.

To the one who loves us and has freed us from our sins by a blood sacrifice ⁶and has made us a nation☆ and priests to God, Jesus' Father [*and Mother**], to whom be glory and dominion forever and ever. Amen. ⁷That very one is coming with the clouds, and will be seen by every eye, by those who pierced that one, and on account of whom all tribes of the earth will wail. Even so. Amen.

⁸ "I am the Alpha and the Omega," says the Sovereign [or Lord] God, who is and who was and who is to come, the Almighty.

---

☆RSV *kingdom*. See Appendix.
*Addition to the text. RSV *priests to his God and Father*. See "Metaphor" and "God the Father and Mother" in the Appendix.

## Gospel ~ John 20:19-31

*The risen Christ appears to Thomas.*

19 On the evening of that day, the first day of the week, the doors being shut where the disciples were, for fear of the religious authorities,▽ Jesus came and stood among them and said to them, "Peace be with you." 20 Having said this, Jesus showed them Jesus' hands and side. Then the disciples were glad when they saw the Sovereign [[or Lord]]. 21 Jesus said to them again, "Peace be with you. As [God] the Father [and Mother*] has sent me, even so I send you." 22 Having said this, Jesus breathed on them, and said to them, "Receive the Holy Spirit. 23 If you forgive the sins of any, they are forgiven; if you retain the sins of any, they are retained."

24 Now Thomas, one of the twelve, called the Twin, was not with them when Jesus came. 25 So the other disciples told him, "We have seen the Sovereign [[or Lord]]." But Thomas said to them, "Unless I see in Jesus' hands the print of the nails, and place my finger in the mark of the nails, and place my hand in Jesus' side, I will not believe."

26 Eight days later, the disciples were again in the house, and Thomas was with them. The doors were shut, but Jesus came and stood among them, and said, "Peace be with you." 27 Then Jesus said to Thomas, "Put your finger here, and see my hands; and put out your hand, and place it in my side; do not be faithless, but believing." 28 Thomas answered, "My Sovereign [[or Lord]] and my God!" 29 Jesus said to Thomas, "Have you believed because you have seen me? Blessed are those who have not seen and yet believe."

30 Now Jesus did many other signs in the presence of the disciples, which are not written in this book; 31 but these are written that you may believe that Jesus is the Christ, the Child◇ of God, and that believing you may have life in Christ's name.

---

▽RSV *the Jews*. See Appendix.
*Addition to the text. See "Metaphor" and "God the Father and Mother" in the Appendix.
◇RSV *Son*. See Appendix.

# EASTER 3

## Lesson 1 ~ Acts 9:1-20

*Saul is chosen to carry Christ's name to the Gentiles.*

[1] But Saul, still breathing threats and murder against the disciples of the Sovereign [or Lord], went to the high priest [2] and asked for letters to the synagogues at Damascus, so that if Saul found any belonging to the Way, men or women, he might bring them bound to Jerusalem. [3] Now as Saul journeyed he approached Damascus, and suddenly a light from heaven flashed about him. [4] And he fell to the ground and heard a voice saying to him, "Saul, Saul, why do you persecute me?" [5] And Saul said, "Who are you, Sovereign [or Lord]?" And the answer came, "I am Jesus, whom you are persecuting; [6] but rise and enter the city, and you will be told what you are to do." [7] The men who were traveling with Saul stood speechless, hearing the voice but seeing no one. [8] Saul arose from the ground; and when his eyes were opened, he could see nothing; so they led him by the hand and brought him into Damascus. [9] And for three days Saul was without sight, and neither ate nor drank.

[10] Now there was a disciple at Damascus named Ananias. The Sovereign [or Lord] said to him in a vision, "Ananias." And he said, "Here I am, Sovereign [or Lord]." [11] And the Sovereign [or Lord] said to him, "Rise and go to the street called Straight, and inquire in the house of Judas for a man of Tarsus named Saul; for he is praying, [12] and he has seen a man named Ananias come in and lay his hands on him so that he might regain his sight." [13] But Ananias answered, "Sovereign [or Lord], I have heard from many about this man, how much evil he has done to your saints at Jerusalem; [14] and here Saul has authority from the chief priests to bind all who call upon your name." [15] But the Sovereign [or Lord] said to Ananias, "Go, for Saul is a chosen instrument of mine to carry my name before the Gentiles and rulers☐ and the children of Israel; [16] for I will show Saul how much he must suffer for the sake of my name." [17] So Ananias departed and entered the house. And laying his hands on Saul he said, "Brother Saul, the Sovereign [or Lord] Jesus who appeared to you on the road by which you came, has sent me that you may regain your sight and be filled with the Holy Spirit." [18] And immediately something like scales fell from Saul's eyes and he regained his sight. Then he rose and was baptized, [19] and took food and was strengthened.

For several days Saul was with the disciples at Damascus. [20] And in the synagogues immediately he proclaimed Jesus, saying, "This one is the Child◇ of God."

---

☐RSV *kings*. See Appendix.
◇RSV *Son*. See Appendix.

⁴ Sing praises to GOD [[or the LORD]], O you saints of God,
  and give thanks to God's holy name.
⁵ For God's anger is but for a moment,
  and God's favor is for a lifetime.
 Weeping may continue for the night,
  but joy comes with the morning.
⁶ As for me, I said in my prosperity,
  "I shall never be moved."
⁷ By your favor, O GOD [[or LORD]],
  you had established me as a strong mountain;
 you hid your face,
  I was dismayed.
⁸ To you, O GOD [[or LORD]], I cried;
  and to GOD [[or the LORD]] I made supplication:
⁹ "What profit is there in my death,
  if I go down to the Pit?
 Will the dust praise you?
  Will it tell of your faithfulness?
¹⁰ Hear, O GOD [[or LORD]], and be gracious to me!
  O GOD [[or LORD]], be my helper!"
¹¹ You have turned for me my mourning into dancing;
  you have loosed my sackcloth
  and girded me with gladness,
¹² that my soul may praise you and not be silent.
  O SOVEREIGN [[or LORD]] my God, I will give thanks to you forever.

## Lesson 2 ~ Revelation 5:11-14

*All creatures in heaven and on earth praise the Lamb and the one seated on the throne.*

[11] Then I looked, and I heard around the throne and the living creatures and the elders the voice of many angels, numbering myriads of myriads and thousands of thousands, [12] saying with a loud voice, "Worthy is the Lamb who was slain, to receive power and wealth and wisdom and might and honor and glory and blessing!" [13] And I heard every creature in heaven and on earth and under the earth and in the sea, and all therein, saying, "To the one who sits upon the throne and to the Lamb be blessing and honor and glory and might forever and ever!" [14] And the four living creatures said, "Amen!" and the elders fell down and worshiped.

## Gospel ~ John 21:1-19 (or 15-19)

*The risen Jesus appears to the disciples and commissions Simon Peter to care for the community.*

[1] Jesus appeared again to the disciples by the Sea of Tiberias, and appeared in this way. [2] Simon Peter, Thomas called the Twin, Nathanael of Cana in Galilee, the sons of Zebedee, and two other disciples were together. [3] Simon Peter said to them, "I am going fishing." They said to him, "We will go with you." They went out and got into the boat; but that night they caught nothing.

[4] Just as the day was breaking, Jesus stood on the beach; yet the disciples did not know that it was Jesus. [5] Jesus said to them, "Children, have you any fish?" They answered, "No." [6] Jesus said to them, "Cast the net on the right side of the boat, and you will find some." So they cast it, and now they were not able to haul it in, for the quantity of fish. [7] That disciple whom Jesus loved said to Peter, "It is the Sovereign [[or Lord]]!" When Simon Peter heard that it was the Sovereign [[or Lord]], he put on his clothes, for he was stripped for work, and sprang into the sea. [8] But the other disciples came in the boat, dragging the net full of fish, for they were not far from the land, but about a hundred yards off.

[9] When they got out on land, they saw a charcoal fire there, with fish lying on it, and bread. [10] Jesus said to them, "Bring some of the fish that you have just caught." [11] So Simon Peter went aboard and hauled the net ashore, full of large fish, a hundred and fifty-three of them; and although

there were so many, the net was not torn. [12] Jesus said to them, "Come and have breakfast." Now none of the disciples dared ask, "Who are you?" They knew it was the Sovereign [or Lord]. [13] Jesus came and took the bread and gave it to them, and so with the fish. [14] This was now the third time that Jesus was revealed to the disciples after being raised from the dead.

[15] When they had finished breakfast, Jesus said to Simon Peter, "Simon, son of John, do you love me more than these?" He said to Jesus, "Yes, Sovereign [or Lord]; you know that I love you." Jesus said to him, "Feed my lambs." [16] A second time Jesus said to him, "Simon, son of John, do you love me?" He replied, "Yes, Sovereign [or Lord]; you know that I love you." Jesus said to him, "Tend my sheep." [17] Jesus said to him the third time, "Simon, son of John, do you love me?" Peter was grieved because Jesus said to him the third time, "Do you love me?" And he said to Jesus, "Sovereign [or Lord], you know everything; you know that I love you." Jesus said to him, "Feed my sheep. [18] Truly, truly, I say to you, when you were young, you girded yourself and walked where you would; but when you are old, you will stretch out your hands, and another will gird you and carry you where you do not wish to go." [19] (This Jesus said to show by what death Peter was to glorify God.) And after this Jesus said to him, "Follow me."

# EASTER 4

## Lesson 1 ~ Acts 13:15-16, 26-33

*Paul and his companions proclaim the message of salvation through Christ.*

¹⁵ After the reading of the law and the prophets, the rulers of the synagogue sent to them, saying, "Friends, if you have any word of exhortation for the people, say it." ¹⁶ So Paul stood up, and motioning with his hand said:

²⁶ "Friends, descendants of the family of Abraham [*and Sarah*\*], and those among you that fear God, to us has been sent the message of this salvation. ²⁷ For those who live in Jerusalem and their rulers, because they did not recognize Jesus nor understand the utterances of the prophets which are read every sabbath, fulfilled these by condemning him. ²⁸ Though they could charge him with nothing deserving death, yet they asked Pilate to have him killed. ²⁹ And when they had fulfilled all that was written of him, they took the body down from the tree, and laid it in a tomb. ³⁰ But God raised Jesus from the dead, ³¹ who appeared for many days to those who came up with him from Galilee to Jerusalem, who are now Jesus' witnesses to the people. ³² And we bring you the good news that what God promised to our ancestors, ³³ God has fulfilled to us, their children, by raising Jesus; as also it is written in the second psalm,

'You are my Child,◇
today I have begotten you.' "

## Psalm 23

¹ GOD [*or* The LORD] is my shepherd, I shall not want;
²    God makes me lie down in green pastures,
and leads me beside still waters;
³    God restores my soul.
God leads me in paths of righteousness
   for God's name's sake.
⁴ Even though I walk through the valley of the shadow of death,
   I fear no evil;
for you are with me;
   your rod and your staff,
   they comfort me.

---

\*Addition to the text. See "Addition of Women's Names to the Text" in the Appendix.
◇RSV *Son*. See Appendix.

⁵ You prepare a table before me
    in the presence of my enemies;
  you anoint my head with oil,
    my cup overflows.
⁶ Surely goodness and mercy shall follow me
    all the days of my life;
  and I shall dwell in the house of GOD [[*or* the LORD]]
    forever.


### Lesson 2 ~ Revelation 7:9-17

*Survivors of great suffering praise God and the Lamb.*

⁹ After this I looked, and there was a great multitude which no one could number, from every nation, from all tribes and peoples and tongues, standing before the throne and before the Lamb, clothed in white robes, with palm branches in their hands, ¹⁰ and crying out with a loud voice, "Salvation belongs to our God who sits upon the throne, and to the Lamb!" ¹¹ And all the angels stood round the throne and round the elders and the four living creatures, and they fell on their faces before the throne and worshiped God, ¹² saying, "Amen! Blessing and glory and wisdom and thanksgiving and honor and power and might be to our God forever and ever! Amen."

¹³ Then one of the elders addressed me, saying, "Who are these, clothed in white robes, and from where have they come?" ¹⁴ I answered, "Sir, you know." And he said to me, "These are they who have come out of the great tribulation; they have washed their robes and made them pure in the blood of the Lamb.

¹⁵ Therefore they are before the throne of God,
    and serve God day and night within the temple;
    and the one who sits upon the throne will dwell with them.
¹⁶ They shall hunger no more, neither thirst anymore;
    the sun shall not strike them, nor any scorching heat.
¹⁷ For the Lamb in the midst of the throne will be their shepherd,
    and will guide them to springs of living water;
  and God will wipe away every tear from their eyes."

## Gospel ~ John 10:22-30

*At Hanukkah the religious authorities question Jesus about being the Christ.*

²² It was the feast of the Dedication at Jerusalem; ²³ it was winter, and Jesus was walking in the temple, in the portico of Solomon. ²⁴ So the religious authorities▽ gathered round Jesus and said to him, "How long will you keep us in suspense? If you are the Christ, tell us plainly." ²⁵ Jesus answered them, "I told you, and you do not believe. The works that I do in the name of [God] my Father [and Mother*], they bear witness to me; ²⁶ but you do not believe, because you do not belong to my sheep. ²⁷ My sheep hear my voice, and I know them, and they follow me; ²⁸ and I give them eternal life, and they shall never perish, and no one shall snatch them out of my hand. ²⁹ God,⊗ who has given them to me, is greater than all, and no one is able to snatch them out of God's⊗ hand. ³⁰ I and [God] the [Mother and*] Father are one."

---

▽RSV *the Jews*. See Appendix.

*Addition to the text. RSV *in my Father's name*. See "Metaphor" and "God the Father and Mother" in the Appendix.

⊗RSV v. 29a *My Father;* v. 29b *the Father's*. See Appendix.

# EASTER 5

## Lesson 1 (alternate) ~ Acts 16:11-15 +

*Paul preaches the gospel among the women of Philippi.*

[11] Setting sail therefore from Troas, we made a direct voyage to Samothrace, and the following day to Neapolis, [12] and from there to Philippi, which is the leading city of the district of Macedonia, and a Roman colony. We remained in this city some days; [13] and on the sabbath day we went outside the gate to the riverside, where we supposed there was a place of prayer; and we sat down and spoke to the women who had come together. [14] One who heard us was a woman named Lydia, from the city of Thyatira, a seller of purple goods, who was a worshiper of God. The Sovereign [or Lord] opened Lydia's heart to give heed to what was said by Paul. [15] And when she was baptized, with her household, she besought us, saying, "If you have judged me to be faithful to the Sovereign [or Lord], come to my house and stay." And she prevailed upon us.

## Lesson 1 ~ Acts 14:8-18

*Paul tells the people of Lystra that God is the source of all good things.*

[8] Now at Lystra there was a man sitting, who could not use his feet; he was lame from birth, and had never walked. [9] He listened to Paul speaking; and Paul, looking intently at him and seeing that he had faith to be made well, [10] said in a loud voice, "Stand upright on your feet." And he sprang up and walked. [11] And when the crowds saw what Paul had done, they lifted up their voices, saying in Lycaonian, "The gods have come down to us in the likeness of human beings!" [12] Barnabas they called Zeus, and Paul, because he was the chief speaker, they called Hermes. [13] And the priest of Zeus, whose temple was in front of the city, brought oxen and garlands to the gates and wanted to offer sacrifice with the people. [14] But when the apostles Barnabas and Paul heard of it, they tore their garments and rushed out among the multitude, crying, [15] "People, why are you doing this? We also are human, of like nature with you, and bring you good news, that you should turn from these vain things to a living God who made the heaven and the earth and the sea and all that is in them, [16] who in past generations allowed all the nations to walk in their own ways. [17] Yet God was not left without witness, bestowing benefits, giving you rains from heaven and fruitful seasons, satisfying your hearts with food and gladness." [18] With these words they scarcely restrained the people from offering sacrifice to them.

---

+ Lection added. See Appendix, p. 263.

¹³ GOD [[*or* The LORD]] is faithful in every word,
    and gracious in every deed.
¹⁴ GOD [[*or* The LORD]] upholds all who are falling,
    and raises up all who are bowed down.
¹⁵ The eyes of all look to you,
    and you give them their food in due season.
¹⁶ You open your hand,
    and satisfy the desire of every living thing.
¹⁷ GOD [[*or* The LORD]] is just in all God's ways,
    and kind in every act.
¹⁸ GOD [[*or* The LORD]] is near to all who call upon God,
    to all who call upon God in truth.
¹⁹ God fulfills the desire of all who fear God,
    and hears their cry, and saves them.
²⁰ GOD [[*or* The LORD]] preserves all who love God,
    but will destroy all the wicked.
²¹ My mouth will speak the praise of GOD [[*or* the LORD]],
    and let all flesh bless God's holy name forever and ever.

## Lesson 2 ~ Revelation 21:1-6

*The seer envisions a new heaven and a new earth.*

¹ Then I saw a new heaven and a new earth; for the first heaven and the first earth had passed away, and the sea was no more. ² And I saw the holy city, new Jerusalem, coming down out of heaven from God, prepared as a bride adorned for her husband; ³ and I heard a loud voice from the throne saying, "The dwelling of God is with human beings. God will dwell with them, and they shall be God's people, and God will indeed be with them. ⁴ God will wipe away every tear from their eyes, and death shall be no more, neither shall there be mourning nor crying nor pain anymore, for the former things have passed away."

⁵ And the one who sat upon the throne said, "See, I make all things new," to which was added, "Write this, for these words are trustworthy and true." ⁶ And the one who sat upon the throne said to me, "It is done! I am the Alpha and the Omega, the beginning and the end. To the thirsty I will give water without price from the fountain of the water of life."

# Gospel ~ John 13:31-35

*Jesus teaches the disciples to love one another.*

[31] When Judas had gone out, Jesus said, "Now is the Human One°
glorified, and in that one God is glorified; [32] if God is glorified in the
Human One, God will also glorify that very one in God's self, and will
glorify that one immediately. [33] Little children, yet a little while I am with
you. You will seek me; and as I said to the religious authorities▽ so now I
say to you, 'Where I am going you cannot come.' [34] A new commandment
I give to you, that you love one another; even as I have loved you, that you
also love one another. [35] By this all will know that you are my disciples, if
you have love for one another."

---

°RSV *Son of man*. See Appendix.
▽RSV *the Jews*. See Appendix.

# EASTER 6

## Lesson 1 ~ Acts 15:1-2, 22-29

*Delegates are sent from Jerusalem to Antioch to help resolve a dispute.*

[1] Some people came down from Judea and were teaching the believers, "Unless you are circumcised according to the custom of Moses, you cannot be saved." [2] And when Paul and Barnabas had no small dissension and debate with them, Paul and Barnabas and some of the others were appointed to go up to Jerusalem to the apostles and the elders about this question.

[22] Then it seemed good to the apostles and the elders, with the whole church, to choose delegates from among them and send them to Antioch with Paul and Barnabas. They sent Judas called Barsabbas, and Silas, leaders among them, [23] with the following letter: "The believers, both the apostles and the elders, to the believers who are of the Gentiles in Antioch and Syria and Cilicia, greeting. [24] Since we have heard that some persons from us have troubled you with words, unsettling your minds, although we gave them no instructions, [25] it has seemed good to us, having come to one accord, to choose delegates and send them to you with our beloved Barnabas and Paul, [26] men who have risked their lives for the sake of our Sovereign [or Lord] Jesus Christ. [27] We have therefore sent Judas and Silas, who themselves will tell you the same things by word of mouth. [28] For it has seemed good to the Holy Spirit and to us to lay upon you no greater burden than these necessary things: [29] that you abstain from what has been sacrificed to idols and from blood and from what is strangled and from unchastity. If you keep yourselves from these, you will do well. Farewell."

## Psalm 67

[1] May God be gracious to us and bless us
and make God's face to shine upon us,
[2] that your way may be known upon earth,
your saving power among all nations.
[3] Let the people praise you, O God;
let all the people praise you!
[4] Let the nations be glad and sing for joy,
for you judge the people with equity
and guide the nations upon earth.

$^5$ Let the people praise you, O God;
    let all the people praise you!
$^6$ The earth has yielded its increase;
    God, our God, has blessed us.
$^7$ God has blessed us;
    let all the ends of the earth fear God!


## Lesson 2 ~ Revelation 21:10, 22-27

*In a vision, the holy city of Jerusalem is seen coming down from heaven.*

$^{10}$ And in the Spirit the angel carried me away to a great, high mountain, and showed me the holy city Jerusalem coming down out of heaven from God.

$^{22}$ And I saw no temple in the city, for its temple is the Sovereign [[*or* Lord]] God the Almighty, and the Lamb. $^{23}$ And the city has no need of sun or moon to shine upon it, for the glory of God is its light, and its lamp is the Lamb. $^{24}$ By its light shall the nations walk; and the rulers□ of the earth shall bring their glory into it, $^{25}$ and its gates shall never be shut by day—and there shall be no night there; $^{26}$ they shall bring into it the glory and the honor of the nations. $^{27}$ But nothing unclean shall enter it, nor anyone who practices abomination or falsehood, but only those who are written in the Lamb's book of life.

---

□RSV *kings.* See Appendix.

## Gospel ~ John 14:23-29

*Those who love Jesus will not be left without comfort.*

²³ Jesus said, "If any love me, they will keep my word, and [*God*] my Father [*and Mother\**] will love them, and we will come to them and make our home with them. ²⁴ Those who do not love me do not keep my words; and the word which you hear is not mine but God's⊗ who sent me.

²⁵ "These things I have spoken to you, while I am still with you. ²⁶ But the Counselor, the Holy Spirit, whom God⊗ will send in my name, will teach you all things, and bring to your remembrance all that I have said to you. ²⁷ Peace I leave with you; my peace I give to you; not as the world gives do I give to you. Let not your hearts be troubled, neither let them be afraid. ²⁸ You heard me say to you, 'I go away, and I will come to you.' If you loved me, you would have rejoiced, because I go to God;⊗ for [*God*] the [*Mother and\**] Father is greater than I. ²⁹ And now I have told you before it takes place, so that when it does take place, you may believe."

---

\*Addition to the text. See "Metaphor" and "God the Father and Mother" in the Appendix.
⊗RSV v. 24 *the Father's;* vs. 26, 28 *the Father.* See Appendix.

# ASCENSION

*(Or on Easter 7)*

## Lesson 1 ~ Acts 1:1-11

*The risen Jesus is taken up into heaven.*

¹ In the first book, O Theophilus, I have dealt with all that Jesus began to do and teach, ² until the day when Jesus was taken up, having given commandment through the Holy Spirit to the apostles whom Jesus had chosen. ³ After the passion Jesus was seen alive by the apostles through many proofs, appearing to them during forty days, and speaking of the realm☆ of God. ⁴ And while staying with the apostles, Jesus charged them not to depart from Jerusalem, but to wait for the promise of God,⊗ which, Jesus said, "you heard from me, ⁵ for John baptized with water, but before many days you shall be baptized with the Holy Spirit."

⁶ So when the apostles had come together, they asked Jesus, "Sovereign [[*or* Lord]], will you at this time restore the realm☆ to Israel?" ⁷ Jesus said, "It is not for you to know times or seasons which have been fixed by God's⊗ own authority. ⁸ But you shall receive power when the Holy Spirit has come upon you; and you shall be my witnesses in Jerusalem and in all Judea and Samaria and to the end of the earth." ⁹ And having said this, as the apostles were looking on, Jesus was lifted up and carried on a cloud out of their sight. ¹⁰ And while they were gazing into heaven as Jesus went, two figures stood by them in white robes, ¹¹ and said, "People of Galilee, why do you stand looking into heaven? This Jesus, who was taken up from you into heaven, will come in the same way as you saw Jesus go into heaven."

## Psalm 47

¹ Clap your hands, all you people!
   Shout to God with loud songs of joy!
² For GOD [[*or* the LORD]], the Most High, is terrible,
   a great ruler⊡ over all the earth,
³ subduing all people under us,
   and nations under our feet,

---

☆RSV *kingdom*. See Appendix.
⊗RSV v. 4 *the Father;* v. 7 *the Father has fixed by his own authority.* See Appendix.
⊡RSV *king*. See Appendix.

$^4$ choosing our heritage for us,
     the pride of Jacob whom God loves.
$^5$ God has gone up with a shout,
     the SOVEREIGN [[or LORD]] with the sound of a trumpet.
$^6$ Sing praises to God, sing praises!
     Sing praises to our Ruler,□ sing praises!
$^7$ For God is the ruler□ of all the earth;
     sing praises with a psalm!
$^8$ God reigns over the nations,
     God sits on the holy throne.
$^9$ The nobles of the nations gather
     as the people of the God of Abraham.
For the shields of the earth belong to God,
     who is highly exalted!

## Lesson 2 ~ Ephesians 1:15-23

*The risen Christ is exalted as head over all.*

$^{15}$ For this reason, because I have heard of your faith in the Sovereign [[or Lord]] Jesus and your love toward all the saints, $^{16}$ I do not cease to give thanks for you, remembering you in my prayers, $^{17}$ that the God of our Sovereign [[or Lord]] Jesus Christ, the Father [and Mother*] of glory, may give you a spirit of wisdom and of revelation in the knowledge of God, $^{18}$ having the eyes of your hearts enlightened, that you may know what is the hope to which you have been called, what are the riches of God's glorious inheritance in the saints, $^{19}$ and what is the immeasurable greatness of God's power in us who believe, according to the working of God's great might $^{20}$ which was accomplished in Christ when God raised Christ from the dead and made Christ sit at God's right hand in the heavenly places, $^{21}$ far above all rule and authority and power and dominion, and above every name that is named, not only in this age but also in that which is to come; $^{22}$ and God has put all things under Christ's feet and has made Christ the head over all things for the church, $^{23}$ which is Christ's body, the fullness of the one who fills all in all.

---

□RSV v. 6 *King;* v. 7 *king.* See Appendix.
*Addition to the text. See "Metaphor" and "God the Father and Mother" in the Appendix.

## Gospel ~ Luke 24:46-53

*Jesus commissions the disciples and is parted from them.*

[46] And Jesus said to them, "Thus it is written, that the Christ should suffer and on the third day rise from the dead, [47] and that repentance and forgiveness of sins should be preached in Christ's name to all nations, beginning from Jerusalem. [48] You are witnesses of these things. [49] And I am sending the promise of [*God*] my Father [*and Mother*\*] upon you; but stay in the city until you are clothed with power from on high."

[50] Then Jesus led them out as far as Bethany, and with uplifted hands blessed them. [51] While blessing them, Jesus parted from them, and was carried up into heaven. [52] And they returned to Jerusalem with great joy, [53] and were continually in the temple blessing God.

## Gospel (alternate) ~ Mark 16:9-16, 19-20

*The risen Jesus appears first to Mary Magdalene and then to others, sending the disciples to preach the gospel.*

[9] Now having risen early on the first day of the week, Jesus appeared first to Mary Magdalene, from whom Jesus had cast out seven demons. [10] She went and told those who had been with Jesus, as they mourned and wept. [11] But when they heard that Jesus was alive and had been seen by her, they would not believe it.

[12] After this Jesus appeared in another form to two of them, as they were walking into the country. [13] And they went back and told the rest, but they did not believe them.

[14] Afterward Jesus appeared to the eleven themselves as they sat at table, and upbraided them for their unbelief and hardness of heart, because they had not believed those who saw Jesus after Jesus had risen. [15] And Jesus said to them, "Go into all the world and preach the gospel to the whole creation. [16] Whoever believes and is baptized will be saved; but whoever does not believe will be condemned."

[19] So then the Sovereign [[*or* Lord]] Jesus, after speaking to them, was taken up into heaven, and sat down at the right hand of God. [20] And they went forth and preached everywhere, while the Sovereign [[*or* Lord]] worked with them and confirmed the message by the signs that attended it. Amen.

---

\*Addition to the text. See "Metaphor" and "God the Father and Mother" in the Appendix.

# EASTER 7

## Lesson 1 ~ Acts 16:16-34

*After healing a girl who was a soothsayer, Paul and Silas are arrested for disturbing the city of Philippi.*

16 As we were going to the place of prayer, we were met by a slave girl who had a spirit of divination and brought her owners much gain by soothsaying. 17 She followed Paul and us, crying, "These men are servants of the Most High God, who proclaim to you the way of salvation." 18 And this she did for many days. But Paul was annoyed, and turned and said to the spirit, "I charge you in the name of Jesus Christ to come out of her." And it came out that very hour.

19 But when her owners saw that their hope of gain was gone, they seized Paul and Silas and dragged them into the market place before the rulers; 20 and when they had brought them to the magistrates they said, "These men are Jews and they are disturbing our city. 21 They advocate customs which it is not lawful for us Romans to accept or practice." 22 The crowd joined in attacking them; and the magistrates tore the garments off them and gave orders to beat them with rods. 23 And when they had inflicted many blows upon them, they threw them into prison, charging the jailer to keep them safely. 24 Having received this charge, he put them into the inner prison and fastened their feet in the stocks.

25 But about midnight Paul and Silas were praying and singing hymns to God, and the prisoners were listening to them, 26 and suddenly there was a great earthquake, so that the foundations of the prison were shaken; and immediately all the doors were opened and everyone's fetters were unfastened. 27 When the jailer woke and saw that the prison doors were open, he drew his sword and was about to kill himself, supposing that the prisoners had escaped. 28 But Paul cried with a loud voice, "Do not harm yourself, for we are all here." 29 And the jailer called for lights and rushed in, and trembling with fear he fell down before Paul and Silas, 30 and brought them out and said, "Sirs, what must I do to be saved?" 31 And they said, "Believe in the Sovereign [[*or* Lord]] Jesus, and you will be saved, you and your household." 32 And they spoke the word of the Sovereign [[*or* Lord]] to the jailer and to all that were in his house. 33 And he took them the same hour of the night, and washed their wounds, and he was baptized at once, with all his family. 34 Then he brought them up into his house, and set food before them, and rejoiced with all his household that he had believed in God.

# Psalm 97

¹ GOD [or The LORD] reigns; let the earth rejoice;
   let the many coastlands be glad!
² Clouds and thick darkness are round about God;
   righteousness and justice are the foundation of God's throne.
³ Fire goes before God,
   and burns up God's adversaries round about.
⁴ God's lightnings lighten the world;
   the earth sees and trembles.
⁵ The mountains melt like wax before the SOVEREIGN [or LORD],
   before the God [or Lord] of all the earth.
⁶ The heavens proclaim God's righteousness;
   and all people behold God's glory.
⁷ All worshipers of images are put to shame,
   who make their boast in worthless idols;
   all gods bow down before God.
⁸ Zion hears and is glad,
   and the daughters of Judah rejoice,
   because of your judgments, O GOD [or LORD].
⁹ For you, O GOD [or LORD], are most high over all the earth;
   you are exalted far above all gods.
¹⁰ GOD [or The LORD] loves those who hate evil,
   preserves the lives of the saints,
   and delivers them from the hand of the wicked.
¹¹ Light dawns for the righteous,
   and joy for the upright in heart.
¹² Rejoice in GOD [or the LORD], O you righteous,
   and give thanks to God's holy name!

## Lesson 2 ~ Revelation 22:12-14, 16-17, 20

*Jesus, the Alpha and the Omega, is coming soon.*

¹² "I am coming soon, bringing my recompense, to repay everyone for what they have done. ¹³ I am the Alpha and the Omega, the first and the last, the beginning and the end."

¹⁴ Blessed are those who wash their robes, so that they may have the right to the tree of life and that they may enter the city by the gates.

¹⁶ "I Jesus have sent my angel to you with this testimony for the churches. I am the root and the offspring of David, the bright morning star."

[17] The Spirit and the Bride say, "Come." And let whoever hears say, "Come." And let whoever is thirsty come; let whoever desires take the water of life without price.

[20] The one who testifies to these things says, "Surely I am coming soon." Amen. Come, Sovereign [[*or* Lord]] Jesus!

## Gospel ~ John 17:20-26

*Jesus commends the disciples to God's care.*

[20] I do not pray for these only, but also for those who believe in me through their word, [21] that they may all be one; even as you, [*O God, my Mother and*\*] Father, are in me, and I in you, that they also may be in us, so that the world may believe that you have sent me. [22] The glory which you have given me I have given to them, that they may be one even as we are one, [23] I in them and you in me, that they may become perfectly one, so that the world may know that you have sent me and have loved them even as you have loved me. [24] O God,⊗ I desire that they also, whom you have given me, may be with me where I am, to behold my glory which you have given me in your love for me before the foundation of the world. [25] O righteous God,⊗ the world has not known you, but I have known you; and these know that you have sent me. [26] I made known to them your name, and I will make it known, that the love with which you have loved me may be in them, and I in them.

---

\*Addition to the text. See "Metaphor" and "God the Father and Mother" in the Appendix.
⊗RSV v. 24 *Father;* v. 25 *O righteous Father.*

# PENTECOST

*(If the first lesson is read from the Old Testament, the lection from Acts should be read as Lesson 2.)*

## Lesson 1 ~ Acts 2:1-21

*Luke describes the day of Pentecost, when worshipers were filled with the Holy Spirit.*

[1] When the day of Pentecost had come, they were all together in one place. [2] And suddenly a sound came from heaven like the rush of a mighty wind, and it filled all the house where they were sitting. [3] And there appeared to them tongues as of fire, distributed and resting on each one of them. [4] And they were all filled with the Holy Spirit and began to speak in other tongues, as the Spirit gave them utterance.

[5] Now there were dwelling in Jerusalem devout Jews from every nation under heaven. [6] And at this sound the multitude came together, and they were bewildered, because they heard them speaking each in their own language. [7] And they were amazed and wondered, saying, "Are not all these who are speaking Galileans? [8] And how is it that we hear, each of us in our own native language? [9] Parthians and Medes and Elamites and residents of Mesopotamia, Judea and Cappadocia, Pontus and Asia, [10] Phrygia and Pamphylia, Egypt and the parts of Libya belonging to Cyrene, and visitors from Rome, both Jews and proselytes, [11] Cretans and Arabians, we hear them telling in our own tongues the mighty works of God." [12] And all were amazed and perplexed, saying to one another, "What does this mean?" [13] But others mocking said, "They are filled with new wine."

[14] But Peter, standing with the eleven, lifted up his voice and addressed them, "People of Judea and all who dwell in Jerusalem, let this be known to you, and give ear to my words. [15] For these people are not drunk, as you suppose, since it is only the third hour of the day; [16] but this is what was spoken by the prophet Joel:

[17] 'And in the last days it shall be, God declares,
that I will pour out my Spirit upon all flesh,
and your sons and your daughters shall prophesy,
and the young shall see visions,
and the old shall dream dreams;
[18] and in those days I will pour out my Spirit
on my servants, both men and women; and they shall prophesy.
[19] And I will show wonders in the heaven above
and signs on the earth beneath,
blood, and fire, and vapor of smoke;

²⁰ the sun shall be turned into night
    and the moon into blood,
    before the day of the Sovereign ⟦*or* Lord⟧ comes,
    the great and manifest day.
²¹ And it shall be that whoever calls on the name of the Sovereign ⟦*or*
    Lord⟧ shall be saved.'"


## Lesson 1 (alternate) ~ Genesis 11:1-9

*The tower of Babel is built.*

¹ Now the whole earth had one language and few words. ² And as people migrated from the east, they found a plain in the land of Shinar and settled there. ³ And they said to one another, "Come, let us make bricks, and burn them thoroughly." And they had brick for stone, and bitumen for mortar. ⁴ Then they said, "Come, let us build ourselves a city, and a tower with its top in the heavens, and let us make a name for ourselves, lest we be scattered abroad upon the face of the whole earth." ⁵ And GOD ⟦*or* the LORD⟧ came down to see the city and the tower, which the people had built. ⁶ And GOD ⟦*or* the LORD⟧ said, "Look, they are one people, and they have all one language; and this is only the beginning of what they will do; and nothing that they propose to do will now be impossible for them. ⁷ Come, let us go down, and there confuse their language, that they may not understand one another's speech." ⁸ So GOD ⟦*or* the LORD⟧ scattered them abroad from there over the face of all the earth, and they left off building the city. ⁹ Therefore its name was called Babel, because there GOD ⟦*or* the LORD⟧ confused the language of all the earth; and from there GOD ⟦*or* the LORD⟧ scattered them abroad over the face of all the earth.


## Psalm 104:24-34

²⁴ O GOD ⟦*or* LORD⟧, how manifold are your works!
    In wisdom you have made them all;
    the earth is full of your creatures.
²⁵ Yonder is the sea, great and wide,
    which teems with things innumerable,
    living things both small and great.
²⁶ There go the ships,
    and Leviathan which you formed to sport in it.
²⁷ These all look to you,
    to give them their food in due season.
²⁸ When you give to them, they gather it up;
    when you open your hand, they are filled with good things.

29 When you hide your face, they are dismayed;
    when you take away their breath, they die
    and return to their dust.
30 When you send forth your Spirit, they are created;
    and you renew the face of the ground.
31 May the glory of GOD [[or the LORD]] endure forever,
    may GOD [[or the LORD]] rejoice in the works of God,
32 who looks on the earth and it trembles,
    who touches the mountains and they smoke!
33 I will sing to GOD [[or the LORD]] as long as I live;
    I will sing praise to my God while I have being.
34 May my meditation be pleasing to God,
    in whom I rejoice.

### Lesson 2 ~ Romans 8:14-17

*Paul writes to the Christians at Rome about the Spirit.*

14 For all who are led by the Spirit of God are daughters and sons of God. 15 For you did not receive the spirit of slavery to fall back into fear, but you have received the spirit of adoption as children of God. When we cry, "[*God! my Mother and**] Father!" 16 it is the Spirit bearing witness with our spirit that we are children of God, 17 and if children, then heirs, heirs of God and joint heirs with Christ, provided we suffer with Christ in order that we may also be glorified with Christ.

---

*Addition to the text. RSV "Abba!" See "God the Father and Mother" in the Appendix.

156

# Gospel ~ John 14:8-17, 25-27

*Jesus promises to send the Counselor, the Spirit of truth.*

⁸ Philip said to Jesus, "Sovereign [[*or* Lord]], show us God,⊗ and we shall be satisfied." ⁹Jesus replied, "Have I been with you so long, and yet you do not know me, Philip? Whoever has seen me has seen God;⊗ how can you say, 'Show us God'⊗? ¹⁰Do you not believe that I am in God⊗ and God⊗ in me? The words that I say to you I do not speak on my own authority; but God⊗ who dwells in me does God's works. ¹¹Believe me that I am in God⊗ and God⊗ in me; or else believe me for the sake of the works themselves.

¹² "Truly, truly, I say to you, all who believe in me will also do the works that I do; and greater works than these will they do, because I go to God.⊗ ¹³Whatever you ask in my name, I will do it, that [*God*] the Father [*and Mother**] may be glorified in God's** Child◇; ¹⁴if you ask anything in my name, I will do it.

¹⁵ "If you love me, you will keep my commandments. ¹⁶And I will pray [*to God*] the [*Mother and**] Father, who will give you another Counselor, to be with you forever—¹⁷the Spirit of truth, whom the world cannot receive, because it neither sees nor knows this Spirit. But you know the Spirit, who dwells with you, and will be in you.

²⁵ "These things I have spoken to you, while I am still with you. ²⁶But the Counselor, the Holy Spirit, whom God⊗ will send in my name, will teach you all things, and bring to your remembrance all that I have said to you. ²⁷Peace I leave with you; my peace I give to you; not as the world gives do I give to you. Let not your hearts be troubled, neither let them be afraid."

---

⊗RSV *the Father.*
*Addition to the text. See "Metaphor" and "God the Father and Mother" in the Appendix.
**Addition to the text.
◇RSV *glorified in the Son.* See Appendix.

# TRINITY

## Lesson 1 ~ Proverbs 8:22-31

*Wisdom is present at creation.*

²² GOD [[*or* The LORD]] created me at the beginning of God's way, the
  first of the acts of old.
²³ Ages ago I was set up,
  at the first, before the beginning of the earth.
²⁴ When there were no depths I was brought forth,
  when there were no springs abounding with water.
²⁵ Before the mountains had been shaped,
  before the hills, I was brought forth;
²⁶ before God had made the earth with its fields,
  or the first of the dust of the world.
²⁷ When God established the heavens, I was there,
  when God drew a circle on the face of the deep,
²⁸ and made firm the skies above,
  when God established the fountains of the deep,
²⁹ and assigned to the sea its limit,
  so that the waters might not transgress God's command,
when God marked out the foundations of the earth,
³⁰  then I was beside God, like a skilled artisan;
and I was daily God's delight,
  rejoicing before God always,
³¹ rejoicing in God's inhabited world
  and delighting in humankind.


## Psalm 8

¹ O SOVEREIGN [[*or* LORD]], our God,
  how majestic is your name in all the earth!
You whose glory above the heavens is chanted
²  by the mouth of babies and infants,
you have founded a bulwark because of your foes,
  to still the enemy and the avenger.
³ When I look at your heavens, the work of your fingers,
  the moon and the stars which you have established;
⁴ what are human beings that you are mindful of them,
  and mortals that you care for them?
⁵ Yet you have made them little less than God,
  and crowned them with glory and honor.

<sup>6</sup> You have given them dominion over the works of your hands;
    you have put all things under their feet,
<sup>7</sup> all sheep and oxen,
    and also the beasts of the field,
<sup>8</sup> the birds of the air, and the fish of the sea,
    whatever passes along the paths of the sea.
<sup>9</sup> O SOVEREIGN [[or LORD]], our God,
    how majestic is your name in all the earth!

### Lesson 2 ~ Romans 5:1-5

*Paul writes to the Christians at Rome about the greatness of God's love for us.*

<sup>1</sup> Therefore, since we are justified by faith, we have peace with God through our Sovereign [[or Lord]] Jesus Christ, <sup>2</sup> through whom we have obtained access to this grace in which we stand, and we rejoice in our hope of sharing the glory of God. <sup>3</sup> More than that, we rejoice in our sufferings, knowing that suffering produces endurance, <sup>4</sup> and endurance produces character, and character produces hope, <sup>5</sup> and hope does not disappoint us, because God's love has been poured into our hearts through the Holy Spirit who has been given to us.

### Gospel ~ John 16:12-15

*The Spirit will come and complete the work of Jesus.*

<sup>12</sup> I have yet many things to say to you, but you cannot bear them now. <sup>13</sup> When the Spirit of truth comes, that Spirit will guide you into all the truth; for the Spirit will not speak independently, but will speak only what the Spirit hears, and will declare to you the things that are to come. <sup>14</sup> The Spirit will glorify me, by taking what is mine and declaring it to you. <sup>15</sup> All that [*God*] the Father [*and Mother**] has is mine; therefore I said that the Spirit will take what is mine and declare it to you.

---

*Addition to the text. See "Metaphor" and "God the Father and Mother" in the Appendix.

# PENTECOST 2

## Lesson 1 ~ 1 Kings 8:22-23, 41-43

*Solomon prays before the altar of God.*

²² Then Solomon stood before the altar of GOD [[or the LORD]] in the presence of all the assembly of Israel, and spread forth his hands toward heaven; ²³ and said, "O SOVEREIGN [[or LORD]], God of Israel, there is no God like you, in heaven above or on earth beneath, keeping covenant and showing steadfast love to your servants who walk before you with all their heart.

⁴¹ "Likewise when a foreigner, who is not of your people Israel, comes from a far country for your name's sake ⁴² (for they shall hear of your great name, and your mighty hand, and of your outstretched arm), when a foreigner comes and prays toward this house, ⁴³ hear in heaven your dwelling place, and do according to all for which the foreigner calls to you; in order that all the peoples of the earth may know your name and fear you, as do your people Israel, and that they may know that this house which I have built is called by your name."

## Psalm 100

¹ Make a joyful noise to GOD [[or the LORD]], all the lands!
²     Serve GOD [[or the LORD]] with gladness!
    Come into God's presence with singing!
³ Know that the SOVEREIGN [[or LORD]] is God!
    It is God who made us, and to God we belong;
    we are God's people, and the sheep of God's pasture.
⁴ Enter God's gates with thanksgiving,
    and God's courts with praise!
    Give thanks to God, bless God's name!
⁵ For GOD [[or the LORD]] is good;
    God's steadfast love endures forever,
    and God's faithfulness to all generations.

## Lesson 2 ~ Galatians 1:1-10

*Paul reminds the Galatians to heed the gospel of Christ which he has proclaimed to them.*

¹ Paul an apostle—not from human beings nor through any person, but through Jesus Christ and God the Father [*and Mother**], who raised Christ from the dead—²and all the co-workers who are with me,

To the churches of Galatia:

³ Grace to you and peace from God the Father [*and Mother**] and our Sovereign [[*or* Lord]] Jesus Christ, ⁴who gave up Christ's self for our sins to deliver us from the present evil age, according to the will of our God [*the Mother**] and Father; ⁵to whom be the glory forever and ever. Amen.

⁶ I am astonished that you are so quickly deserting the one who called you in the grace of Christ and turning to a different gospel—⁷not that there is another gospel, but there are some who trouble you and want to pervert the gospel of Christ. ⁸But even if we, or an angel from heaven, should preach to you a gospel contrary to that which we preached to you, let them be accursed. ⁹As we have said before, so now I say again, If anyone is preaching to you a gospel contrary to that which you received, let them be accursed.

¹⁰ Am I now seeking human favor, or the favor of God? Or am I trying to please human beings? If I were still pleasing them, I should not be a servant of Christ.

---

*Addition to the text. See "Metaphor" and "God the Father and Mother" in the Appendix.

# Gospel ~ Luke 7:1-10

*Jesus heals the slave of a centurion.*

[1] After Jesus had ended all his sayings in the hearing of the people, he entered Capernaum. [2] Now a centurion had a slave who was dear to him, who was sick and at the point of death. [3] After hearing about Jesus, the centurion sent elders of the Jews to ask Jesus to come and heal his slave. [4] And when they came to Jesus, they begged earnestly, saying, "The centurion is worthy to have you do this for him, [5] for he loves our nation and built us our synagogue." [6] And Jesus went with them. When he was not far from the house, the centurion sent friends to him, saying, "Sovereign [*or* Lord], do not trouble yourself, for I am not worthy to have you come under my roof; [7] therefore I did not presume to come to you. But say the word, and let my servant be healed. [8] For I am a man set under authority, with soldiers under me: and I say to one, 'Go,' and he goes; and to another, 'Come,' and he comes; and to my slave, 'Do this,' and the slave does it." [9] When Jesus heard this he marveled at the centurion, and turned and said to the multitude that followed, "I tell you, not even in Israel have I found such faith." [10] And when those who had been sent returned to the house, they found the slave well.

# PENTECOST 3

## Lesson 1 ~ 1 Kings 17:17-24

*Elijah raises the son of the widow.*

<sup>17</sup> After this the son of the woman, the mistress of the house, became ill; and the illness was so severe that there was no breath left in him. <sup>18</sup> And the woman said to Elijah, "What have you against me, O man of God? You have come to me to bring my sin to remembrance, and to cause the death of my child!" <sup>19</sup> And Elijah said to her, "Give me your son." And Elijah took him from her bosom, and carried him up into the upper chamber, where Elijah lodged, and laid the child upon his own bed. <sup>20</sup> And Elijah cried to GOD [*or* the LORD], "O SOVEREIGN [*or* LORD] my God, have you brought calamity even upon the widow with whom I sojourn, by slaying her son?" <sup>21</sup> Then Elijah stretched himself upon the child three times, and cried to GOD [*or* the LORD], "O SOVEREIGN [*or* LORD] my God, let this child's breath come into him again." <sup>22</sup> And GOD [*or* the LORD] listened to the voice of Elijah; and the breath of the child came into him again, and he revived. <sup>23</sup> And Elijah took the child, and brought him down from the upper chamber into the house, and delivered him to his mother; and Elijah said, "See, your son lives." <sup>24</sup> And the woman said to Elijah, "Now I know that you are a man of God, and that the word of GOD [*or* the LORD] in your mouth is truth."

## Psalm 113

<sup>1</sup> Praise GOD [*or* the LORD]!
  Praise, O servants of GOD [*or* the LORD],
    praise the name of the SOVEREIGN [*or* LORD]!
<sup>2</sup> Blessed be the name of the SOVEREIGN [*or* LORD]
    from this time forth and for evermore!
<sup>3</sup> From the rising of the sun to its setting
    the name of the SOVEREIGN [*or* LORD] is to be praised!
<sup>4</sup> GOD [*or* The LORD] is high above all nations,
    and God's glory above the heavens!
<sup>5</sup> Who is like the SOVEREIGN [*or* LORD] our God,
    who is seated on high,
<sup>6</sup> who looks far down
    upon the heavens and the earth?
<sup>7</sup> God raises the poor from the dust,
    and lifts the needy from the ash heap,

<sup>8</sup> to make them sit with nobles,
　　with the nobles of God's people.
<sup>9</sup> God gives the barren woman a home,
　　making her the joyous mother of children.
　Praise GOD [[*or* the LORD]]!


## Lesson 2 ~ Galatians 1:11-24

*Paul defends the gospel which he received and his call to preach the faith.*

<sup>11</sup> For I would have you know, sisters and brothers, that the gospel which was preached by me is not a human gospel. <sup>12</sup> For I did not receive it from a human being, nor was I taught it, but it came through a revelation of Jesus Christ. <sup>13</sup> For you have heard of my former life in Judaism, how I persecuted the church of God violently and tried to destroy it; <sup>14</sup> and I advanced in Judaism beyond many of my own age among my people, so extremely zealous was I for the traditions of my ancestors. <sup>15</sup> But when God who had set me apart before I was born, and had called me through grace, <sup>16</sup> was pleased to reveal God's Child<sup>◇</sup> to me, in order that I might preach that one among the Gentiles, I did not confer with flesh and blood, <sup>17</sup> nor did I go up to Jerusalem to those who were apostles before me, but I went away into Arabia; and again I returned to Damascus.

<sup>18</sup> Then after three years I went up to Jerusalem to visit Cephas, and remained with him fifteen days. <sup>19</sup> But I saw none of the other apostles except James the Sovereign's [[*or* Lord's]] brother. <sup>20</sup> (In what I am writing to you, before God, I do not lie!) <sup>21</sup> Then I went into the regions of Syria and Cilicia. <sup>22</sup> And I was still not known by sight to the churches of Christ in Judea; <sup>23</sup> they only heard it said, "He who once persecuted us is now preaching the faith he once tried to destroy." <sup>24</sup> And they glorified God because of me.

---

<sup>◇</sup>RSV *his Son*. See Appendix.

164

## Gospel ~ Luke 7:11-17

*Jesus raises the son of the widow.*

<sup>11</sup> Soon afterward Jesus went to a city called Nain, and the disciples and a great crowd went with him. <sup>12</sup> As he drew near to the gate of the city, a man who had died was being carried out, the only son of his mother, and she was a widow; and a large crowd from the city was with her. <sup>13</sup> And when the Sovereign [[*or* Lord]] saw her, he had compassion on her and said to her, "Do not weep." <sup>14</sup> And Jesus came and touched the bier, and the bearers stood still. And he said, "Young man, I say to you, arise." <sup>15</sup> And the dead man sat up, and began to speak. And Jesus gave him to his mother. <sup>16</sup> Fear seized them all; and they glorified God, saying, "A great prophet has arisen among us!" and "God has visited God's people!" <sup>17</sup> And this report concerning Jesus spread through the whole of Judea and all the surrounding country.

# PENTECOST 4

*Elijah is fortified for the journey to Mount Horeb.*

¹ Ahab told Jezebel all that Elijah had done, and how he had slain all the prophets with the sword. ² Then Jezebel sent a messenger to Elijah, saying, "So may the gods do to me, and more also, if I do not make your life as the life of one of them by this time tomorrow." ³ Then Elijah was afraid, and arose and fled for his life, and came to Beer-sheba, which belongs to Judah, and left his servant there.

⁴ But Elijah went a day's journey into the wilderness, and came and sat down under a broom tree, and asked that he might die, saying, "It is enough; now, O GOD [*or* LORD], take away my life; for I am no better than my ancestors." ⁵ And Elijah lay down and slept under a broom tree; and an angel touched him, and said, "Arise and eat." ⁶ And Elijah looked, and there was at his head a cake baked on hot stones and a jar of water. And he ate and drank, and lay down again. ⁷ And the angel of GOD [*or* the LORD] came again a second time, and touched him, and said, "Arise and eat, else the journey will be too great for you." ⁸ And Elijah arose, and ate and drank, and went in the strength of that food forty days and forty nights to Horeb, the mount of God.

## Psalm 42

¹ As a hart longs
    for flowing streams,
  so longs my soul
    for you, O God.
² My soul thirsts for God,
    for the living God.
  When shall I come and behold
    the face of God?
³ My tears have been my food
    day and night,
  while people say to me continually,
    "Where is your God?"
⁴ These things I remember,
    as I pour out my soul:
  how I went with the throng,
    and led them in procession to the house of God,

with glad shouts and songs of thanksgiving,
 a multitude keeping festival.
⁵ Why are you cast down, O my soul,
 and why are you disquieted within me?
Hope in God; for I shall again praise God,
 my help ⁶ and my God.
My soul is cast down within me,
 therefore I remember you
from the land of Jordan and of Hermon,
 from Mount Mizar.
⁷ Deep calls to deep
 at the thunder of your cataracts;
all your waves and your billows
 have gone over me.
⁸ By day GOD [[or the LORD]] commands God's steadfast love;
 and at night God's song is with me,
 a prayer to the God of my life.
⁹ I say to God, my rock:
 "Why have you forgotten me?
Why go I mourning
 because of the oppression of the enemy?"
¹⁰ As with a deadly wound in my body,
 my adversaries taunt me,
while they say to me continually,
 "Where is your God?"
¹¹ Why are you cast down, O my soul,
 and why are you disquieted within me?
Hope in God; for I shall again praise God,
 my help and my God.


## Lesson 2 ~ Galatians 2:15-21

*Paul proclaims justification through faith in Christ Jesus.*

¹⁵ We ourselves, who are Jews by birth and not Gentile sinners, ¹⁶ yet who know that a person is not justified by works of the law but through faith in Jesus Christ, even we have believed in Christ Jesus, in order to be justified by faith in Christ, and not by works of the law, because by works of the law shall no one be justified. ¹⁷ But if, in our endeavor to be justified in Christ, we ourselves were found to be sinners, is Christ then an agent of sin? Certainly not! ¹⁸ But if I build up again those things which I tore down, then I prove myself a transgressor. ¹⁹ For I through the law died to the law, that I might live to God. ²⁰ I have been crucified with Christ; it is

no longer I who live, but Christ who lives in me; and the life I now live in the flesh, I live by faith in the Child◇ of God, who loved me and gave up self for me. ²¹I do not nullify the grace of God; for if justification were through the law, then Christ died to no purpose.

## Gospel ~ Luke 7:36–8:3

*A woman anoints Jesus, and Jesus teaches about love and forgiveness.*

³⁶One of the Pharisees asked Jesus to eat with him, and he went into the Pharisee's house, and sat at table. ³⁷And a woman of the city, who was a sinner, when she learned that Jesus was sitting at table in the Pharisee's house, brought an alabaster flask of ointment, ³⁸and standing behind Jesus at his feet, weeping, she began to wet his feet with her tears, and wiped them with the hair of her head, and kissed his feet, and anointed them with the ointment. ³⁹Now when the Pharisee who had invited Jesus saw it, he said to himself, "If this man were a prophet, he would have known who and what sort of woman this is who is touching him, for she is a sinner." ⁴⁰And Jesus answering said to him, "Simon, I have something to say to you." And Simon answered, "What is it, Teacher?" ⁴¹"A certain creditor had two debtors; one owed five hundred denarii, and the other fifty. ⁴²When they could not pay, the creditor forgave them both. Now which of them will love the creditor more?" ⁴³Simon answered, "The one, I suppose, to whom the creditor forgave more." And Jesus said to Simon, "You have judged rightly." ⁴⁴Then turning toward the woman, he said to Simon, "Do you see this woman? When I entered your house, you gave me no water for my feet, but she has wet my feet with her tears and wiped them with her hair. ⁴⁵You gave me no kiss, but from the time I came in she has not ceased to kiss my feet. ⁴⁶You did not anoint my head with oil, but she has anointed my feet with ointment. ⁴⁷Therefore I tell you, her sins, which are many, are forgiven, for she loved much; but whoever is forgiven little, loves little." ⁴⁸And Jesus said to her, "Your sins are forgiven." ⁴⁹Then those who were at table with him began to say among themselves, "Who is this, who even forgives sins?" ⁵⁰And Jesus said to the woman, "Your faith has saved you; go in peace."

⁸:¹Soon afterward Jesus went on through cities and villages, preaching and bringing the good news of the realm☆ of God. And the twelve were with him, ²and also some women who had been healed of evil spirits and infirmities: Mary, called Magdalene, from whom seven demons had gone out, ³and Joanna, the wife of Chuza, Herod's steward, and Susanna, and many others, who provided for them out of their means.

---

◇RSV *Son*. See Appendix.
☆RSV *kingdom*. See Appendix.

# PENTECOST 5

## Lesson 1 ~ 1 Kings 19:9-14

*The story is told of Elijah in a cave of Mount Horeb.*

⁹ Elijah came to a cave, and lodged there; and the word of GOD [[*or* the LORD]] came to him, saying, "What are you doing here, Elijah?" ¹⁰ He said, "I have been very jealous for the SOVEREIGN [[*or* LORD]], the God of hosts; for the people of Israel have forsaken your covenant, thrown down your altars, and slain your prophets with the sword; and I, even I only, am left; and they seek my life, to take it away." ¹¹ The answer came, "Go forth, and stand upon the mount before GOD [[*or* the LORD]]." And GOD [[*or* the LORD]] passed by, and a great and strong wind rent the mountains, and broke in pieces the rocks before GOD [[*or* the LORD]], but GOD [[*or* the LORD]] was not in the wind; and after the wind an earthquake, but GOD [[*or* the LORD]] was not in the earthquake; ¹² and after the earthquake a fire, but GOD [[*or* the LORD]] was not in the fire; and after the fire a still small voice. ¹³ And when Elijah heard it, he wrapped his face in his mantle and went out and stood at the entrance of the cave. And there came a voice saying, "What are you doing here, Elijah?" ¹⁴ He answered, "I have been very jealous for the SOVEREIGN [[*or* LORD]], the God of hosts; for the people of Israel have forsaken your covenant, thrown down your altars, and slain your prophets with the sword; and I, even I only, am left; and they seek my life, to take it away."

## Psalm 43

¹ Vindicate me, O God, and defend my cause
    against an ungodly people;
  from deceitful and unjust people
    deliver me!
² For you are the God in whom I take refuge;
    why have you cast me off?
Why do I mourn
    because of the oppression of the enemy?
³ Oh send out your light and your truth;
    let them lead me,
  let them bring me to your holy hill
    and to your dwelling!
⁴ Then I will go to the altar of God,
    to God my exceeding joy;

and I will praise you with the lyre,
O God, my God.
5 Why are you cast down, O my soul,
and why are you disquieted within me?
Hope in God; for I shall again praise God,
my help and my God.

## Lesson 2 ~ Galatians 3:23-29

*Paul interprets the consequences of justification by faith.*

23 Now before faith came, we were confined under the law, kept under restraint until faith should be revealed. 24 So that the law was our custodian until Christ came, that we might be justified by faith. 25 But now that faith has come, we are no longer under a custodian; 26 for in Christ Jesus you are all sons and daughters of God, through faith. 27 For as many of you as were baptized into Christ have put on Christ. 28 There is neither Jew nor Greek, there is neither slave nor free, there is neither male nor female; for you are all one in Christ Jesus. 29 And if you are Christ's, then you are offspring of Abraham [*and Sarah**], heirs according to promise.

## Gospel ~ Luke 9:18-24

*Peter confesses Jesus to be the Christ, and Jesus teaches about the cost of discipleship.*

18 Now it happened that as Jesus was praying alone the disciples were with him; and Jesus asked them, "Who do the people say that I am?" 19 And they answered, "John the Baptist; but others say, Elijah; and others, that one of the old prophets has risen." 20 And Jesus said to them, "But who do you say that I am?" And Peter answered, "The Christ of God." 21 But Jesus charged and commanded them to tell this to no one, 22 saying, "The Human One° must suffer many things, and be rejected by the elders and chief priests and scribes, and be killed, and on the third day be raised."

23 And Jesus said to all, "If any would come after me, let them deny themselves and take up their cross daily and follow me. 24 For those who would save their life will lose it; and those who lose their life for my sake, they will save it."

---

*Addition to the text. See "Addition of Women's Names to the Text" in the Appendix.
°RSV *Son of man*. See Appendix.

# PENTECOST 6

## Lesson 1 ~ 1 Kings 19:15-21

*Elisha receives the mantle of prophecy from Elijah.*

¹⁵ GOD [*or* The LORD] said to Elijah, "Go, return on your way to the wilderness of Damascus; and when you arrive, you shall anoint Hazael to be king over Syria; ¹⁶ and Jehu the son of Nimshi you shall anoint to be king over Israel; and Elisha the son of Shaphat of Abel-meholah you shall anoint to be prophet in your place. ¹⁷ And whoever escapes from the sword of Hazael shall Jehu slay; and whoever escapes from the sword of Jehu shall Elisha slay. ¹⁸ Yet I will leave seven thousand in Israel, all the knees that have not bowed to Baal, and every mouth that has not kissed Baal."

¹⁹ So Elijah departed from there, and found Elisha the son of Shaphat, who was plowing, with twelve yoke of oxen before him, and he was with the twelfth. Elijah passed by Elisha and cast his mantle upon him. ²⁰ And Elisha left the oxen, and ran after Elijah, and said, "Let me kiss my father and my mother, and then I will follow you." And Elijah said to him, "Go back again; for what have I done to you?" ²¹ And Elisha returned from following Elijah, and took the yoke of oxen, and slew them, and boiled their flesh with the yokes of the oxen, and gave it to the people, and they ate. Then he arose and went after Elijah, and ministered to him.

## Psalm 44:1-8

¹ We have heard with our ears, O God,
    our ancestors have told us,
  what deeds you performed in their days,
    in the days of old:
² you with your own hand drove out the nations,
    but them you planted;
  you afflicted the peoples,
    but them you set free;
³ for not by their own sword did they win the land,
    nor did their own arm give them victory;
  but by your right hand, and your arm,
    and the light of your countenance;
    for you delighted in them.

⁴ You are my Ruler□ and my God,
  who ordains victories for Jacob.
⁵ Through you we push down our foes;
  through your name we tread down our assailants.
⁶ For not in my bow do I trust,
  nor can my sword save me.
⁷ But you have saved us from our foes,
  and have put to confusion those who hate us.
⁸ In God we have boasted continually,
  and we will give thanks to your name forever.

## Lesson 2 ~ Galatians 5:1, 13-25

*Paul interprets the freedom for which Christ has set us free.*

¹ For freedom Christ has set us free; stand fast therefore, and do not submit again to a yoke of slavery.

¹³ For you were called to freedom, sisters and brothers; only do not use your freedom as an opportunity for the flesh, but through love be servants of one another. ¹⁴ For the whole law is fulfilled in one word, "You shall love your neighbor as yourself." ¹⁵ But if you bite and devour one another, take heed that you are not consumed by one another.

¹⁶ But I say, walk by the Spirit, and do not gratify the desires of the flesh. ¹⁷ For the desires of the flesh are against the Spirit, and the desires of the Spirit are against the flesh; for these are opposed to each other, to prevent you from doing what you would. ¹⁸ But if you are led by the Spirit, you are not under the law. ¹⁹ Now the works of the flesh are plain: fornication, impurity, licentiousness, ²⁰ idolatry, sorcery, enmity, strife, jealousy, anger, selfishness, dissension, party spirit, ²¹ envy, drunkenness, carousing, and the like. I warn you, as I warned you before, that those who do such things shall not inherit the realm☆ of God. ²² But the fruit of the Spirit is love, joy, peace, patience, kindness, goodness, faithfulness, ²³ gentleness, self-control; against such there is no law. ²⁴ And those who belong to Christ Jesus have crucified the flesh with its passions and desires.

²⁵ If we live by the Spirit, let us also walk by the Spirit.

---

□RSV *King*. See Appendix.
☆RSV *kingdom*. See Appendix.

# Gospel ~ Luke 9:51-62

*Jesus begins the journey to Jerusalem and teaches about discipleship.*

[51] When the days drew near for Jesus to be received up, he set his face to go to Jerusalem. [52] And Jesus sent messengers ahead, who went and entered a village of the Samaritans, to make ready for him; [53] but the people would not receive him, because his face was set toward Jerusalem. [54] And when the disciples James and John saw it, they said, "Sovereign [or Lord], do you want us to bid fire come down from heaven and consume them?" [55] But Jesus turned and rebuked them. [56] And they went on to another village.

[57] As they were going along the road, someone said to Jesus, "I will follow you wherever you go." [58] And Jesus replied, "Foxes have holes, and birds of the air have nests; but the Human One° has nowhere to lie down and sleep." [59] To another Jesus said, "Follow me." But the answer came, "Sovereign [or Lord], let me first go and bury my father." [60] But Jesus said, "Leave the dead to bury their own dead; but as for you, go and proclaim the realm☆ of God." [61] Another said, "I will follow you, Sovereign [or Lord]; but let me first say farewell to those at my home." [62] Jesus replied, "No one who puts a hand to the plow and looks back is fit for the realm☆ of God."

---

°RSV *Son of man*. See Appendix.
☆RSV *kingdom*. See Appendix.

*5 Jul 92 Peace Sunday.*

# PENTECOST 7

## Lesson 1 ~ 1 Kings 21:1-3, 17-21

*Elijah prophesies the punishment for King Ahab's evildoing.*

¹ Now Naboth the Jezreelite had a vineyard in Jezreel, beside the palace of Ahab king of Samaria. ² And after this Ahab said to Naboth, "Give me your vineyard, that I may have it for a vegetable garden, because it is near my house; and I will give you a better vineyard for it; or, if it seems good to you, I will give you its value in money." ³ But Naboth said to Ahab, "GOD [*or* The LORD] forbid that I should give you the inheritance of my ancestors."

¹⁷ Then the word of GOD [*or* the LORD] came to Elijah the Tishbite, saying, ¹⁸ "Arise, go down to meet Ahab king of Israel, who is in Samaria; he is in the vineyard of Naboth, where he has gone to take possession. ¹⁹ And you shall say to Ahab, 'Thus says the SOVEREIGN [*or* LORD]: "Have you killed, and also taken possession?"' And you shall say to Ahab, 'Thus says the SOVEREIGN [*or* LORD]: "In the place where dogs licked up the blood of Naboth shall dogs lick your own blood."'"

²⁰ Ahab said to Elijah, "Have you found me, O my enemy?" Elijah answered, "I have found you, because you have sold yourself to do what is evil in the sight of GOD [*or* the LORD]. ²¹ I will bring evil upon you; I will utterly sweep you away, and will cut off from Ahab every male, bond or free, in Israel."

## Psalm 5:1-8

¹ Give ear to my words, O GOD [*or* LORD];
  give heed to my groaning.
² Hearken to the sound of my cry,
  my Ruler□ and my God,
  for to you do I pray.
³ O GOD [*or* LORD], in the morning you hear my voice;
  in the morning I prepare a sacrifice for you, and watch.
⁴ For you are not a God who delights in wickedness;
  evil may not sojourn with you.
⁵ The boastful may not stand before your eyes;
  you hate all evildoers.

---

□RSV *King*. See Appendix.

174

<sup>6</sup> You destroy those who speak lies;

GOD [[*or* the LORD]] abhors those who are bloodthirsty and deceitful.

<sup>7</sup> But as for me, through the abundance of your steadfast love,
I will enter your house;

I will worship toward your holy temple
in the fear of you.

<sup>8</sup> Lead me, O GOD [[*or* LORD]], in your righteousness
because of my enemies;

make your way straight before me.

## Lesson 2 ~ Galatians 6:7-18

*Paul advises the Galatians on how to conduct their lives.*

<sup>7</sup> Do not be deceived; God is not mocked, for whatever one sows, one will also reap. <sup>8</sup> For whoever sows to their own flesh will from the flesh reap corruption; but whoever sows to the Spirit will from the Spirit reap eternal life. <sup>9</sup> And let us not grow weary in well-doing, for in due season we shall reap, if we do not lose heart. <sup>10</sup> So then, as we have opportunity, let us do good to all people, and especially to those who are of the house-hold of faith.

<sup>11</sup> See with what large letters I am writing to you with my own hand. <sup>12</sup> It is those who want to make a good showing in the flesh that would compel you to be circumcised, and only in order that they may not be persecuted for the cross of Christ. <sup>13</sup> For even those who receive circumci-sion do not themselves keep the law, but they desire to have you circum-cised that they may glory in your flesh. <sup>14</sup> But far be it from me to glory except in the cross of our Sovereign [[*or* Lord]] Jesus Christ, by which the world has been crucified to me, and I to the world. <sup>15</sup> For neither circum-cision counts for anything, nor uncircumcision, but a new creation. <sup>16</sup> Peace and mercy be upon all who walk by this rule, upon the Israel of God.

<sup>17</sup> Henceforth let no one trouble me; for I bear on my body the marks of Jesus.

<sup>18</sup> The grace of our Sovereign [[*or* Lord]] Jesus Christ be with your spirit, my friends. Amen.

# Gospel ~ Luke 10:1-12, 17-20

*Jesus sends seventy people on a missionary journey to proclaim God's realm.*

[1] After this the Sovereign [*or* Lord] appointed seventy others, and sent them on ahead, two by two, into every town and place where he himself was about to come. [2] And he said to them, "The harvest is plentiful, but the laborers are few; pray therefore the Sovereign [*or* Lord] of the harvest to send out laborers into the harvest. [3] Go your way; I send you out as lambs in the midst of wolves. [4] Carry no purse, no bag, no sandals; and salute no one on the road. [5] Whatever house you enter, first say, 'Peace be to this house!' [6] And if a person of peace is there, your peace shall rest on it; but if not, it shall return to you. [7] And remain in the same house, eating and drinking what they provide, for a laborer deserves wages; do not go from house to house. [8] Whenever you enter a town and they receive you, eat what is set before you; [9] heal the sick in it and say to them, 'The realm☆ of God has come near to you.' [10] But whenever you enter a town and they do not receive you, go into its streets and say, [11] 'Even the dust of your town that clings to our feet, we wipe off against you; nevertheless know this, that the realm☆ of God has come near.' [12] I tell you, it shall be more tolerable on that day for Sodom than for that town."

[17] The seventy returned with joy, saying, "Sovereign [*or* Lord], even the demons are subject to us in your name!" [18] And he said to them, "I saw Satan fall like lightning from heaven. [19] And now I have given you authority to tread upon serpents and scorpions, and over all the power of the enemy; and nothing shall hurt you. [20] Nevertheless do not rejoice in this, that the spirits are subject to you; but rejoice that your names are written in heaven."

---

☆RSV *kingdom*. See Appendix.

# PENTECOST 8

## Lesson 1 ~ 2 Kings 2:1, 6-14

*Elijah is taken up to heaven by a whirlwind, and Elisha becomes God's prophet.*

¹ Now when GOD [*or* the LORD] was about to take Elijah up to heaven by a whirlwind, Elijah and Elisha were on their way from Gilgal.

⁶ Then Elijah said to Elisha, "Wait here, please; for GOD [*or* the LORD] has sent me to the Jordan." But Elisha said, "As GOD [*or* the LORD] lives, and as you yourself live, I will not leave you." So the two of them went on. ⁷ Fifty of the prophets also went, and stood at some distance from them, as they both were standing by the Jordan. ⁸ Then Elijah took his mantle, and rolled it up, and struck the water, and the water was parted to the one side and to the other, till the two of them could go over on dry ground.

⁹ When they had crossed, Elijah said to Elisha, "Ask what I shall do for you, before I am taken from you." And Elisha said, "Please, let me inherit a double share of your spirit." ¹⁰ And Elijah said, "You have asked a hard thing; yet, if you see me as I am being taken from you, it shall be so for you; but if you do not see me, it shall not be so." ¹¹ And as they still went on and talked, a chariot of fire and horses of fire separated the two of them. And Elijah went up by a whirlwind into heaven. ¹² And Elisha saw it and cried out, "My teacher, my teacher! the chariots of Israel and its riders!" And Elisha saw Elijah no more.

Then Elisha took hold of his own clothes and rent them in two pieces. ¹³ And he took up the mantle of Elijah that had fallen from him, and went back and stood on the bank of the Jordan. ¹⁴ Then Elisha took the mantle of Elijah that had fallen from him, and struck the water, saying, "Where is the SOVEREIGN [*or* LORD], the God of Elijah?" And when he had struck the water, the water was parted to the one side and to the other; and Elisha went over.

## Psalm 139:1-12

¹ O GOD [*or* LORD], you have searched me and known me!
² You know when I sit down and when I rise up;
 you discern my thoughts from afar.
³ You search out my path and my lying down,
 and are acquainted with all my ways.
⁴ Even before a word is on my tongue,
 O GOD [*or* LORD], you know it altogether.

⁵ You beset me behind and before,
　　and lay your hand upon me.
⁶ Such knowledge is too wonderful for me;
　　it is high, I cannot attain it.
⁷ Where shall I go from your Spirit?
　　Or where shall I flee from your presence?
⁸ If I ascend to heaven, you are there!
　　If I make my bed in Sheol, you are there!
⁹ If I take the wings of the morning
　　and dwell in the uttermost parts of the sea,
¹⁰ even there your hand shall lead me,
　　and your right hand shall hold me.
¹¹ If I say, "Let only darkness cover me,
　　and the light about me be night,"
¹² even the darkness is not dark to you,
　　the night is bright as the day;
　　for darkness is as light with you.


### Lesson 2 ~ Colossians 1:1-14

*The Christians at Colossae are reminded of the gospel of Jesus Christ.*

¹ Paul, an apostle of Christ Jesus by the will of God, and Timothy our brother,

² To the saints and faithful brothers and sisters in Christ at Colossae:
　　Grace to you and peace from God our Father [*and Mother**].

³ When we pray for you, we always thank God, the Father [*and Mother**] of our Sovereign [[*or* Lord]] Jesus Christ, ⁴ because we have heard of your faith in Christ Jesus and of the love which you have for all the saints, ⁵ because of the hope laid up for you in heaven. Of this you have heard before in the word of the truth, the gospel ⁶ which has come to you, as indeed in the whole world it is bearing fruit and growing—so among yourselves, from the day you heard and understood the grace of God in truth, ⁷ as you learned it from our beloved Epaphras, a servant with us. He is a faithful minister of Christ on our behalf ⁸ and has made known to us your love in the Spirit.

⁹ And so, from the day we heard of it, we have not ceased to pray for you, asking that you may be filled with the knowledge of God's will in all spiritual wisdom and understanding, ¹⁰ to lead a life worthy of the Sovereign [[*or* Lord]], pleasing in everything, bearing fruit in every good work and increasing in the knowledge of God. ¹¹ May you be strengthened with

---

*Addition to the text. See "Metaphor" and "God the Father and Mother" in the Appendix.

all power, according to God's glorious might, for all endurance and patience with joy, [12] giving thanks to [God] the [Mother and*] Father, who has qualified us to share in the inheritance of the saints in light. [13] God has delivered us from the power of evil and transferred us to the dominion☆ of God's beloved Child,◇ [14] in whom we have redemption, the forgiveness of sins.

## Gospel ~ Luke 10:25-37

*Jesus teaches about being a neighbor.*

[25] A lawyer stood up to put Jesus to the test, saying, "Teacher, what shall I do to inherit eternal life?" [26] Jesus said to him, "What is written in the law? How do you read?" [27] And the lawyer answered, "You shall love the Sovereign [[or Lord]] your God with all your heart, and with all your soul, and with all your strength, and with all your mind; and your neighbor as yourself." [28] And Jesus said to the lawyer, "You have answered right; do this, and you will live."

[29] But the lawyer, desiring to justify himself, said to Jesus, "And who is my neighbor?" [30] Jesus replied, "A man was going down from Jerusalem to Jericho and fell among robbers, who stripped him and beat him, and departed, leaving him half dead. [31] Now by chance a priest was going down that road; and when he saw him, the priest passed by on the other side. [32] So likewise a Levite, when he came to the place and saw him, passed by on the other side. [33] But a Samaritan, as he journeyed, came to where the man was; and when he saw the man, he had compassion, [34] and went to him and bound up his wounds, pouring on oil and wine; then the Samaritan set him on his own beast and brought him to an inn, and took care of him. [35] And the next day the Samaritan took out two denarii and gave them to the innkeeper, saying, 'Take care of him; and whatever more you spend, I will repay you when I come back.' [36] Which of these three, do you think, proved neighbor to the man who fell among the robbers?" [37] The lawyer said, "The one who showed mercy on him." And Jesus replied, "Go and do likewise."

---

*Addition to the text. See "Metaphor" and "God the Father and Mother" in the Appendix.
☆RSV *kingdom*. See Appendix.
◇RSV *Son*. See Appendix.

# PENTECOST 9

## Lesson 1 ~ 2 Kings 4:8-17

*A Shunammite woman cares for Elisha and receives a blessing.*

⁸ One day Elisha went on to Shunem, where a wealthy woman lived, who urged him to eat some food. So whenever Elisha passed that way, he would turn in there to eat food. ⁹ And she said to her husband, "Now I perceive that this is a holy man of God, who is continually passing our way. ¹⁰ Let us make a small roof chamber with walls, and put there for him a bed, a table, a chair, and a lamp, so that whenever Elisha comes to us, he can go in there."

¹¹ One day Elisha came there, and turned into the chamber and rested there. ¹² And he said to Gehazi his servant, "Call this Shunammite." When Gehazi had called her, she stood before him. ¹³ And Elisha said to Gehazi, "Say now to her, See, you have taken all this trouble for us; what is to be done for you? Would you have a word spoken on your behalf to the king or to the commander of the army?" She answered, "I dwell among my own people." ¹⁴ And Elisha said, "What then is to be done for her?" Gehazi answered, "Well, she has no heir, and her husband is old." ¹⁵ Elisha said, "Call her." And when Gehazi had called her, she stood in the doorway. ¹⁶ And Elisha said, "At this season, when the time comes round, you shall embrace a son." And she said, "No, my lord, O man of God; do not lie to your servant." ¹⁷ But the woman conceived, and she bore a son about that time the following spring, as Elisha had said to her.

## Psalm 139:13-18

¹³ For you formed my inward parts,
    you knit me together in my mother's womb.
¹⁴ I praise you, for you are fearful and wonderful.
    Wonderful are your works!
    You know me right well;
¹⁵    my frame was not hidden from you,
    when I was being made in secret,
        intricately wrought in the depths of the earth.
¹⁶ Your eyes beheld my unformed substance;
    in your book were written, every one of them,
    the days that were formed for me,
        when as yet there was none of them.

<sup>17</sup> How precious to me are your thoughts, O God!
   How vast is the sum of them!
<sup>18</sup> If I would count them, they are more than the sand.
   When I awake, I am still with you.


## Lesson 2 ~ Colossians 1:21-29

*Christ's work of reconciliation is continued in the ministry of the gospel.*

<sup>21</sup> And you, who once were estranged and hostile in mind, doing evil deeds, <sup>22</sup> have now been reconciled in Christ's body of flesh by Christ's death, in order to present you holy and blameless and irreproachable before God, <sup>23</sup> provided that you continue in the faith, stable and steadfast, not shifting from the hope of the gospel which you heard, which has been preached to every creature under heaven, and of which I, Paul, became a minister.

<sup>24</sup> Now I rejoice in my sufferings for your sake, and in my flesh I complete what is lacking in Christ's afflictions for the sake of Christ's body, that is, the church, <sup>25</sup> of which I became a minister according to the divine office which was given to me for you, to make the word of God fully known, <sup>26</sup> the mystery hidden for ages and generations but now made manifest to the saints. <sup>27</sup> To them God chose to make known how great among the Gentiles are the riches of the glory of this mystery, which is Christ in you, the hope of glory. <sup>28</sup> Christ we proclaim, warning everyone and teaching everyone in all wisdom, that we may present everyone mature in Christ. <sup>29</sup> For this I toil, striving with all the energy which God mightily inspires within me.


## Gospel ~ Luke 10:38-42

*Jesus visits at the home of Mary and Martha.*

<sup>38</sup> Now as they went on their way, Jesus entered a village; and a woman named Martha received him into her house. <sup>39</sup> And she had a sister called Mary, who sat at the Sovereign's [*or* Lord's] feet and listened to his teaching. <sup>40</sup> But Martha was distracted with much serving; and she went to Jesus and said, "Sovereign [*or* Lord], do you not care that my sister has left me to serve alone? Tell her then to help me." <sup>41</sup> But the Sovereign [*or* Lord] answered her, "Martha, Martha, you are anxious and troubled about many things; <sup>42</sup> one thing is needful. Mary has chosen the good portion, which shall not be taken away from her."

# PENTECOST 10

## Lesson 1 ~ 2 Kings 5:1-15ab

*Naaman is cured of leprosy.*

¹ Naaman, commander of the army of the king of Syria, was a great man with his ruler and in high favor, because by Naaman GOD [*or* the LORD] had given victory to Syria. Naaman was a mighty man of valor, but he had leprosy. ² Now the Syrians on one of their raids had carried off a young girl from the land of Israel, and she waited on Naaman's wife, ³ and said to her, "Would that my lord were with the prophet who is in Samaria! The prophet would cure Naaman of leprosy." ⁴ So Naaman went in and told his lord, "Thus and so spoke the girl from the land of Israel." ⁵ And the king of Syria said, "Go now, and I will send a letter to the king of Israel."

So Naaman went, taking ten talents of silver, six thousand shekels of gold, and ten festal garments. ⁶ And Naaman brought the letter to the king of Israel, which read, "When this letter reaches you, know that I have sent to you Naaman my servant, that you may cure him of leprosy." ⁷ And when the king of Israel read the letter, he rent his clothes and said, "Am I God, to kill and to make alive, that the king of Syria sends word to me to cure someone of leprosy? Only consider, and see how that king is seeking a quarrel with me."

⁸ But when Elisha the prophet of God heard that the king of Israel had rent his clothes, Elisha sent to the king, saying, "Why have you rent your clothes? Let Naaman come now to me, that he may know that there is a prophet in Israel." ⁹ So Naaman came with horses and chariots, and halted at the door of Elisha's house. ¹⁰ And Elisha sent a messenger to Naaman, saying, "Go and wash in the Jordan seven times, and your flesh shall be restored, and you shall be clean." ¹¹ But Naaman was angry, and went away, saying, "I thought that Elisha would surely come out to me, and stand, and call on the name of the SOVEREIGN [*or* LORD] his God, and wave his hand over the place, and cure the one with leprosy. ¹² Are not Abana and Pharpar, the rivers of Damascus, better than all the waters of Israel? Could I not wash in them, and be clean?" So Naaman turned and went away in a rage. ¹³ But his servants came near and said to Naaman, "My father, if the prophet had commanded you to do some great thing, would you not have done it? How much rather, then, when Elisha says to you, 'Wash, and be clean'?" ¹⁴ So Naaman went down and dipped himself seven times in the Jordan, according to the word of the prophet of God; and Naaman's flesh was restored like the flesh of a little child, and he was clean.

¹⁵ Then Naaman and all his company returned to the prophet of God, and he came and stood before Elisha and said, "I know that there is no God in all the earth but in Isreal."

### Psalm 21:1-7

¹ In your strength the monarch⊡ rejoices, O GOD [[or LORD]];
  and in your help how greatly the ruler exults!
² You have satisfied the desire of the ruler's heart,
  and have not withheld the request of the ruler's lips.
³ For with goodly blessings you meet the monarch,
  upon whose head you set a crown of fine gold.
⁴ The ruler asked life of you; you gave it,
  length of days forever and ever.
⁵ Through your help, great is the glory of the monarch,
  upon whom you bestow splendor and majesty.
⁶ You make the ruler most blessed forever,
  glad with the joy of your presence.
⁷ For the monarch⊡ trusts in GOD [[or the LORD]],
  and through the steadfast love of the Most High shall not be moved.

### Lesson 2 ~ Colossians 2:6-15

*The Colossians are reminded about the meaning of faith in Christ.*

⁶ As therefore you received Christ Jesus the Sovereign [[or Lord]], so live in Christ, ⁷ rooted and built up in Christ and established in the faith, just as you were taught, abounding in thanksgiving.

⁸ See to it that no one makes a prey of you by philosophy and empty deceit, according to human tradition, according to the elemental spirits of the universe, and not according to Christ. ⁹ For in Christ the whole fulness of deity dwells bodily, ¹⁰ and you have come to fulness of life in Christ, who is the head of all rule and authority, ¹¹ and in whom also you were circumcised with a circumcision made without hands, by putting off the body of flesh in the circumcision of Christ; ¹² and you were buried with Christ in baptism, in which you were also raised with Christ through faith in the working of God, who raised Christ from the dead. ¹³ And you, who were dead in trespasses and the uncircumcision of your flesh, God made alive together with Christ, having forgiven us all our trespasses, ¹⁴ having canceled the bond which stood against us with its legal demands; this God set aside, nailing it to the cross, ¹⁵ disarming the principalities and powers, and making a public example of them, triumphing over them in Christ.

---

⊡RSV *king*. See Appendix.

# Gospel ~ Luke 11:1-13

*Jesus teaches the disciples how they should pray.*

¹ Jesus was praying in a certain place, and when he ceased, one of the disciples said to him, "Sovereign [[or Lord]], teach us to pray, as John taught his disciples." ² And Jesus said to them, "When you pray, say:

"[O God,] Father [and Mother*], hallowed be your name. May your dominion☆ come. ³ Give us each day our daily bread; ⁴ and forgive us our sins, for we ourselves forgive everyone who is indebted to us; and lead us not into temptation."

⁵ And Jesus said to them, "Which of you who has a friend will go to that friend at midnight and say, 'Friend, lend me three loaves; ⁶ for a friend of mine has arrived on a journey, and I have nothing to serve'; ⁷ and your friend will answer from within, 'Do not bother me; the door is now shut, and my children are with me in bed; I cannot get up and give you anything'? ⁸ I tell you, though your friend will not get up and give you anything because of being a friend, yet because of being pressured, the friend will rise and give whatever is needed. ⁹ And I tell you, Ask, and it will be given you; seek, and you will find; knock, and it will be opened to you. ¹⁰ For everyone who asks receives, and the one who seeks finds, and to the one who knocks it will be opened. ¹¹ What mother or father among you, if a child asks for a fish, instead of a fish will give a serpent; ¹² or if a child asks for an egg, will give a scorpion? ¹³ If you then, who are evil, know how to give good gifts to your children, how much more will [God] the heavenly Father [and Mother*] give the Holy Spirit to those who ask!"

---

*Addition to the text. See "Metaphor" and "God the Father and Mother" in the Appendix.
☆RSV *kingdom*. See Appendix.

2 AUG 92

# PENTECOST 11

## Lesson 1 ~ 2 Kings 13:14-20a

*Elisha gives a final message to Joash, the king of Israel.*

14 Now when Elisha had fallen sick with the illness of which he was to die, Joash king of Israel went down to him, and wept before him, crying, "My father, my father! The chariots of Israel and its riders!" 15 And Elisha said to Joash, "Take a bow and arrows"; so he took a bow and arrows. 16 Then he said to the king of Israel, "Draw the bow"; and he drew it. And Elisha laid his hands upon the king's hands. 17 And Elisha said, "Open the window eastward"; and Joash opened it. Then Elisha said, "Shoot"; and Joash shot. And Elisha said, "GOD's [or The LORD's] arrow of victory, the arrow of victory over Syria! For you shall fight the Syrians in Aphek until you have made an end of them." 18 And Elisha said, "Take the arrows"; and Joash took them. And Elisha said to the king of Israel, "Strike the ground with them"; and he struck three times, and stopped. 19 Then the man of God was angry with Joash, and said, "You should have struck five or six times; then you would have struck down Syria until you had made an end of it, but now you will strike down Syria only three times."

20 So Elisha died, and they buried him.

## Psalm 28

1 To you, O GOD [or LORD], I call;
   my rock, be not deaf to me,
  lest, if you be silent to me,
    I become like those who go down to the Pit.
2 Hear the voice of my supplication,
   as I cry to you for help,
  as I lift up my hands
   toward your most holy sanctuary.
3 Take me not off with the wicked,
   with those who are workers of evil,
  who speak peace with their neighbors,
   while mischief is in their hearts.
4 Requite them according to their work,
   and according to the evil of their deeds;
  requite them according to the work of their hands;
   render them their due reward.

⁵ Because they do not regard the works of GOD [[*or* the LORD]],
    or the work of God's hands,
  God will break them down and build them up no more.
⁶ Blessed be GOD [[*or* the LORD]],
    who has heard the voice of my supplications.
⁷ GOD [[*or* The LORD]] is my strength and my shield,
    the one in whom my heart trusts;
  so I am helped and my heart exults,
    and with my song I give thanks to God.
⁸ GOD [[*or* The LORD]] is the strength of the people,
    the saving refuge of God's anointed.
⁹ O save your people, and bless your heritage;
    be their shepherd, and carry them for ever.

### Lesson 2 ~ Colossians 3:1-11

*The Colossians learn about our new life in Christ.*

¹ If then you have been raised with Christ, seek the things that are above, where Christ is, seated at the right hand of God. ² Set your minds on things that are above, not on things that are on earth. ³ For you have died, and your life is hid with Christ in God. ⁴ When Christ who is our life appears, then you also will appear with Christ in glory. ⁵ Put to death therefore what is earthly in you: fornication, impurity, passion, evil desire, and covetousness, which is idolatry. ⁶ On account of these the wrath of God is coming. ⁷ In these you once walked, when you lived in them. ⁸ But now put them all away: anger, wrath, malice, slander, and foul talk from your mouth. ⁹ Do not lie to one another, seeing that you have put off the old nature with its practices ¹⁰ and have put on the new nature, which is being renewed in knowledge after the image of its creator. ¹¹ Here there cannot be Greek and Jew, those who are under the law and those who are not, barbarian, Scythian, slave or free, but Christ is all, and in all.

# Gospel ~ Luke 12:13-21

*Jesus teaches that life does not consist in the abundance of possessions.*

[13] One of the multitude said to Jesus, "Teacher, bid my brother divide the inheritance with me." [14] But Jesus replied, "Who made me a judge or divider over you?" [15] And he said to them, "Take heed, and beware of all covetousness; for one's life does not consist in the abundance of possessions." [16] And Jesus told them a parable, saying, "The land of a rich man brought forth plentifully; [17] and he thought to himself, 'What shall I do, for I have nowhere to store my crops?' [18] And he said, 'I will do this: I will pull down my barns, and build larger ones; and there I will store all my grain and my goods. [19] And I will say to myself, Self, you have ample goods laid up for many years; take your ease, eat, drink, be merry.' [20] But God said to him, 'Fool! This night your life is required of you; and the things you have prepared, whose will they be?' [21] So are those who lay up treasure for themselves, and are not rich toward God."

9 AUG 92

# PENTECOST 12

## Lesson 1 ~ Jeremiah 18:1-11

*Jeremiah is sent to the potter's house to learn of God's intent for Israel.*

¹ The word that came to Jeremiah from GOD [*or* the LORD]: ² "Arise, and go down to the potter's house, and there I will let you hear my words." ³ So I went down to the house of the potter, who was working at the wheel. ⁴ And the vessel, being made of clay, was spoiled in the potter's hand, so the potter reworked it into another vessel, as it seemed good to do.

⁵ Then the word of GOD [*or* the LORD] came to me: ⁶ "O house of Israel, can I not do with you as this potter has done? says the SOVEREIGN [*or* LORD]. Like the clay in the potter's hand, so are you in my hands, O house of Israel. ⁷ If at any time I declare concerning a nation or a kingdom, that I will pluck up and break down and destroy it, ⁸ and if that nation, concerning which I have spoken, turns from its evil, I will repent of the evil that I intended to do to it. ⁹ And if at any time I declare concerning a nation or a kingdom that I will build and plant it, ¹⁰ and if it does evil in my sight, not listening to my voice, then I will repent of the good which I had intended to do to it. ¹¹ Now, therefore, say to the people of Judah and the inhabitants of Jerusalem: "Thus says the SOVEREIGN [*or* LORD]: I am shaping evil against you and devising a plan against you. Return, everyone from your evil way, and amend your ways and your doings.'"

# Psalm 14

<sup>1</sup> The foolish say in their heart,
  "There is no God."
 They are corrupt, they do abominable deeds,
  there is none that does good.
<sup>2</sup> GOD [[*or* The LORD]] looks down from heaven upon humankind,
  to see if there are any that act wisely,
  that seek after God.
<sup>3</sup> They have all gone astray, they are all alike corrupt;
  there is none that does good,
  no, not one.
<sup>4</sup> Have they no knowledge, all the evildoers
  who eat up my people as they eat bread,
  and do not call upon GOD [[*or* the LORD]]?
<sup>5</sup> There they shall be in great terror,
  for God is with the generation of the righteous.
<sup>6</sup> You would confound the plans of the poor,
  but GOD [[*or* the LORD]] is their refuge.
<sup>7</sup> O that deliverance for Israel would come out of Zion!
  When GOD [[*or* the LORD]] restores the fortunes of God's people,
  Jacob shall rejoice, Israel shall be glad.

## Lesson 2 ~ Hebrews 11:1-3, 8-19

*Abraham and Sarah provide an example of a faithful relationship to God.*

[1] Now faith is the assurance of things hoped for, the conviction of things not seen. [2] For by it our ancestors received divine approval. [3] By faith we understand that the world was created by the word of God, so that what is seen was made out of things which do not appear.

[8] By faith Abraham obeyed when he was called to go out to a place which he was to receive as an inheritance; and he went out, not knowing where he was to go. [9] By faith he sojourned in the land of promise, as in a foreign land, living in tents with Isaac and Jacob, heirs with him of the same promise. [10] For he looked forward to the city which has foundations, whose builder and maker is God. [11] By faith Sarah herself received power to conceive, even when she was past the age, since she considered faithful the one who had promised. [12] Therefore from one as good as dead were born descendants, as many as the stars of heaven and as innumerable as the grains of sand by the seashore.

[13] These all died in faith, not having received what was promised, but having seen it and greeted it from afar, and having acknowledged that they were strangers and exiles on the earth. [14] For people who speak thus make it clear that they are seeking a homeland. [15] If they had been thinking of that land from which they had gone out, they would have had opportunity to return. [16] But as it is, they desire a better country, that is, a heavenly one. Therefore God is not ashamed to be called their God, having prepared for them a city.

[17] By faith Abraham, when he was tested, offered up Isaac, and he who had received the promises was ready to offer up his only son, [18] of whom it was said, "Through Isaac shall your descendants be named." [19] Abraham considered that God was able even to raise the dead; hence, figuratively speaking, Abraham did receive Isaac back.

# Gospel ~ Luke 12:32-40

*Jesus urges people to be prepared for the coming of God's dominion.*

[32] Fear not, little flock, for it is God's⊗ good pleasure to give you the dominion. ☆ [33] Sell your possessions, and give alms; provide yourselves with purses that do not grow old, with a treasure in the heavens that does not fail, where no thief approaches and no moth destroys. [34] For where your treasure is, there will your heart be also.

[35] Let your loins be girded and your lamps burning, [36] and be like those who are waiting for their sovereign [[*or* lord]] to come home from the marriage feast, so that they may open the door at once when the sovereign [[*or* lord]] comes and knocks. [37] Blessed are those servants who are then found awake; truly, I say to you, the sovereign [[*or* lord]] will be girded and have them sit at table, and will come and serve them. [38] If the sovereign [[*or* lord]] comes in the second watch, or in the third, and finds them so, blessed are those servants!

[39] But know this, that if the householder had known at what hour the thief was coming, that householder would not have left the house to be broken into. [40] You also must be ready; for the Human One○ is coming at an unexpected hour.

---

⊗RSV *your Father's*. See Appendix.
☆RSV *kingdom*. See Appendix.
○RSV *Son of man*. See Appendix.

# PENTECOST 13

### Lesson 1 ~ Jeremiah 20:7-13

*Jeremiah is compelled to speak for God, and is denounced by the people.*

⁷ O GOD [*or* LORD], you have deceived me,
and I was deceived;
you are stronger than I,
and you have prevailed.
I have become a laughingstock all the day;
everyone mocks me.
⁸ For whenever I speak, I cry out,
I shout, "Violence and destruction!"
For the word of GOD [*or* the LORD] has become for me
a reproach and derision all day long.
⁹ If I say, "I will not mention God,
or speak anymore in God's name,"
there is in my heart as it were a burning fire
shut up in my bones,
and I am weary with holding it in,
and I cannot.
¹⁰ For I hear many whispering.
Terror is on every side!
"Denounce him! Let us denounce Jeremiah!"
say all my familiar friends,
watching for my fall.
"Perhaps he will be deceived;
then we can overcome him,
and take our revenge on him."
¹¹ But GOD [*or* the LORD] is with me as a dread warrior;
therefore my persecutors will stumble,
they will not overcome me.
They will be greatly shamed,
for they will not succeed.
Their eternal dishonor
will never be forgotten.
¹² O GOD [*or* LORD] of hosts, you try the righteous,
you see the heart and the mind,
let me see your vengeance upon them,
for to you have I committed my cause.
¹³ Sing to GOD [*or* the LORD];
praise GOD [*or* the LORD]!
For God has delivered the life of the needy
from the hand of evildoers.

[12] Arise, O SOVEREIGN [[*or* LORD]]; O God, lift up your hand;
  forget not those who are afflicted.
[13] Why does the wicked renounce God,
  and think, "You will not call to account"?
[14] You see; you take note of trouble and vexation,
  that you may take it into your hands;
 those who have misfortune commit themselves to you;
  you have been the helper of the orphan.
[15] Break the arm of the wicked and evildoer;
  seek out their wickedness till you find none.
[16] GOD [[*or* The LORD]] is ruler□ forever and ever;
  the nations shall perish from God's land.
[17] O GOD [[*or* LORD]], you will hear the desire of the meek;
  you will strengthen their heart, you will incline your ear
[18] to do justice to the orphan and the oppressed,
  so that people who are of the earth may strike terror no more.

## Lesson 2 ~ Hebrews 12:1-2, 12-17

*Jesus is the pioneer and perfecter of our faith.*

[1] Therefore, since we are surrounded by so great a cloud of witnesses, let us also lay aside every weight, and sin which clings so closely, and let us run with perseverance the race that is set before us, [2] looking to Jesus the pioneer and perfecter of our faith, who for the joy that was set before him endured the cross, despising the shame, and is seated at the right hand of the throne of God.

[12] Therefore lift your drooping hands and strengthen your weak knees, [13] and make straight paths for your feet, so that what is lame may not be put out of joint but rather be healed. [14] Strive for peace with all people, and for the holiness without which no one will see the Sovereign [[*or* Lord]]. [15] See to it that no one fail to obtain the grace of God; that no "root of bitterness" spring up and cause trouble, and by it the many become defiled; [16] that no one be immoral or irreligious like Esau, who sold his birthright for a single meal. [17] For you know that afterward, when Esau desired to inherit the blessing, he was rejected, for he found no chance to repent, though he sought it with tears.

---

□RSV *king*. See Appendix.

# Gospel ~ Luke 12:49-56

*Jesus warns people of the signs of the times.*

[49] "I came to cast fire upon the earth; and would that it were already kindled! [50] I have a baptism to be baptized with; and how I am constrained until it is accomplished! [51] Do you think that I have come to give peace on earth? No, I tell you, but rather division; [52] For henceforth in one house there will be five divided, three against two and two against three; [53] they will be divided, father against son and son against father, mother against daughter and daughter against mother, mother-in-law against daughter-in-law and daughter-in-law against mother-in-law."

[54] Jesus also said to the multitudes, "When you see a cloud rising in the west, you say at once, 'A shower is coming'; and so it happens. [55] And when you see the south wind blowing, you say, 'There will be scorching heat'; and it happens. [56] You hypocrites! You know how to interpret the appearance of earth and sky; but why do you not know how to interpret the present time?"

# PENTECOST 14

## Lesson 1 ~ Jeremiah 28:1-9

*Jeremiah and Hananiah differ about God's intent for Israel.*

¹ In that same year, at the beginning of the reign of Zedekiah king of Judah, in the fifth month of the fourth year, Hananiah the son of Azzur, the prophet from Gibeon, spoke to me in the house of GOD [[*or* the LORD]], in the presence of the priests and all the people, saying, ² "Thus says the GOD [[*or* LORD]] of hosts, the God of Israel: I have broken the yoke of the king of Babylon. ³ Within two years I will bring back to this place all the vessels of GOD's [[*or* the LORD's]] house, which Nebuchadnezzar king of Babylon took away from this place and carried to Babylon. ⁴ I will also bring back to this place Jeconiah the son of Jehoiakim, king of Judah, and all the exiles from Judah who went to Babylon, says the SOVEREIGN [[*or* LORD]], for I will break the yoke of the king of Babylon."

⁵ Then the prophet Jeremiah spoke to Hananiah the prophet in the presence of the priests and all the people who were standing in the house of GOD [[*or* the LORD]]; ⁶ and the prophet Jeremiah said, "Amen! May GOD [[*or* the LORD]] do so; may GOD [[*or* the LORD]] make the words which you have prophesied come true, and bring back to this place from Babylon the vessels of the house of GOD [[*or* the LORD]], and all the exiles. ⁷ Yet hear now this word which I speak in your hearing and in the hearing of all the people. ⁸ The prophets who preceded you and me from ancient times prophesied war, famine, and pestilence against many countries and great kingdoms. ⁹ As for the prophet who prophesies peace, when the word of that prophet comes to pass, then it will be known that GOD [[*or* the LORD]] has truly sent that prophet."

## Psalm 84

¹ How lovely is your dwelling place,
   O GOD [[*or* LORD]] of hosts!
² My soul longs, even faints
      for the courts of GOD [[*or* the LORD]];
   my heart and flesh sing for joy
      to the living God.
³ Even the sparrow finds a home,
      and the swallow a nest for herself,
      where she may lay her young,
   at your altars, O GOD [[*or* LORD]] of hosts,
      my Ruler⌑ and my God.

---

⌑RSV *King*. See Appendix.

⁴ Blessed are those who dwell in your house,
    ever singing your praise!
⁵ Blessed are those whose strength is in you,
    in whose heart are the highways to Zion.
⁶ As they go through the valley of Baca
    they make it a place of springs;
    the early rain also covers it with pools.
⁷ They go from strength to strength;
    the God of gods will be seen in Zion.
⁸ O SOVEREIGN [or LORD] God of hosts, hear my prayer;
    give ear, O God of Jacob!
⁹ Behold our shield, O God;
    look upon the face of your anointed!
¹⁰ For a day in your courts is better
    than a thousand elsewhere.
  I would rather be a doorkeeper in the house of my God
    than dwell in the tents of wickedness.
¹¹ For the SOVEREIGN [or LORD] God is a sun and shield,
    who bestows favor and honor.
  No good thing does GOD [or the LORD] withhold
    from those who walk uprightly.
¹² O GOD [or LORD] of hosts,
    blessed is the one who trusts in you!

## Lesson 2 ~ Hebrews 12:18-29

*Jesus has mediated a new covenant and has brought a realm that cannot be shaken.*

¹⁸ For you have not come to what may be touched, a blazing fire, and darkness, and gloom, and a tempest, ¹⁹ and the sound of a trumpet, and a voice whose words made the hearers entreat that no further messages be spoken to them. ²⁰ For they could not endure the order that was given, "If even a beast touches the mountain, it shall be stoned." ²¹ Indeed, so terrifying was the sight that Moses said, "I tremble with fear." ²² But you have come to Mount Zion and to the city of the living God, the heavenly Jerusalem, and to innumerable angels in festal gathering, ²³ and to the assembly of the firstborn who are enrolled in heaven, and to a judge who is God of all, and to the spirits of the just, who are made perfect, ²⁴ and to Jesus, the mediator of a new covenant, and to the sprinkled blood that speaks more graciously than the blood of Abel.

[25] See that you do not refuse the one who is speaking. For if they did not escape when they refused the one who warned them on earth, much less shall we escape if we reject the one who warns from heaven, [26] whose voice then shook the earth. But now it has been promised, "Yet once more I will shake not only the earth but also the heaven." [27] This phrase, "Yet once more," indicates the removal of what is shaken, as of what has been made, in order that what cannot be shaken may remain. [28] Therefore let us be grateful for receiving a realm✩ that cannot be shaken, and thus let us offer to God acceptable worship, with reverence and awe; [29] for our God is a consuming fire.

## Gospel ~ Luke 13:22-30

*Jesus speaks of the coming time of judgment.*

[22] Jesus went on his way through towns and villages, teaching, and journeying toward Jerusalem. [23] And someone said to him, "Sovereign [[or Lord]], will those who are saved be few?" And Jesus said to them, [24] "Strive to enter by the narrow door; for many, I tell you, will seek to enter and will not be able. [25] When once the householder has risen up and shut the door, you will begin to stand outside and to knock at the door, saying, 'Sovereign [[or Lord]], open to us.' You will be answered, 'I do not know where you come from.' [26] Then you will begin to say, 'We ate and drank in your presence, and you taught in our streets.' [27] But you will be told, 'I tell you, I do not know where you come from; depart from me, all you workers of iniquity!' [28] There you will weep and gnash your teeth, when you see Abraham and Isaac and Jacob and all the prophets in the realm✩ of God and you yourselves thrust out. [29] And people will come from east and west, and from north and south, and sit at table in the realm✩ of God. [30] And some are last who will be first, and some are first who will be last."

---

✩RSV *kingdom*. See Appendix.

# PENTECOST 15

## Lesson 1 ~ Ezekiel 18:1-9, 25-29

*Ezekiel speaks about individual responsibility.*

[1] The word of GOD [[*or* the LORD]] came to me again: [2] "What do you mean by repeating this proverb concerning the land of Israel, 'The parents have eaten sour grapes, and the children's teeth are set on edge'? [3] As I live, says the Sovereign [[*or* Lord]] GOD, this proverb shall no more be used by you in Israel. [4] All people are mine; the parents themselves as well as the children themselves are mine: the one that sins shall die.

[5] "If a person is righteous and does what is lawful and right— [6] does not eat upon the mountains nor look up to the idols of the house of Israel, and does not defile a neighbor's spouse nor approach anyone who is ritually impure; [7] if a person does not oppress anyone, but restores a debtor's pledge; if a person commits no robbery, gives bread to the hungry and covers the naked with a garment, [8] does not lend at interest or take any increase, shuns iniquity, executes true justice between one person and another, [9] walks in my statutes, and is careful to observe my ordinances— that one is righteous and shall surely live, says the Sovereign [[*or* Lord]] GOD.

[25] "Yet you say, 'The way of God [[*or* the Lord]] is not just.' Hear now, O house of Israel: Is my way not just? Is it not your ways that are not just? [26] When someone righteous turns away from righteousness and commits iniquity, that one shall die for it; for the iniquity which has been committed that one shall die. [27] Again, when someone wicked turns away from the wickedness that has been committed and does what is lawful and right, that one shall be saved. [28] Having considered and turned away from all these transgressions which have been committed, that one shall surely live and shall not die. [29] Yet the house of Israel says, 'The way of the Sovereign [[*or* Lord]] is not just.' O house of Israel, are my ways not just? Is it not your ways that are not just?"

## Psalm 15

[1] O GOD [[*or* LORD]], who shall sojourn in your tent?
   Who shall dwell on your holy hill?
[2] The one who walks blamelessly, and does what is right,
   and speaks truth from the heart;
[3] who does not slander with the tongue,
   and does no evil to a friend,
   nor takes up a reproach against a neighbor;

⁴in whose eyes a reprobate is despised,
   but who honors those who fear GOD [[or the LORD]];
who swears to one's own hurt and does not change;
⁵who does not put out money at interest,
   and does not take a bribe against the innocent.
Whoever does these things shall never be moved.


### Lesson 2 ~ Hebrews 13:1-8

*The author of Hebrews gives us specific exhortations.*

¹Let your love for one another continue. ²Do not neglect to show hospitality to strangers, for thereby some have entertained angels unawares. ³Remember those who are in prison, as though in prison with them; and those who are ill-treated, since you also are in the body. ⁴Let marriage be held in honor among all, and let the marriage bed be undefiled; for God will judge the immoral and adulterous. ⁵Keep your life free from love of money, and be content with what you have; for God has said, "I will never fail you nor forsake you." ⁶Hence we can confidently say,

"The Sovereign [[or Lord]] is my helper,
I will not be afraid;
what can a human being do to me?"

⁷Remember your leaders, those who spoke to you the word of God; consider the outcome of their life, and imitate their faith. ⁸Jesus Christ is the same yesterday and today and forever.

# Gospel ~ Luke 14:1, 7-14

*Jesus tells a story that illustrates humility.*

¹ One sabbath when Jesus went to dine at the house of a ruler who belonged to the Pharisees, they were watching him.

⁷ Noticing how they chose the places of honor, Jesus told a parable to those who were invited, saying to them, ⁸ "When you are invited by anyone to a marriage feast, do not sit down in a place of honor, lest a more eminent person than you be invited; ⁹ and the one who invited you both will come and say to you, 'Give place to this person,' and then you will begin with shame to take the lowest place. ¹⁰ But when you are invited, go and sit in the lowest place, so that your host, having come, may say to you, 'Friend, go up higher'; then you will be honored in the presence of all who sit at table with you. ¹¹ For all who exalt themselves will be humbled, and all who humble themselves will be exalted."

¹² Jesus said also to the person who had invited him, "When you give a dinner or a banquet, do not invite your friends or your brothers and sisters or your relatives or rich neighbors, lest they also invite you in return, and you be repaid. ¹³ But when you give a feast, invite those who are poor and maimed and lame and blind, ¹⁴ and you will be blessed, because they cannot repay you. You will be repaid at the resurrection of the just."

# PENTECOST 16

## Lesson 1 ~ Ezekiel 33:1-11

*The prophet Ezekiel functions as a sentry for Israel.*

¹ The word of GOD [[*or* the LORD]] came to me: ² "O mortal,° speak to
your people and say to them, If I bring the sword upon a land, and the
people of the land take a person from among them, and make that person
their sentry; ³ and if the sentry sees the sword coming upon the land and
blows the trumpet and warns the people; ⁴ then if any who hear the sound
of the trumpet do not take warning, and the sword comes and takes them
away, their blood shall be upon their own heads. ⁵ They heard the sound of
the trumpet and did not take warning; their blood shall be upon themselves. But if they had taken warning, they would have saved their lives.
⁶ But if the sentry sees the sword coming and does not blow the trumpet,
so that the people are not warned, and the sword comes and takes any of
them, they are taken away in their iniquity, but their blood I will require
at the sentry's hand.

⁷ "So you, O mortal,° I have made a sentry for the house of Israel;
whenever you hear a word from my mouth, you shall give them warning
from me. ⁸ If I say to the wicked, O wicked one, you shall surely die, and
you do not speak to warn the wicked to turn from their way, the wicked
shall die in their iniquity, but their blood I will require at your hand. ⁹ But
if you warn the wicked to turn from their wicked ways, and they do not
turn from their wicked ways, they shall die in their iniquity, but you will
have saved your life.

¹⁰ "And you, O mortal,° say to the house of Israel, Thus have you said:
'Our transgressions and our sins are upon us, and we waste away because
of them; how then can we live?' ¹¹ Say to them, As I live, says the Sovereign [[*or* Lord]] GOD, I have no pleasure in the death of the wicked, but
that the wicked turn from their ways and live; turn back, turn back from
your evil ways; for why will you die, O house of Israel?"

### Psalm 94:12-22

¹² Blessed are those whom you chasten, O GOD [[*or* LORD]],
　　and whom you teach out of your law
¹³ to give them respite from days of trouble,
　　until a pit is dug for the wicked.

---

°RSV v. 2 *Son of man;* vs. 7, 10 *son of man*. See Appendix.

201

<sup>14</sup> For GOD [[*or* the LORD]] will not forsake God's people,
>    and will not abandon God's heritage;
<sup>15</sup> for justice will return to the righteous,
>    and all the upright in heart will follow it.
<sup>16</sup> Who rises up for me against the wicked?
>    Who stands up for me against the evildoers?
<sup>17</sup> If GOD [[*or* the LORD]] had not been my help,
>    my soul would soon have dwelt in the land of silence.
<sup>18</sup> When I thought, "My foot slips,"
>    your steadfast love, O GOD [[*or* LORD]], held me up.
<sup>19</sup> When the cares of my heart are many,
>    your consolations cheer my soul.
<sup>20</sup> Can wicked rulers be allied with you,
>    who frame mischief by statute?
<sup>21</sup> They band together against the life of the righteous,
>    and condemn the innocent to death.
<sup>22</sup> But the SOVEREIGN [[*or* LORD]] has become my stronghold,
>    and my God the rock of my refuge.

## Lesson 2 (alternate) ~ Hebrews 13:8-16, 20-21 [+]

*The author exhorts us continually to offer up a sacrifice of praise.*

[8] Jesus Christ is the same yesterday and today and forever. [9] Do not be led away by diverse and strange teachings; for it is well that the heart be strengthened by grace, not by foods, which have not benefited their adherents. [10] We have an altar from which those who serve the tent have no right to eat. [11] For the bodies of those animals whose blood is brought into the sanctuary by the high priest as a sacrifice for sin are burned outside the camp. [12] So Jesus also suffered outside the gate in order to sanctify the people through Jesus' own blood. [13] Therefore let us go forth to Jesus outside the camp, and bear the abuse Jesus endured. [14] For here we have no lasting city, but we seek the city which is to come. [15] Through Jesus then let us continually offer up a sacrifice of praise to God, that is, the fruit of lips that acknowledge Jesus' name. [16] Do not neglect to do good and to share what you have, for such sacrifices are pleasing to God.

[20] Now may the God of peace who brought again from the dead our Sovereign [[*or* Lord]] Jesus, the great shepherd of the sheep, by the blood of the eternal covenant, [21] equip you with everything good that you may do God's will, working in you through Jesus Christ that which is pleasing in God's sight, to whom be glory forever and ever. Amen.

---

[+] Lection added. See Appendix, p. 263.

## Lesson 2 ~ Philemon 1-20

*Paul urges Philemon to take Onesimus back as a brother in Christ.*

¹ Paul, a prisoner for Christ Jesus, and Timothy our brother,

To Philemon our beloved co-worker ²and Apphia our sister and Archippus our companion in struggle, and the church in your house:

³ Grace to you and peace from God our Father [*and Mother**] and from the Sovereign [[*or* Lord]] Jesus Christ.

⁴ I thank my God always when I remember you in my prayers, ⁵because I hear of your love and of the faith which you have toward the Sovereign [[*or* Lord]] Jesus and all the saints, ⁶and I pray that the sharing of your faith may promote the knowledge of all the good that is ours in Christ. ⁷For I have derived much joy and comfort from your love, my brother, because the hearts of the saints have been refreshed through you.

⁸ Accordingly, though I am bold enough in Christ to command you to do what is required, ⁹yet for love's sake I prefer to appeal to you—I, Paul, an ambassador and now a prisoner also for Christ Jesus— ¹⁰I appeal to you for my child, Onesimus, whose father I have become in my imprisonment. ¹¹(Formerly he was useless to you, but now he is indeed useful to you and to me.) ¹²I am sending Onesimus back to you, sending my very heart. ¹³I would have been glad to keep him with me, in order that he might serve me on your behalf during my imprisonment for the gospel; ¹⁴but I preferred to do nothing without your consent in order that your goodness might not be by compulsion but of your own free will.

¹⁵ Perhaps this is why Onesimus was parted from you for a while, that you might have him back forever, ¹⁶no longer as a slave but more than a slave, as a beloved brother, especially to me but how much more to you, both in the flesh and in the Sovereign [[*or* Lord]]. ¹⁷So if you consider me your partner, receive Onesimus as you would receive me. ¹⁸If he has wronged you at all, or owes you anything, charge that to my account. ¹⁹I, Paul, write this with my own hand, I will repay it—to say nothing of your owing me even your own self. ²⁰Yes, brother, I want some benefit from you in the Sovereign [[*or* Lord]]. Refresh my heart in Christ.

---

*Addition to the text. See "Metaphor" and "God the Father and Mother" in the Appendix.

*Jesus speaks about the cost of discipleship.*

25 Now great multitudes accompanied Jesus; and he turned and said to them, 26 "Whoever comes to me and does not hate their own father and mother and wife [*and husband**] and children and brothers and sisters, yes, and even life itself, cannot be my disciple. 27 Whoever does not bear their own cross and come after me, cannot be my disciple. 28 For which of you, desiring to build a tower, does not first sit down and count the cost, whether there is enough to complete it? 29 Otherwise, when the foundation is laid and the tower cannot be finished, all who see it begin to mock, 30 saying, 'This person began to build, and was not able to finish.' 31 Or what king, going to encounter another king in war, will not sit down first and take counsel whether he is able with ten thousand to meet the one who comes against him with twenty thousand? 32 And if not, while the other is yet a great way off, he sends an embassy and asks terms of peace. 33 So therefore, whoever of you does not renounce all possessions cannot be my disciple."

---

*Addition to the text.

# PENTECOST 17

## Lesson 1 ~ Hosea 4:1-3; 5:15–6:6

*Hosea reminds the people that God desires steadfast love and faithfulness.*

¹ Hear the word of GOD [*or* the LORD], O people of Israel;
  for GOD [*or* the LORD] has a controversy with the inhabitants of the
    land.
There is no faithfulness or kindness,
  and no knowledge of God in the land;
² there is swearing, lying, killing, stealing, and committing adultery;
  they break all bounds and murder follows murder.
³ Therefore the land mourns,
  and all who dwell in it languish,
and also the beasts of the field,
  and the birds of the air;
  and even the fish of the sea are taken away.
5:15 I will return again to my place,
  until they acknowledge their guilt and seek my face,
  and in their distress they seek me, saying,
6:1 "Come, let us return to GOD [*or* the LORD];
  for God has torn, and will heal us,
  has stricken, and will bind us up.
² After two days God will revive us,
  and on the third day will raise us up,
  that we may live in the presence of God.
³ Let us know, let us press on to know GOD [*or* the LORD];
  God's going forth is sure as the dawn;
God will come to us as the showers,
  as the spring rains that water the earth."
⁴ What shall I do with you, O Ephraim?
  What shall I do with you, O Judah?
Your love is like a morning cloud,
  like the dew that goes early away.
⁵ Therefore I have hewn them by the prophets,
  I have slain them by the words of my mouth,
  and my judgment goes forth as the light.
⁶ For I desire steadfast love and not sacrifice,
  the knowledge of God, rather than burnt offerings.

<sup>11</sup> I will call to mind the deeds of GOD [[*or* the LORD]];
   I will remember your wonders of old.
<sup>12</sup> I will meditate on all your work,
   and muse on your mighty deeds.
<sup>13</sup> Your way, O God, is holy.
   What god is great like our God?
<sup>14</sup> You are the God who works wonders,
   who has manifested your might among the nations.
<sup>15</sup> With your arm you redeemed your people,
   the offspring of Jacob and Joseph.
<sup>16</sup> When the waters saw you, O God,
   when the waters saw you, they were afraid;
   the deep trembled.
<sup>17</sup> The clouds poured out water;
   the skies gave forth thunder;
   your arrows flashed on every side.
<sup>18</sup> The crash of your thunder was in the whirlwind;
   your lightnings lighted up the world;
   the earth trembled and shook.
<sup>19</sup> Your way was through the sea,
   your path through the great waters;
   yet your footprints were unseen.
<sup>20</sup> You led your people like a flock
   by the hand of Moses and Aaron.

## Lesson 2 ~ 1 Timothy 1:12-17

*The author is grateful that though formerly a sinner, by grace he is now a minister of Christ.*

¹² I thank the one who has given me strength for this, Christ Jesus our Sovereign [or Lord], for having judged me faithful by appointing me to Christ's service, ¹³ though I was formerly a blasphemer, a persecutor, and a bully; but I received mercy because I had acted ignorantly in unbelief, ¹⁴ and the grace of our Sovereign [or Lord] overflowed for me with the faith and love that are in Christ Jesus. ¹⁵ The saying is sure and worthy of full acceptance, that Christ Jesus came into the world to save sinners. And I am the foremost of sinners; ¹⁶ but I received mercy for this reason, that in me, as the foremost, Jesus Christ might display perfect patience for an example to those who were to believe in Christ for eternal life. ¹⁷ To the Ruler☐ of ages, immortal, invisible, the only God, be honor and glory forever and ever. Amen.

## Gospel ~ Luke 15:1-10

*Jesus tells the parables of the lost sheep and the lost coin.*

¹ Now the tax collectors and sinners were all drawing near to hear Jesus. ² And the Pharisees and the scribes murmured, saying, "This man receives sinners and eats with them."

³ So Jesus told them this parable: ⁴ "Which one of you, having a hundred sheep, if he has lost one of them, does not leave the ninety-nine in the wilderness and go after the one which is lost, until he finds it? ⁵ And having found it, he lays it on his shoulders, rejoicing. ⁶ And when he comes home, he calls together his friends and neighbors, saying to them, 'Rejoice with me, for I have found my sheep which was lost.' ⁷ Just so, I tell you, there will be more joy in heaven over one sinner who repents than over ninety-nine righteous persons who need no repentance.

⁸ "Or what woman, having ten silver coins, if she loses one coin, does not light a lamp and sweep the house and seek diligently until she finds it? ⁹ And when she has found it, she calls together her friends and neighbors, saying, 'Rejoice with me, for I have found the coin which I had lost.' ¹⁰ Just so, I tell you, there is joy before the angels of God over one sinner who repents."

---

☐RSV *King*. See Appendix.

# PENTECOST 18

## Lesson 1 ~ Hosea 11:1-11

*Hosea tells of God's tender and compassionate love for Israel.*

[1] When Israel was young, I loved them,
and out of Egypt I called my child.
[2] The more I called them,
the more they went from me;
they kept sacrificing to the Baals,
and burning incense to the idols.
[3] Yet it was I who taught Ephraim to walk,
I took them up in my arms;
but they did not know that I healed them.
[4] I led them with cords of compassion,
with the bands of love,
and I became to them as one
who eases the yoke on their jaws,
and I bent down to them and fed them.
[5] They shall return to the land of Egypt,
and Assyria shall be their king,
because they have refused to return to me.
[6] The sword shall rage against their cities,
consume the bars of their gates,
and devour them in their fortresses.
[7] My people are bent on turning away from me;
so they are appointed to the yoke,
and none shall remove it.
[8] How can I give you up, O Ephraim!
How can I hand you over, O Israel!
How can I make you like Admah!
How can I treat you like Zeboiim!
My heart recoils within me,
my compassion grows warm and tender.
[9] I will not execute my fierce anger,
I will not again destroy Ephraim;
for I am God and not a human being,
the Holy One in your midst,
and I will not come to destroy.
[10] They shall go after GOD [[*or* the LORD]],
who will roar like a lion;
yea, God will roar,
and God's children shall come trembling from the west;

<sup>11</sup> they shall come trembling like birds from Egypt,
and like doves from the land of Assyria;
and I will return them to their homes, says the SOVEREIGN [[*or*
LORD]].


## Psalm 107:1-9

<sup>1</sup> O give thanks to GOD [[*or* the LORD]], for God is good;
God's steadfast love endures for ever!
<sup>2</sup> Let the redeemed of GOD [[*or* the LORD]] say so,
whom God has redeemed from trouble
<sup>3</sup> and gathered in from the lands,
from the east and from the west,
from the north and from the south.
<sup>4</sup> Some wandered in desert wastes,
finding no way to a city to dwell in;
<sup>5</sup> hungry and thirsty,
their soul fainted within them.
<sup>6</sup> Then in their trouble they cried to GOD [[*or* the LORD]],
who delivered them from their distress,
<sup>7</sup> and led them by a straight way,
till they reached a city to dwell in.
<sup>8</sup> Let them thank GOD [[*or* the LORD]] for God's steadfast love,
for God's wonderful works to humankind!
<sup>9</sup> For God satisfies the thirsty,
and fills the hungry with good things.


## Lesson 2 ~ 1 Timothy 2:1-7

*The writer urges prayer for people in high places, in the name of God and
the one mediator Christ Jesus.*

<sup>1</sup> First of all, then, I urge that supplications, prayers, intercessions,
and thanksgivings be made for all people, <sup>2</sup> for rulers□ and all who are in
high positions, that we may lead a quiet and peaceable life, godly and
respectful in every way. <sup>3</sup> This is good, and it is acceptable in the sight of
God our Savior, <sup>4</sup> who desires all people to be saved and to come to the

---

□RSV *kings*. See Appendix.

knowledge of the truth. ⁵ For there is one God, and there is one mediator between God and humankind, Christ Jesus, ⁶ who sacrificed self as a ransom for all, the testimony to which was borne at the proper time. ⁷ For this I was appointed a preacher and apostle (I am telling the truth, I am not lying), a teacher of the Gentiles in faith and truth.

## Gospel ~ Luke 16:1-13

*Hear Jesus' story of the unjust steward.*

¹ Jesus also said to the disciples, "There was a rich man who had a steward accused of wasting his goods. ² And the rich man called the steward and said, 'What is this that I hear about you? Turn in the account of your stewardship, for you can no longer be steward.' ³ And the steward thought, 'What shall I do, since my master is taking the stewardship away from me? I am not strong enough to dig, and I am ashamed to beg. ⁴ I have decided what to do, so that people may receive me into their houses when I am put out of the stewardship.' ⁵ So, summoning the master's debtors one by one, the steward said to the first, 'How much do you owe my master?' ⁶ The answer came, 'A hundred measures of oil.' And the steward said, 'Take your bill, and sit down quickly and write fifty.' ⁷ Then the steward said to another, 'And how much do you owe?' The answer came, 'A hundred measures of wheat.' The steward said, 'Take your bill, and write eighty.' ⁸ The master commended the dishonest steward for acting shrewdly; for the children of this world are more shrewd in dealing with their own generation than the children of light. ⁹ And I tell you, make friends for yourselves by means of unrighteous mammon, so that when it fails they may receive you into the eternal habitations.

¹⁰ "One who is faithful in a very little is faithful also in much; and one who is dishonest in a very little is dishonest also in much. ¹¹ If then you have not been faithful in the unrighteous mammon, who will entrust to you the true riches? ¹² And if you have not been faithful in that which is another's, who will give you that which is your own? ¹³ No servant can serve two masters; for the servant will either hate the one and love the other, or be devoted to the one and despise the other. You cannot serve God and mammon."

# PENTECOST 19

## Lesson 1 ~ Joel 2:23-30

*The prophet Joel praises God for the promise of an abundant harvest.*

²³ Be glad, O children of Zion,
and rejoice in the SOVEREIGN [*or* LORD], your God,
who has given the early rain for your vindication,
and has poured down for you abundant rain,
the early and the latter rain, as before.
²⁴ The threshing floors shall be full of grain,
the vats shall overflow with wine and oil.
²⁵ I will restore to you the years
which the swarming locust has eaten,
the hopper, the destroyer, and the cutter,
my great army, which I sent among you.
²⁶ You shall eat in plenty and be satisfied,
and praise the name of the SOVEREIGN [*or* LORD] your God,
who has dealt wondrously with you.
And my people shall never again be put to shame.
²⁷ You shall know that I am in the midst of Israel,
and that I, the SOVEREIGN [*or* LORD], am your God and there is
none else.
And my people shall never again be put to shame.
²⁸ And it shall come to pass afterward,
that I will pour out my spirit on all flesh;
your sons and your daughters shall prophesy,
the old shall dream dreams,
and the young shall see visions.
²⁹ Even upon the menservants and womenservants
in those days, I will pour out my spirit.

³⁰ And I will give portents in the heavens and on the earth, blood and
fire and columns of smoke.

## Psalm 107:1, 33-43

¹ O give thanks to GOD [*or* the LORD], for God is good;
God's steadfast love endures for ever!
³³ God turns rivers into a desert,
springs of water into thirsty ground,
³⁴ a fruitful land into a salty waste,
because of the wickedness of its inhabitants.

<sup>35</sup> God turns a desert into pools of water,
 a parched land into springs of water.
<sup>36</sup> And there God lets the hungry dwell,
 and they establish a city to live in;
<sup>37</sup> they sow fields, and plant vineyards,
 and get a fruitful yield.
<sup>38</sup> They multiply greatly by the blessing of God,
 who does not let their cattle decrease.
<sup>39</sup> When they are diminished and brought low
 through oppression, trouble, and sorrow,
<sup>40</sup> God pours contempt upon princes
 and makes them wander in trackless wastes;
<sup>41</sup> but God raises up those who are needy out of affliction,
 and makes their families like flocks.
<sup>42</sup> The upright see it and are glad;
 and all wickedness stops its mouth.
<sup>43</sup> Whoever is wise should give heed to these things;
 let people consider the steadfast love of GOD [or the LORD].

## Lesson 2 ~ 1 Timothy 6:6-19

*The writer urges upon us steadfastness and fidelity.*

<sup>6</sup> There is great gain in godliness with contentment; <sup>7</sup> for we brought nothing into the world, and we cannot take anything out of the world; <sup>8</sup> but if we have food and clothing, with these we shall be content. <sup>9</sup> But those who desire to be rich fall into temptation, into a snare, into many senseless and hurtful desires that plunge people into ruin and destruction. <sup>10</sup> For the love of money is the root of all evils; it is through this craving that some have wandered away from the faith and pierced their hearts with many pangs.

<sup>11</sup> But as for you, O person of God, shun all this; aim at righteousness, godliness, faith, love, steadfastness, gentleness. <sup>12</sup> Fight the good fight of the faith; take hold of the eternal life to which you were called when you made the good confession in the presence of many witnesses. <sup>13</sup> In the presence of God who gives life to all things, and of Christ Jesus who in testifying before Pontius Pilate made the good confession, <sup>14</sup> I charge you to keep the commandment unstained and free from reproach until the appearing of our Sovereign [or Lord] Jesus Christ; <sup>15</sup> and this will be made manifest at the proper time by the blessed and only Sovereign, the Ruler of rulers,<sup>□</sup> and Sovereign of sovereigns [or Lord of lords], <sup>16</sup> who alone has

---

□RSV *King of kings.* See Appendix.

immortality and dwells in unapproachable light, whom no one has ever seen or can see, to whom be honor and eternal dominion. Amen.

[17] As for the rich in this world, charge them not to be haughty, nor to set their hopes on uncertain riches but on God who richly furnishes us with everything to enjoy. [18] They are to do good, to be rich in good deeds, liberal and generous, [19] thus laying up for themselves a good foundation for the future, so that they may take hold of the life which is life indeed.

## Gospel ~ Luke 16:19-31

*Hear now Jesus' story of the rich person and Lazarus.*

[19] There was a rich person, clothed in purple and fine linen, who feasted sumptuously every day. [20] And at the gate lay a poor man named Lazarus, full of sores, [21] who desired to be fed with what fell from the rich person's table; moreover the dogs came and licked his sores. [22] The poor man died and was carried by the angels to Abraham's bosom. The rich person also died and was buried; [23] and being in torment in Hades, looked up, and saw Abraham far off and Lazarus in his bosom. [24] And the rich person called out, "Father Abraham, have mercy upon me, and send Lazarus to dip the end of his finger in water and cool my tongue; for I am in anguish in this flame." [25] But Abraham said, "My child, remember that you in your lifetime received your good things, and Lazarus in like manner evil things; but now he is comforted here, and you are in anguish. [26] And besides all this, between us and you a great chasm has been fixed, in order that those who would pass from here to you may not be able, and none may cross from there to us." [27] And the rich person said, "Then I beg you, father, to send Lazarus to my parents' house, [28] for I have five brothers, so that he may warn them, lest they also come into this place of torment." [29] But Abraham said, "They have Moses and the prophets; let them hear them." [30] And the rich person said, "No, father Abraham; but if someone goes to them from the dead, they will repent." [31] Abraham answered, "If they do not hear Moses and the prophets, neither will they be convinced if someone should rise from the dead."

# PENTECOST 20

## Lesson 1 ~ Amos 5:6-7, 10-15

*Amos warns the people of God's judgment unless they establish justice in their land.*

⁶ Seek GOD [[*or* the LORD]] and live,
    lest God break out like fire in the house of Joseph,
    and it devour, with none to quench it for Bethel,
⁷ O you who turn justice to wormwood,
    and cast down righteousness to the earth!
¹⁰ They hate the one who reproves in the gate,
    and they abhor the one who speaks the truth.
¹¹ Therefore because you trample on those who are poor
    and take from them exactions of wheat,
  you have built houses of hewn stone,
    but you shall not dwell in them;
  you have planted pleasant vineyards,
    but you shall not drink their wine.
¹² For I know how many are your transgressions,
    and how great are your sins—
  you who afflict the righteous, who take a bribe,
    and turn aside those who are needy in the gate.
¹³ Therefore whoever is prudent will keep silent in such a time;
    for it is an evil time.
¹⁴ Seek good, and not evil,
    that you may live;
  and so the SOVEREIGN [[*or* LORD]], the God of hosts, will be with you,
    as you have said.
¹⁵ Hate evil, and love good,
    and establish justice in the gate;
  it may be that the SOVEREIGN [[*or* LORD]], the God of hosts,
    will be gracious to the remnant of Joseph.

## Psalm 101

¹ I will sing of loyalty and of justice;
    to you, O GOD [[*or* LORD]], I will sing.
² I will give heed to the way that is blameless.
    Oh when will you come to me?
  I will walk with integrity of heart
    within my house;

214

3 I will not set before my eyes
   anything that is base.
I hate the work of those who fall away;
   it shall not cleave to me.
4 Perverseness of heart shall be far from me;
   I will know nothing of evil.
5 The one who slanders a neighbor secretly
   I will destroy.
The one of haughty looks and arrogant heart
   I will not endure.
6 I will look with favor on the faithful in the land,
   that they may dwell with me;
one who walks in the way that is blameless
   shall minister to me.
7 No one who practices deceit
   shall dwell in my house;
no one who utters lies
   shall continue in my presence.
8 Morning by morning I will destroy
   all the wicked in the land,
cutting off all the evildoers
   from the city of GOD [or the LORD].


## Lesson 2 ~ 2 Timothy 1:1-14

*Timothy is urged to share in the suffering of the gospel.*

1 Paul, an apostle of Christ Jesus by the will of God according to the promise of the life which is in Christ Jesus,

2 To Timothy, my beloved child:

Grace, mercy, and peace from God the Father [*and Mother**] and Christ Jesus our Sovereign [or Lord].

3 I thank God whom I serve with a clear conscience, as did my ancestors, when I remember you constantly in my prayers. 4 As I remember your tears, I long night and day to see you, that I may be filled with joy. 5 I am reminded of your sincere faith, a faith that dwelt first in your grandmother Lois and your mother Eunice and now, I am sure, dwells in you. 6 Hence I remind you to rekindle the gift of God that is within you through the laying on of my hands; 7 for God did not give us a spirit of timidity but a spirit of power and love and self-control.

---

*Addition to the text. See "Metaphor" and "God the Father and Mother" in the Appendix.

8 Do not be ashamed then of testifying to our Sovereign [[or Lord]], nor of me the Sovereign's [[or Lord's]] prisoner, but share in suffering for the gospel in the power of God, 9who saved us and called us with a holy calling, not in virtue of our works but in virtue of God's own purpose and the grace which was given us in Christ Jesus ages ago, 10and now has been manifested through the appearing of our Savior Christ Jesus, who abolished death and brought life and immortality to light through the gospel. 11For this gospel I was appointed a preacher and apostle and teacher, 12and therefore I suffer as I do. But I am not ashamed, for I know whom I have believed, and I am sure that God is able to guard until that Day what has been entrusted to me. 13 Follow the pattern of the sound words which you have heard from me, in the faith and love which are in Christ Jesus; 14guard the truth that has been entrusted to you by the Holy Spirit who dwells within us.


### Gospel ~ Luke 17:5-10

*Jesus tells us what the wages of a servant are.*

5The apostles said to the Sovereign [[or Lord]], "Increase our faith!" 6And the Sovereign [[or Lord]] said, "If you had faith as a grain of mustard seed, you could say to this mulberry tree, 'Be rooted up, and be planted in the sea,' and it would obey you.

7"Will any one of you, who has a servant plowing or keeping sheep, say, when the servant comes in from the field, 'Come at once and sit down at table'? 8Will you not rather say, 'Prepare supper for me, and gird yourself and serve me, till I eat and drink; and afterward you shall eat and drink'? 9Is the servant thanked for doing what was commanded? 10So you also, when you have done all that is commanded you, say, 'We are unworthy servants; we have only done what was our duty.'"

# PENTECOST 21

## Lesson 1 ~ Micah 1:2; 2:1-10

*Micah accuses the people of evil and injustice.*

² Hear, you nations, all of you;
    hearken, O earth, and all that is in it;
  and let the Sovereign [[*or* Lord]] GOD be a witness against you,
    God [[*or* the Lord]] from the holy temple.
²:¹ Woe to those who devise wickedness
    and work evil upon their beds!
  When the morning dawns, they perform it,
    because it is in the power of their hand.
² They covet fields, and seize them;
    and houses, and take them away;
  they oppress people and their houses,
    people and their inheritance.
³ Therefore thus says the SOVEREIGN [[*or* LORD]]:
  Against this family I am devising evil,
    from which you cannot remove your necks;
  and you shall not walk haughtily,
    for it will be an evil time.
⁴ In that day they shall take up a taunting song against you,
    and wail with bitter lamentation,
  and say, "We are utterly ruined;
    the portion of my people is changed;
  it is removed from me!
    Our fields are divided among our captors."
⁵ Therefore you will have none to cast the line by lot in the assembly of
    GOD [[*or* the LORD]].
⁶ "Do not preach"—thus they preach—
    "one should not preach of such things;
    disgrace will not overtake us."
⁷ Should this be said, O house of Jacob?
    Is the Spirit of GOD [[*or* the LORD]] impatient?
    Are these God's doings?
  Do not my words do good
    to the one who walks uprightly?
⁸ But you rise against my people as an enemy;
    you strip the robe from the peaceful,
  from those who pass by trustingly
    with no thought of war.

⁹ The women of my people you drive out
   from their pleasant houses;
 from their young children you take away
   my glory forever.
¹⁰ Arise and go,
   for this is no place to rest;
 because of uncleanness that destroys
   with a grievous destruction.


## Psalm 26

¹ Vindicate me, O GOD [or LORD], for I have walked in my integrity,
   and I have trusted in GOD [or the LORD] without wavering.
² Prove me, O GOD [or LORD], and try me;
   test my heart and my mind.
³ For your steadfast love is before my eyes,
   and I walk in faithfulness to you.
⁴ I do not sit with those who are false,
   nor do I consort with dissemblers;
⁵ I hate the company of evildoers,
   and I will not sit with the wicked.
⁶ I wash my hands in innocence,
   and go about your altar, O GOD [or LORD],
⁷ singing aloud a song of thanksgiving,
   and telling all your wondrous deeds.
⁸ O GOD [or LORD], I love the habitation of your house,
   and the place where your glory dwells.
⁹ Sweep me not away with sinners,
   nor my life with those who are bloodthirsty,
¹⁰ in whose hands are evil devices,
   and whose right hands are full of bribes.
¹¹ But as for me, I walk in my integrity;
   redeem me, and be gracious to me.
¹² My foot stands on level ground;
   in the great congregation I will bless GOD [or the LORD].

## Lesson 2 ~ 2 Timothy 2:8-15

*The Christian's relationship with Christ is set forth in an early hymn.*

⁸ Remember Jesus Christ, risen from the dead, descended from David, as preached in my gospel, ⁹ the gospel for which I am suffering and wearing fetters like a criminal. But the word of God is not fettered. ¹⁰ Therefore I endure everything for the sake of the elect, that they also may obtain salvation in Christ Jesus with its eternal glory. ¹¹ The saying is sure:

If we have died with Christ, we shall also live with Christ;
¹² if we endure, we shall also reign with Christ;
if we make denial, Christ also will deny us;
¹³ if we are faithless, that one remains faithful—

for there can be no denying of self.
¹⁴ Remind them of this, and charge them before the Sovereign [[or Lord]] to avoid disputing about words, which does no good, but only ruins the hearers. ¹⁵ Do your best to present yourself to God as one approved, a worker who has no need to be ashamed, rightly handling the word of truth.

## Gospel ~ Luke 17:11-19

*Jesus heals the ten people of their leprosy.*

¹¹ On the way to Jerusalem Jesus was passing along between Samaria and Galilee. ¹² And entering a village, he was met by ten people with leprosy, who stood at a distance ¹³ and lifted up their voices and said, "Jesus, Teacher,† have mercy on us." ¹⁴ And seeing them, Jesus said, "Go and show yourselves to the priests." And as they went they were cleansed. ¹⁵ Then one of them, seeing that he was healed, turned back, praising God with a loud voice; ¹⁶ and he fell down at Jesus' feet, giving him thanks. Now that one was a Samaritan. ¹⁷ Then said Jesus, "Were not ten cleansed? Where are the nine? ¹⁸ Was no one found to return and give praise to God except this foreigner?" ¹⁹ And Jesus said to him, "Rise and go your way; your faith has made you well."

---

†RSV *Master.* See Appendix.

# PENTECOST 22

## Lesson 1 ~ Habakkuk 1:1-3; 2:1-4

*Habakkuk cries to God for redemption, and receives a vision of God's plan.*

1 The oracle of God which Habakkuk the prophet saw.
2 GOD [[*or* LORD]], how long shall I cry for help,
 and you will not hear?
Or cry to you, "Violence!"
 and you will not save?
3 Why do you make me see wrongs
 and look upon trouble?
Destruction and violence are before me;
 strife and contention arise.
2:1 I will take my stand to watch,
 and station myself on the tower,
and look forth to see what God will say to me,
 and what I will answer concerning my complaint.
2 And GOD [[*or* the LORD]] answered me:
"Write the vision;
 make it plain upon tablets,
 so the one who reads it may run.
3 For still the vision awaits its time;
 it hastens to the end—it will not lie.
If it seem slow, wait for it;
 it will surely come, it will not delay.
4 The one whose soul is not
 upright within shall fail,
 but the righteous shall live by their faith."

## Psalm 119:137-144

137 Righteous are you, O GOD [[or LORD]],
   and right are your judgments.
138 You have appointed your testimonies in righteousness
   and in all faithfulness.
139 My zeal consumes me,
   because my foes forget your words.
140 Your promise is well tried,
   and your servant loves it.
141 I am small and despised,
   yet I do not forget your precepts.
142 Your righteousness is righteous forever,
   and your law is true.
143 Trouble and anguish have come upon me,
   but your commandments are my delight.
144 Your testimonies are righteous forever;
   give me understanding that I may live.

## Lesson 2 ~ 2 Timothy 3:14–4:5

*Timothy is admonished to follow the teachings of his mother and grand-mother and to be faithful to his ministry.*

14 But as for you, continue in what you have learned and have firmly believed, knowing from whom you learned it 15 and how from childhood you have been acquainted with the sacred writings which are able to instruct you for salvation through faith in Christ Jesus. 16 All scripture is inspired by God and profitable for teaching, for reproof, for correction, and for training in righteousness, 17 that the person who is of God may be complete, equipped for every good work.
4:1 I charge you in the presence of God and of Christ Jesus who is to judge the living and the dead, and by the appearing and reign of Christ✩: 2 preach the word, be urgent in season and out of season, convince, rebuke, and exhort, be unfailing in patience and in teaching. 3 For the time is coming when people will not endure sound teaching, but having itching ears they will accumulate for themselves teachers to suit their own likings, 4 and will turn away from listening to the truth and wander into myths. 5 As for you, always be steady, endure suffering, do the work of an evangelist, fulfill your ministry.

---

✩RSV *by his appearing and his kingdom*. See Appendix.

# Gospel ~ Luke 18:1-8

*Jesus tells the disciples a parable about prayer.*

¹ And Jesus told them a parable, to the effect that they ought always to pray and not lose heart. ² He said, "In a certain city there was a judge who neither feared God nor respected people; ³ and there was a widow in that city who kept coming to the judge and saying, 'Vindicate me against my adversary.' ⁴ For a while the judge refused, but afterward thought, 'Though I neither fear God nor respect people, ⁵ yet because this widow bothers me, I will vindicate her, or she will wear me out by her continual coming.'" ⁶ And the Sovereign ⟦*or* Lord⟧ said, "Hear what the unrighteous judge says. ⁷ And will not God vindicate the elect, who cry to God day and night? Will God delay long over them? ⁸ I tell you, God will vindicate them speedily. Nevertheless, when the Human One° comes, will the Human One find faith on earth?"

---

°RSV *Son of man*. See Appendix.

# PENTECOST 23

### Lesson 1 ~ Zephaniah 3:1-9

*The prophet judges the oppressing city and praises God's justice.*

¹ Woe to the one that is rebellious and defiled,
    the oppressing city!
² It listens to no voice,
    accepts no correction.
It does not trust in GOD [[*or* the LORD]],
    and does not draw near to its God.
³ Its officials within the city
    are roaring lions;
its judges are evening wolves
    that leave nothing till the morning.
⁴ Its prophets are wanton
    and faithless;
its priests profane what is sacred,
    they do violence to the law.
⁵ GOD [[*or* The LORD]] is righteous within it
    and does no wrong,
showing forth justice every morning,
    never failing at dawn;
    but the unjust knows no shame.
⁶ "I have cut off nations;
    their battlements are in ruins;
I have laid waste their streets
    so that none walks in them;
their cities have been made desolate,
    without a single person, without an inhabitant.
⁷ I said, 'Surely the city will fear me,
    and will accept correction;
it will not lose sight
    of all I have enjoined upon it.'
But all the more they were eager
    to make all their deeds corrupt."
⁸ "Therefore wait for me," says the SOVEREIGN [[*or* LORD]],
    "for the day when I arise as a witness.
For my decision is to gather nations,
    to assemble kingdoms,
to pour out upon them my indignation,
    all the heat of my anger;

for in the fire of my jealous wrath
    all the earth shall be consumed.
9 Indeed, at that time I will change the speech of the nations
    to a pure speech,
  that all of them may call on the name of GOD [[*or* the LORD]]
    and serve God with one accord."

## Psalm 3

1 O GOD [[*or* LORD]], how many are my foes!
    Many are rising against me;
2 many are saying of me,
    there is no help for that one in God.
3 But you, O GOD [[*or* LORD]], are a shield about me,
    my glory, and the lifter of my head.
4 I cry aloud to GOD [[*or* the LORD]],
    who answers me from God's holy hill.
5 I lie down and sleep;
    I wake again, for GOD [[*or* the LORD]] sustains me.
6 I am not afraid of ten thousands of people .
    who have set themselves against me round about.
7 Arise, O GOD [[*or* LORD]]!
    Deliver me, O my God!
  For you smite all my enemies on the cheek,
    you break the teeth of the wicked.
8 Deliverance belongs to GOD [[*or* the LORD]];
    your blessing be upon your people!

## Lesson 2 ~ 2 Timothy 4:6-8, 16-18

*The apostle, who is about to be sacrificed, trusts in the Sovereign.*

⁶ For I am already on the point of being sacrificed; the time of my departure has come. ⁷ I have fought the good fight, I have finished the race, I have kept the faith. ⁸ Henceforth there is laid up for me the crown of righteousness, which the Sovereign [[*or* Lord]], the righteous judge, will award to me on that Day, and not only to me but also to all who have loved the Sovereign's [[*or* Lord's]] appearing.

¹⁶ At my first defense no one took my part; all deserted me. May it not be charged against them! ¹⁷ But the Sovereign [[*or* Lord]] stood by me and gave me strength to proclaim the message fully, that all the Gentiles might hear it. So I was rescued from the lion's mouth. ¹⁸ The Sovereign [[*or* Lord]] will rescue me from every evil and save me for the heavenly dominion. ☆ To that one be the glory forever and ever. Amen.

## Gospel ~ Luke 18:9-14

*Hear now Jesus' parable of the Pharisee and the tax collector.*

⁹ Jesus told this parable to some who trusted in themselves that they were righteous and despised others: ¹⁰ "Two people went up into the temple to pray, one a Pharisee and the other a tax collector. ¹¹ The Pharisee stood and prayed thus with himself, 'God, I thank you that I am not like other people, extortioners, unjust, adulterers, or even like this tax collector. ¹² I fast twice a week, I give tithes of all that I get.' ¹³ But the tax collector, standing far off, would not even look up to heaven, but beat his breast and said, 'God, be merciful to me a sinner!' ¹⁴ I tell you, this one went home justified rather than the other; for all who exalt themselves will be humbled, but those who humble themselves will be exalted."

---

☆RSV *kingdom*. See Appendix.

# PENTECOST 24

### Lesson 1 ~ Haggai 2:1-9

*God promises that the splendor of the temple will be restored.*

¹ In the second year of Darius the king, in the seventh month, on the twenty-first day of the month, the word of GOD [[*or* the LORD]] came by Haggai the prophet, ² "Speak now to Zerubbabel the son of Shealtiel, governor of Judah, and to Joshua the son of Jehozadak, the high priest, and to all the remnant of the people, and say, ³ 'Who is left among you that saw this house in its former glory? How do you see it now? Is it not in your sight as nothing? ⁴ Yet now take courage, O Zerubbabel, says the SOVEREIGN [[*or* LORD]]; take courage, O Joshua, son of Jehozadak, the high priest; take courage, all you people of the land, says the SOVEREIGN [[*or* LORD]]; work, for I am with you, says the GOD [[*or* LORD]] of hosts, ⁵ according to the promise that I made you when you came out of Egypt. My Spirit abides among you; fear not. ⁶ For thus says the GOD [[*or* LORD]] of hosts: Once again, in a little while, I will shake the heavens and the earth and the sea and the dry land; ⁷ and I will shake all nations, so that the treasures of all nations shall come in, and I will fill this house with splendor, says the GOD [[*or* LORD]] of hosts. ⁸ The silver is mine, and the gold is mine, says the GOD [[*or* LORD]] of hosts. ⁹ The latter splendor of this house shall be greater than the former, says the GOD [[*or* LORD]] of hosts; and in this place I will give prosperity, says the GOD [[*or* LORD]] of hosts.' "

### Psalm 65:1-8

¹ Praise is due to you,
    O God, in Zion;
  and to you shall vows be performed,
²   O you who hear prayer!
  To you shall all flesh come
³   on account of sins.
  When our transgressions prevail over us,
    you forgive them.
⁴ Blessed is the one whom you choose and bring near,
    to dwell in your courts!
  We shall be satisfied with the goodness of your house,
    your holy temple!

⁵ By dread deeds you answer us with deliverance,
   O God of our salvation,
 who are the hope of all the ends of the earth,
   and of the farthest seas;
⁶ who by your strength have established the mountains,
   being girded with might;
⁷ who still the roaring of the seas,
   the roaring of their waves,
   the tumult of the peoples;
⁸ so that those who dwell at earth's farthest bounds
   are afraid at your signs;
 you make the outgoings of the morning and the evening
   to shout for joy.

### Lesson 2 ~ 2 Thessalonians 1:5-12

*Paul speaks of the righteous judgment of God.*

⁵ This is evidence of the righteous judgment of God, that you may be made worthy of the dominion☆ of God, for which you are suffering— ⁶ since indeed God deems it just to repay with affliction those who afflict you, ⁷ and to grant rest with us to you who are afflicted, when the Sovereign [or Lord] Jesus is revealed from heaven with the mighty angels in flaming fire, ⁸ inflicting vengeance upon those who do not know God and upon those who do not obey the gospel of our Sovereign [or Lord] Jesus. ⁹ They shall suffer the punishment of eternal destruction and exclusion from the Sovereign's [or Lord's] presence and from the glory of the Sovereign's [or Lord's] might, ¹⁰ when on that day the Sovereign [or Lord] comes to be glorified in the saints, and to be marveled at in all who have believed, because our testimony to you was believed. ¹¹ To this end we always pray for you, that our God may make you worthy of the call, and may fulfill every good resolve and work of faith with power, ¹² so that the name of our Sovereign [or Lord] Jesus may be glorified in you, and you in the Sovereign [or Lord], according to the grace of our God and the Sovereign [or Lord] Jesus Christ.

---

☆RSV *kingdom*. See Appendix.

# Gospel ~ Luke 19:1-10

*Salvation comes to the house of Zacchaeus.*

[1] Jesus entered Jericho and was passing through. [2] And there was a man named Zacchaeus, who was a chief tax collector, and rich. [3] And he sought to see who Jesus was, but could not, on account of the crowd, because he was small of stature. [4] So he ran on ahead and climbed up into a sycamore tree to see Jesus, who was to pass that way. [5] And when Jesus came to the place, he looked up and said to him, "Zacchaeus, make haste and come down; for I must stay at your house today." [6] So he made haste and came down, and received Jesus joyfully. [7] And when they saw it they all murmured, "He has gone in to be the guest of a man who is a sinner." [8] And Zacchaeus stood and said to the Sovereign [[*or* Lord]], "Half of my goods I give to the poor; and if I have defrauded anyone of anything, I restore it fourfold." [9] And Jesus said to him, "Today salvation has come to this house, since Zacchaeus also is a descendant of Abraham. [10] For the Human One○ came to seek and to save the lost."

---

○RSV *Son of man*. See Appendix.

# PENTECOST 25

## Lesson 1 ~ Zechariah 7:1-10

*The people who have returned from exile are reminded that justice and mercy are more important to God than the keeping of fasts.*

¹ In the fourth year of King Darius, the word of GOD [[or the LORD]] came to Zechariah in the fourth day of the ninth month, which is Chislev. ² Now the people of Bethel had sent Sharezer and Regem-melech and their men, to entreat the favor of GOD [[or the LORD]] ³ and to ask the priests of the house of the GOD [[or LORD]] of hosts and the prophets, "Should I mourn and fast in the fifth month, as I have done for so many years?" ⁴ Then the word of the GOD [[or LORD]] of hosts came to me: ⁵ "Say to all the people of the land and the priests, When you fasted and mourned in the fifth month and in the seventh, for these seventy years, was it for me that you fasted? ⁶ And when you eat and when you drink, do you not eat for yourselves and drink for yourselves? ⁷ When Jerusalem was inhabited and in prosperity, with its cities round about it, and the South and the lowland were inhabited, were not these the words which GOD [[or the LORD]] proclaimed by the former prophets?"

⁸ And the word of GOD [[or the LORD]] came to Zechariah, saying, ⁹ "Thus says the GOD [[or LORD]] of hosts, Render true judgments, show kindness and mercy each to your neighbor, ¹⁰ do not oppress the widow, the orphan, the resident alien, or the poor; and let none of you devise evil against your neighbor in your heart."

## Psalm 9:11-20

¹¹ Sing praises to GOD [[or the LORD]], who dwells in Zion!
   Tell among the nations the deeds of God!
¹² For the one who avenges blood is mindful of them,
   and does not forget the cry of those who are afflicted.
¹³ Be gracious to me, O GOD [[or LORD]]!
   Look at what I suffer from those who hate me,
   O you who lift me up from the gates of death,
¹⁴ that I may recount all your praises,
   that in the gates of beloved Zion
   I may rejoice in your deliverance.
¹⁵ The nations have sunk in the pit which they made;
   in the net which they hid has their own foot been caught.

<sup>16</sup> GOD [[*or* The LORD]] has made God's self known and has executed
   judgment;
      the wicked are snared in the work of their own hands.
<sup>17</sup> The wicked shall depart to Sheol,
      all the nations that forget God.
<sup>18</sup> For the needy shall not always be forgotten,
      and the hope of the poor shall not perish forever.
<sup>19</sup> Arise, O GOD [[*or* LORD]]! Let no one prevail;
      let the nations be judged before you!
<sup>20</sup> Put them in fear, O GOD [[*or* LORD]]!
      Let the nations know that they are only human!

### Lesson 2 ~ 2 Thessalonians 2:13–3:5

*Paul thanks God for choosing the Thessalonians and sanctifying them by the Spirit.*

<sup>13</sup> But we are bound to give thanks to God always for you, brothers and sisters beloved by the Sovereign [[*or* Lord]], because God chose you from the beginning to be saved, through sanctification by the Spirit and belief in the truth. <sup>14</sup> To this God called you through our gospel, so that you may obtain the glory of our Sovereign [[*or* Lord]] Jesus Christ. <sup>15</sup> So then, beloved, stand firm and hold to the traditions which you were taught by us, either by word of mouth or by letter.

<sup>16</sup> Now may our Sovereign [[*or* Lord]] Jesus Christ, and God our [*Mother and**] Father, who loved us and gave us eternal comfort and good hope through grace, <sup>17</sup> comfort your hearts and establish them in every good work and word.

<sup>3:1</sup> Finally, sisters and brothers, pray for us, that the word of the Sovereign [[*or* Lord]] may speed on and triumph, as it did among you, <sup>2</sup> and that we may be delivered from wicked and evil people; for not all have faith. <sup>3</sup> But the Sovereign [[*or* Lord]] is faithful, and will strengthen you and guard you from evil. <sup>4</sup> And we have confidence in the Sovereign [[*or* Lord]] about you, that you are doing and will do the things which we command. <sup>5</sup> May the Sovereign [[*or* Lord]] direct your hearts to the love of God and to the steadfastness of Christ.

---

*Addition to the text. See "Metaphor" and "God the Father and Mother" in the Appendix.

## Gospel ~ Luke 20:27-38

*Jesus answers a question of the Sadducees concerning the resurrection.*

27 There came to Jesus some Sadducees, those who say that there is no resurrection, 28 and they asked a question, saying, "Teacher, Moses wrote for us that if a man's brother dies, having a wife but no children, the man must take the wife and raise up children for his brother. 29 Now there were seven brothers; the first took a wife, and died without children; 30 and the second 31 and the third took her, and likewise all seven left no children and died. 32 Afterward the woman also died. 33 In the resurrection, therefore, whose wife will the woman be? For the seven had her as wife."

34 And Jesus said to them, "The daughters and sons of this age marry and are given in marriage; 35 but those who are accounted worthy to attain to that age and to the resurrection from the dead neither marry nor are given in marriage, 36 for they cannot die anymore, because they are equal to angels and are children of God, being children of the resurrection. 37 But that the dead are raised, even Moses showed, in the passage about the bush, where he calls the Sovereign [[or Lord]] the God of Abraham and the God of Isaac and the God of Jacob. 38 Now God is not God of the dead, but of the living; for all live to God."

# PENTECOST 26

## Lesson 1 ~ Malachi 4:1-6

*Malachi tells the people of the coming day of God which will bring judgment to evildoers and blessings to the righteous.*

¹ For the day is coming, burning like an oven, when all the arrogant and all evildoers will be stubble; the day that comes shall burn them up, says the GOD [[*or* LORD]] of hosts, so that it will leave them neither root nor branch. ² But for you who fear my name the sun of righteousness shall rise with healing in its wings. You shall go forth leaping like calves from the stall. ³ And you shall tread down the wicked, for they will be ashes under the soles of your feet, on the day when I act, says the GOD [[*or* LORD]] of hosts.

⁴ Remember the law of my servant Moses, the statutes and ordinances that I commanded him at Horeb for all Israel.

⁵ Before the great and terrible day of the SOVEREIGN [[*or* LORD]] comes, I will send you Elijah the prophet. ⁶ And he will turn the hearts of parents to their children and the hearts of children to their parents, lest I come and smite the land with a curse.

## Psalm 82

¹ God stands up in the divine council;
    in the midst of the gods, God holds judgment:
² "How long will you judge unjustly
    and show partiality to the wicked?
³ Give justice to the weak and the orphan;
    maintain the right of the afflicted and the destitute.
⁴ Rescue the weak and the needy;
    deliver them from the hand of the wicked."
⁵ They have neither knowledge nor understanding,
    they walk about in confusion;
    all the foundations of the earth are shaken.
⁶ I say, "You are gods,
    offspring of the Most High, all of you;
⁷ nevertheless, you shall die like human beings,
    and fall like any ruler."
⁸ Arise, O God, judge the earth;
    for to you belong all the nations!

## Lesson 2 ~ 2 Thessalonians 3:6-13

*Paul exhorts the Christians at Thessalonica to work and earn their own living.*

⁶ Now we command you, friends, in the name of our Sovereign [[*or* Lord]] Jesus Christ, that you keep away from any brother or sister who is living in idleness and not in accord with the tradition that you received from us. ⁷ For you yourselves know how you ought to imitate us; we were not idle when we were with you, ⁸ we did not eat anyone's bread without paying, but with toil and labor we worked night and day, that we might not burden any of you. ⁹ It was not because we have not that right, but to give you in our conduct an example to imitate. ¹⁰ For even when we were with you, we gave you this command: Whoever will not work, let them not eat. ¹¹ For we hear that some of you are living in idleness, mere busybodies, not doing any work. ¹² Now such persons we command and exhort in the Sovereign [[*or* Lord]] Jesus Christ to do their work in quietness and to earn their own living. ¹³ Friends, do not be weary in well-doing.

## Gospel ~ Luke 21:5-19

*Jesus speaks about the signs that will accompany the end.*

⁵ And as some spoke of the temple, how it was adorned with noble stones and offerings, Jesus said, ⁶ "As for these things which you see, the days will come when there shall not be left here one stone upon another that will not be thrown down." ⁷ And they asked, "Teacher, when will this be, and what will be the sign when this is about to take place?" ⁸ And Jesus said, "Take heed that you are not led astray; for many will come in my name, saying, 'I am the one!' and, 'The time is at hand!' Do not go after them. ⁹ And when you hear of wars and tumults, do not be terrified; for this must first take place, but the end will not be at once."
¹⁰ Then Jesus said to them, "Nation will rise against nation, and kingdom against kingdom; ¹¹ there will be great earthquakes, and in various places famines and pestilences; and there will be terrors and great signs from heaven. ¹² But before all this they will lay their hands on you and persecute you, delivering you up to the synagogues and prisons, and you will be brought before kings and governors for my name's sake. ¹³ This will be a time for you to bear testimony. ¹⁴ Settle it therefore in your minds, not to meditate beforehand how to answer; ¹⁵ for I will give you a mouth and wisdom, which none of your adversaries will be able to withstand or contradict. ¹⁶ You will be delivered up even by parents and brothers and sisters and relatives and friends, and some of you they will put to death; ¹⁷ you will be hated by all for my name's sake. ¹⁸ But not a hair of your head will perish. ¹⁹ By your endurance you will gain your lives."

# PENTECOST 27

## Lesson 1 ~ 2 Samuel 5:1-5

*David reigns over Israel and Judah.*

¹ Then all the tribes of Israel came to David at Hebron, and said, "We are your bone and flesh. ² In times past, when Saul was king over us, it was you that led out and brought in Israel; and GOD [[*or* the LORD]] said to you, 'You shall be shepherd of my people Israel, and you shall be prince over Israel.'" ³ So all the elders of Israel came to the king at Hebron; and King David made a covenant with them at Hebron before GOD [[*or* the LORD]], and they anointed David king over Israel. ⁴ David was thirty years old when he began to reign, and he reigned forty years. ⁵ At Hebron David reigned over Judah seven years and six months; and at Jerusalem he reigned over all Israel and Judah thirty-three years.

## Psalm 95

¹ O come, let us sing to GOD [[*or* the LORD]];
　　let us make a joyful noise to the rock of our salvation!
² Let us come into God's presence with thanksgiving;
　　let us make a joyful noise to God with songs of praise!
³ For the SOVEREIGN [[*or* LORD]] is a great God,
　　and a great Ruler□ above all gods.
⁴ The depths of the earth are in the hand of God;
　　the heights of the mountains are God's also.
⁵ The sea belongs to God, for God made it;
　　for God's hands formed the dry land.
⁶ O come, let us worship and bow down,
　　let us kneel before GOD [[*or* the LORD]], our Maker!
⁷ For this is our God,
　　and we are the people of God's pasture,
　　and the sheep of God's hand.
　O that today you would hearken to the voice of God!
⁸　Harden not your hearts, as at Meribah,
　　as on the day at Massah in the wilderness,
⁹ when your ancestors tested me,
　　and put me to the proof, though they had seen my work.

---

□RSV *King*. See Appendix.

$^{10}$ For forty years I loathed that generation
and said, "They are a people who err in heart,
and they do not regard my ways."
$^{11}$ Therefore I swore in my anger
that they should not enter my rest.

## Lesson 2 ~ Colossians 1:11-20

*Hear a great christological passage from the letter to the Colossians.*

$^{11}$ May you be strengthened with all power, according to God's glorious might, for all endurance and patience with joy, $^{12}$ giving thanks to [*God*] the [*Mother and**] Father, who has qualified us to share in the inheritance of the saints in light. $^{13}$ God has delivered us from the power of evil and transferred us to the dominion☆ of God's beloved Child,◇ $^{14}$ in whom we have redemption, the forgiveness of sins.

$^{15}$ Christ is the image of the invisible God, the firstborn of all creation. $^{16}$ For in Christ all things were created, in heaven and on earth, visible and invisible, whether thrones or dominions or principalities or authorities—all things were created through Christ and for Christ. $^{17}$ Christ is before all things, the one in whom all things hold together. $^{18}$ Christ is the head of the body, the church, and is the beginning, the firstborn from the dead, that in everything Christ might be preeminent. $^{19}$ For in Christ all the fullness of God was pleased to dwell, $^{20}$ and through Christ to reconcile for Christ all things, whether on earth or in heaven, making peace by the blood of the cross.

---

*Addition to the text. See "Metaphor" and "God the Father and Mother" in the Appendix.
☆RSV *kingdom*. See Appendix.
◇RSV *Son*. See Appendix.

## Gospel ~ John 12:9-19

*John describes Jesus' entry into Jerusalem.*

9 When the great crowd of the Jews learned that Jesus was there, they came, not only on account of Jesus but also to see Lazarus, whom Jesus had raised from the dead. 10 So the chief priests planned to put Lazarus also to death, 11 because on account of him many of the Jews were going away and believing in Jesus.

12 The next day a great crowd who had come to the feast heard that Jesus was coming to Jerusalem. 13 So they took branches of palm trees and went out to meet him, crying, "Hosanna! Blessed is the one who comes in the name of the Sovereign [[or Lord]], even the Ruler□ of Israel!" 14 And Jesus found a young donkey and sat upon it; as it is written,

15 "Fear not, beloved Zion;
   your ruler□ is coming,
   sitting on a donkey's colt!"

16 The disciples did not understand this at first; but when Jesus was glorified, then they remembered that this had been written of Jesus and had been done to him. 17 The crowd that had been with him when he called Lazarus out of the tomb and raised him from the dead bore witness. 18 The reason why the crowd went to meet Jesus was that they heard he had done this sign. 19 The Pharisees then said to one another, "You see that you can do nothing; look, the world has gone after him."

---

□RSV v. 13 *King;* v. 15 *king.* See Appendix.

# PRESENTATION—FEBRUARY 2

## Lesson 1 ~ Malachi 3:1-4

*The messenger goes before God to bring judgment to the people.*

¹ I am sending my messenger to prepare the way before me, and God ⟦*or* the Lord⟧ whom you seek will suddenly come to the temple; the messenger of the covenant in whom you delight—that one is coming, says the GOD ⟦*or* LORD⟧ of hosts. ² But who can endure the day of that coming, and who can stand when the messenger appears?

For my messenger is like a refiner's fire and like launderers' bleach, ³ who will sit as a refiner and purifier of silver, and will purify the tribe of Levi and refine them like gold and silver, till they present right offerings to GOD ⟦*or* the LORD⟧. ⁴ Then the offering of Judah and Jerusalem will be pleasing to GOD ⟦*or* the LORD⟧ as in the days of old and as in former years.

## Psalm 84

¹ How lovely is your dwelling place,
    O GOD ⟦*or* LORD⟧ of hosts!
² My soul longs, even faints
    for the courts of GOD ⟦*or* the LORD⟧;
  my heart and flesh sing for joy
    to the living God.
³ Even the sparrow finds a home,
    and the swallow a nest for herself,
    where she may lay her young,
  at your altars, O GOD ⟦*or* LORD⟧ of hosts,
    my Ruler⬚ and my God.
⁴ Blessed are those who dwell in your house,
    ever singing your praise!
⁵ Blessed are those whose strength is in you,
    in whose heart are the highways to Zion.
⁶ As they go through the valley of Baca
    they make it a place of springs;
    the early rain also covers it with pools.
⁷ They go from strength to strength;
    the God of gods will be seen in Zion.
⁸ O SOVEREIGN ⟦*or* LORD⟧ God of hosts, hear my prayer;
    give ear, O God of Jacob!

---

⬚RSV *King*. See Appendix.

<sup>9</sup> Behold our shield, O God;
    look upon the face of your anointed!
<sup>10</sup> For a day in your courts is better
    than a thousand elsewhere.
  I would rather be a doorkeeper in the house of my God
    than dwell in the tents of wickedness.
<sup>11</sup> For the SOVEREIGN [[*or* LORD]] God is a sun and shield,
    who bestows favor and honor.
  No good thing does GOD [[*or* the LORD]] withhold
    from those who walk uprightly.
<sup>12</sup> O GOD [[*or* LORD]] of hosts,
    blessed is the one who trusts in you!

### Psalm 24:7-10 (alternate)

<sup>7</sup> Lift up your heads, O gates!
    and be lifted up, O ancient doors!
    that the Ruler<sup>□</sup> of glory may come in.
<sup>8</sup> Who is the Ruler<sup>□</sup> of glory?
    GOD [[*or* The LORD]], strong and mighty,
    GOD [[*or* the LORD]], mighty in battle!
<sup>9</sup> Lift up your heads, O gates!
    and be lifted up, O ancient doors!
    that the Ruler<sup>□</sup> of glory may come in.
<sup>10</sup> Who is this Ruler<sup>□</sup> of glory?
    The GOD [[*or* LORD]] of hosts,
    that one is the Ruler<sup>□</sup> of glory!

---

□RSV *King*. See Appendix.

## Lesson 2 ~ Hebrews 2:14-18

*Jesus, by becoming a human being, delivers the people by making expiation for their sins.*

[14] Since therefore the children share in flesh and blood, Jesus likewise partook of the same nature in order to destroy through death the one who has the power of death, that is, the devil, [15] and to deliver all those who through fear of death were subject to lifelong bondage. [16] For surely it is not with angels that Jesus is concerned but with the descendants of Abraham [and Sarah*]. [17] Therefore Jesus had to be made like human beings in every respect, in order to become a merciful and faithful high priest in the service of God, to make expiation for the sins of the people. [18] For because Jesus also has suffered and been tempted, Jesus is able to help those who are tempted.

## Gospel ~ Luke 2:22-40

*Mary and Joseph take the infant Jesus to the temple in Jerusalem, and the child is met there by Simeon and Anna.*

[22] And when the time came for their purification according to the law of Moses, they brought the child Jesus up to Jerusalem to be presented to God [or the Lord], [23] (as it is written in the law of God [or the Lord], "Every male that opens the womb shall be called holy to God [or the Lord]"), [24] and to offer a sacrifice according to what is said in the law of God [or the Lord], "a pair of turtledoves, or two young pigeons." [25] Now there was a man in Jerusalem, whose name was Simeon, who was righteous and devout, looking for the consolation of Israel, and the Holy Spirit was upon him. [26] And it had been revealed to Simeon by the Holy Spirit that he should not see death before he had seen the Christ of God [or the Lord]. [27] And inspired by the Spirit, Simeon came into the temple; and when the parents brought in the child Jesus, to do for him according to the custom of the law, [28] Simeon took the child in his arms and blessed God and said,

[29] "Sovereign [or Lord], now let your servant depart in peace,
   according to your word;
[30] for my eyes have seen your salvation
[31] which you have prepared in the presence of all people,
[32] a light for revelation to the Gentiles,
   and for glory to your people Israel."

---

*Addition to the text. See "Addition of Women's Names to the Text" in the Appendix.

<sup>33</sup> And the father and mother of Jesus marveled at what was said about their child; <sup>34</sup> and Simeon blessed them and said to Mary, Jesus' mother,

"This child is set for the fall and rising of many in Israel,
and for a sign that is spoken against
<sup>35</sup> (and a sword will pierce through your own soul also),
that thoughts out of many hearts may be revealed."

<sup>36</sup> And there was a prophet, Anna, the daughter of Phanuel, of the tribe of Asher; she was of a great age, having lived with her husband seven years, <sup>37</sup> and as a widow till she was eighty-four. She did not depart from the temple, worshiping with fasting and prayer night and day. <sup>38</sup> And coming up at that very hour she gave thanks to God, and spoke about the child to all who were looking for the redemption of Jerusalem.

<sup>39</sup> And when Mary and Joseph had performed everything according to the law of God [[*or* the Lord]], they returned into Galilee, to their own city, Nazareth. <sup>40</sup>And the child grew and became strong, filled with wisdom; and the favor of God was upon the child.

# ANNUNCIATION—MARCH 25

## Lesson 1 ~ Isaiah 7:10-14

*Isaiah brings a word of assurance from God to Ahaz, ruler of Judah, in the face of a threat from the rulers of Syria.*

[10] Again GOD [[*or* the LORD]] spoke to Ahaz, [11] "Ask a sign of the SOVEREIGN [[*or* LORD]] your God; let it be deep as Sheol or high as heaven." [12] But Ahaz said, "I will not ask, and I will not put GOD [[*or* the LORD]] to the test." [13] And Isaiah said, "Hear then, O house of David! Is it too little for you to weary human beings, that you weary my God also? [14] Therefore God [[*or* the Lord]] will give you a sign: a young woman shall conceive and bear a child, whom she shall call Immanuel."

## Psalm 40:6-10 +

[6] Sacrifice and offering you do not desire;
　　but you have given me an open ear.
Burnt offering and sin offering
　　you have not required.
[7] Then I said, "I am coming;
　　in the scroll of the book it is written of me;
[8] I delight to do your will, O my God;
　　your law is within my heart."
[9] I have told the glad news of deliverance
　　in the great congregation;
I have not restrained my lips,
　　as you know, O GOD [[*or* LORD]].
[10] I have not hid your saving help within my heart,
　　I have spoken of your faithfulness and your salvation;
I have not concealed your steadfast love and your faithfulness
　　from the great congregation.

## Lesson 2 ~ Hebrews 10:4-10

*Jesus Christ, the high priest, is the single sacrifice for sins.*

[4] For it is impossible that the blood of bulls and goats should take away sins.
[5] Consequently, Christ, having come into the world, said,

"Sacrifices and offerings you have not desired,
　　but a body you have prepared for me;

---

+ Alternate Ps. 45 not included. See Appendix, p. 263.

⁶ in burnt offerings and sin offerings you have taken no pleasure.

⁷ Then I said, 'I have come to do your will, O God,'
   as it is written of me in the scroll of the book.''

⁸ When Christ said above, "You have neither desired nor taken pleasure in sacrifices and offerings and burnt offerings and sin offerings" (these are offered according to the law), ⁹ then Christ added, "I have come to do your will." Christ abolishes the first in order to establish the second. ¹⁰ And by that will we have been sanctified through the offering of the body of Jesus Christ once for all.

### Gospel ~ Luke 1:26-38

*The angel Gabriel announces to Mary that she will bear the child of God.*

²⁶ In the sixth month the angel Gabriel was sent from God to a city of Galilee named Nazareth, ²⁷ to a virgin betrothed to a man whose name was Joseph, of the house of David; and her name was Mary. ²⁸ And the angel came to her and said, "Hail, O favored one, God [[or the Lord]] is with you!" ²⁹ But she was greatly troubled at the saying, and considered in her mind what sort of greeting this might be. ³⁰ And the angel said to her, "Do not be afraid, Mary, for you have found favor with God. ³¹ You will conceive in your womb and bear a child, whose name you shall call Jesus.

³² This one will be great, and will be called the Child◇ of the Most
   High;
   and the Sovereign [[or Lord]] God will give to that Child the throne of
   David, the ancestor of the Child,
³³ to reign over the house of Jacob forever;
   and of that reign☆ there will be no end.''

³⁴ And Mary said to the angel, "How shall this be, since I have no husband?" ³⁵ And the angel said to her,

   "The Holy Spirit will come upon you,
   and the power of the Most High will overshadow you;
   therefore the child to be born will be called holy,
   the Child◇ of God.

³⁶ And your kinswoman Elizabeth in her old age has also conceived a child; and this is the sixth month with her who was called barren. ³⁷ For with God nothing will be impossible." ³⁸ And Mary said, "I am the servant of God [[or the Lord]]; let it be to me according to your word." And the angel departed from her.

---

◇RSV *Son*. See Appendix.
☆RSV *kingdom*. See Appendix.

# VISITATION—MAY 31

*Hannah offers a prayer to God.*

<sup>1</sup> Hannah also prayed and said,
"My heart exults in GOD [[*or* the LORD]];
  my strength is exalted in GOD [[*or* the LORD]].
My mouth derides my enemies,
  because I rejoice in your salvation.
<sup>2</sup> There is none holy like GOD [[*or* the LORD]],
  there is none besides you;
  there is no rock like our God.
<sup>3</sup> Talk no more so very proudly,
  let not arrogance come from your mouth;
for GOD [[*or* the LORD]] is a God of knowledge,
  by whom actions are weighed.
<sup>4</sup> The bows of the mighty are broken,
  but the feeble gird on strength.
<sup>5</sup> Those who were full have hired themselves out for bread,
  but those who were hungry have ceased to hunger.
The barren has borne seven,
  but she who has many children is forlorn.
<sup>6</sup> It is GOD [[*or* the LORD]] who kills and brings to life,
  who brings down to Sheol and raises up,
<sup>7</sup> who makes poor and makes rich,
  who brings low and also exalts.
<sup>8</sup> It is God who raises up the poor from the dust,
  and lifts the needy from the ash heap,
to make them sit with nobles
  and inherit a seat of honor.
For the pillars of the earth belong to GOD [[*or* the LORD]],
  and on them God has set the world.
<sup>9</sup> God will guard the feet of the faithful ones;
  but the wicked shall be removed from sight;
  for not by might shall any one prevail.
<sup>10</sup> The adversaries of GOD [[*or* the LORD]] shall be broken to pieces;
  against them God will thunder in heaven.
GOD [[*or* The LORD]] will judge the ends of the earth,
  giving strength to God's ruler,□
  and exalting the power of the anointed one."

---

□ RSV *his king*. See Appendix.

# Psalm 113

<sup>1</sup> Praise GOD [[*or* the LORD]]!
  Praise, O servants of GOD [[*or* the LORD]],
    praise the name of the SOVEREIGN [[*or* LORD]]!
<sup>2</sup> Blessed be the name of the SOVEREIGN [[*or* LORD]]
    from this time forth and forevermore!
<sup>3</sup> From the rising of the sun to its setting
    the name of the SOVEREIGN [[*or* LORD]] is to be praised!
<sup>4</sup> GOD [[*or* The LORD]] is high above all nations,
    and God's glory above the heavens!
<sup>5</sup> Who is like the SOVEREIGN [[*or* LORD]] our God,
    who is seated on high,
<sup>6</sup> who looks far down
    upon the heavens and the earth?
<sup>7</sup> God raises the poor from the dust,
    and lifts the needy from the ash heap,
<sup>8</sup> to make them sit with nobles,
    with the nobles of God's people.
<sup>9</sup> God gives the barren woman a home,
    making her the joyous mother of children.
  Praise GOD [[*or* the LORD]]!

### Lesson 2 ~ Romans 12:9-16b

*Paul writes to the Christians at Rome about their relationships with one another.*

<sup>9</sup> Let love be genuine; hate what is evil, hold fast to what is good; <sup>10</sup> be affectionately devoted to one another; outdo one another in showing honor. <sup>11</sup> Never flag in zeal, be aglow with the Spirit, serve the Sovereign [[*or* Lord]]. <sup>12</sup> Rejoice in your hope, be patient in tribulation, be constant in prayer. <sup>13</sup> Contribute to the needs of the saints, practice hospitality.

<sup>14</sup> Bless those who persecute you; bless and do not curse them. <sup>15</sup> Rejoice with those who rejoice, weep with those who weep. <sup>16</sup> Live in harmony with one another; do not be haughty, but associate with the lowly.

## Gospel ~ Luke 1:39-57

*Mary greets Elizabeth and sings a song of praise to God.*

39 In those days Mary arose and went with haste into the hill country, to a city of Judah, 40 and she entered the house of Zechariah and greeted Elizabeth. 41 And when Elizabeth heard the greeting of Mary, the baby leaped in her womb; and Elizabeth was filled with the Holy Spirit 42 and she exclaimed with a loud cry, "Blessed are you among women, and blessed is the fruit of your womb! 43 And why is this granted me, that the mother of my Sovereign [or Lord] should come to me? 44 For when the voice of your greeting came to my ears, the baby in my womb leaped for joy. 45 And blessed is she who believed that there would be a fulfillment of what was spoken to her from God [or the Lord]." 46 And Mary said,

"My soul magnifies the Sovereign [or Lord],
47 and my spirit rejoices in God my Savior,
48 who has regarded the low estate of God's servant.
For henceforth all generations will call me blessed;
49 for the one who is mighty has done great things for me,
and holy is God's name.
50 And God's mercy is on those who fear God
from generation to generation.
51 God has shown strength with God's arm,
and has scattered the proud in the imagination of their hearts,
52 God has put down the mighty from their thrones,
and exalted those of low degree;
53 God has filled the hungry with good things,
and has sent the rich empty away.
54 God has helped God's servant Israel,
in remembrance of God's mercy,
55 as God spoke to our ancestors,
to Abraham [*and Sarah,**] and to their posterity forever."

56 And Mary remained with Elizabeth about three months, and returned to her home.

57 Now the time came for Elizabeth to be delivered, and she gave birth to a son.

---

*Addition to the text. RSV *to Abraham and to his posterity.* See "Addition of Women's Names to the Text" in the Appendix.

# HOLY CROSS—SEPTEMBER 14

## Lesson 1 ~ Numbers 21:4b-9

*Moses makes a bronze serpent to heal victims of the plague of fiery serpents.*

[4] The people became impatient on the way, [5] and they spoke against God and against Moses, "Why have you brought us up out of Egypt to die in the wilderness? For there is no food and no water, and we loathe this worthless food." [6] Then GOD [*or* the LORD] sent fiery serpents among the people, and they bit the people, so that many people of Israel died. [7] And the people came to Moses, and said, "We have sinned, for we have spoken against GOD [*or* the LORD] and against you; pray to GOD [*or* the LORD] to take away the serpents from us." So Moses prayed for the people. [8] And GOD [*or* the LORD] said to Moses, "Make a fiery serpent, and set it on a pole; and all who are bitten, when they see it, shall live." [9] So Moses made a bronze serpent, and set it on a pole; and anyone whom a serpent bit would look at the bronze serpent and live.

## Psalm 98:1-5

[1] O sing a new song to GOD [*or* the LORD],
    who has done marvelous things,
  whose right hand and holy arm
    have gained the victory!
[2] GOD [*or* The LORD] has made known the victory,
    and has revealed God's vindication in the sight of the nations.
[3] God has remembered God's steadfast love and faithfulness
    to the house of Israel.
  All the ends of the earth have seen
    the victory of our God.
[4] Make a joyful noise to GOD [*or* the LORD], all the earth;
    break forth into joyous song and sing praises!
[5] Sing praises to GOD [*or* the LORD] with the lyre,
    with the lyre and the sound of melody!

## Psalm 78:1-2, 34-38 (alternate)

1 Give ear, O my people, to my teaching;
    incline your ears to the words of my mouth!
2 I will open my mouth in a parable;
    I will utter obscure sayings from of old.
34 When God slew them, they sought for God;
    they repented and sought God earnestly.
35 They remembered that God was their rock,
    the Most High God their redeemer.
36 But they flattered God with their mouths;
    they lied to God with their tongues.
37 Their heart was not steadfast toward God;
    they were not true to God's covenant.
38 Yet God, being compassionate,
    forgave their iniquity,
    and did not destroy them,
  restraining God's anger often,
    and not arousing all God's wrath.

## Lesson 2 ~ 1 Corinthians 1:18-24

*Paul writes to the Christians at Corinth about the wisdom of God.*

18 For the word of the cross is folly to those who are perishing, but to us who are being saved it is the power of God. 19 For it is written,

"I will destroy the wisdom of the wise,
and the cleverness of the clever I will thwart."

20 Where is the wise one? Where is the scribe? Where is the debater of this age? Has not God made foolish the wisdom of the world? 21 For since, in the wisdom of God, the world did not know God through wisdom, it pleased God through the folly of what we preach to save those who believe. 22 For Jews demand signs and Greeks seek wisdom, 23 but we preach Christ crucified, a stumbling block to Jews and folly to Gentiles, 24 but to those who are called, both Jews and Greeks, Christ the power of God and the wisdom of God.

# Gospel ~ John 3:13-17

*Those who believe in the Child of God will have eternal life.*

¹³ "No one has ascended into heaven but the one who descended from heaven, the Human One.° ¹⁴ And as Moses lifted up the serpent in the wilderness, so must the Human One° be lifted up, ¹⁵ that whoever believes in that one may have eternal life."

¹⁶ For God so loved the world that God gave God's only Child,◇ that whoever believes in that Child should not perish but have eternal life. ¹⁷ For God sent that Child◇ into the world, not to condemn the world, but that through that Child the world might be saved.

---

°RSV *Son of man*. See Appendix.
◇RSV v. 16 *his only Son;* v. 17 *the Son.* See Appendix.

# ALL SAINTS—NOVEMBER 1

*(Or the first Sunday in November)*

## Lesson 1 ~ Daniel 7:1-3, 15-18

*Daniel receives an interpretation of his dream about the four beasts coming up out of the sea.*

¹ In the first year of Belshazzar king of Babylon, Daniel had a dream and visions of his head as he lay in his bed. Then he wrote down the dream, and told the sum of the matter. ² Daniel said, "I saw in my vision by night, and the four winds of heaven were stirring up the great sea. ³ And four great beasts came up out of the sea, different from one another.

¹⁵ "As for me, Daniel, my spirit within me was anxious and the visions of my head alarmed me. ¹⁶ I approached one of those who stood there and asked the truth concerning all this. So I was told, and the interpretation of the things was made known to me. ¹⁷ 'These four great beasts are four kings who shall arise out of the earth. ¹⁸ But the saints of the Most High shall receive the dominion,☆ and possess it forever, forever and ever.' "

## Psalm 149

¹ Praise GOD [[*or* the LORD]]!
  Sing to GOD [[*or* the LORD]] a new song,
    God's praise in the assembly of the faithful!
² Let Israel be glad in its Maker,
    let the children of Zion rejoice in their Ruler!⊡
³ Let them praise God's name with dancing,
    making melody with timbrel and lyre!
⁴ For GOD [[*or* the LORD]] takes pleasure in God's people,
    and adorns the humble with victory.
⁵ Let the faithful exult in glory;
    let them sing for joy on their couches.
⁶ Let the high praises of God be in their throats
    and two-edged swords in their hands,
⁷ to wreak vengeance on the nations
    and chastisement on the peoples,

---

☆RSV *kingdom*. See Appendix.
⊡RSV *King*. See Appendix.

<sup>8</sup> to bind their rulers<sup>☐</sup> with chains
  and their nobles with fetters of iron,
<sup>9</sup> to execute on them the judgment written!
  This is glory for all God's faithful ones.
  Praise GOD ⟦*or* the LORD⟧!

## Lesson 2 ~ Ephesians 1:11-23

*The risen Christ is exalted as head over all.*

<sup>11</sup> In Christ, according to the purpose of the one who accomplishes all things according to the counsel of God's will, <sup>12</sup>we who first hoped in Christ have been destined and appointed to live for the praise of God's glory. <sup>13</sup> In Christ you also, who have heard the word of truth, the gospel of your salvation, and have believed in Christ, were sealed with the promised Holy Spirit, <sup>14</sup>which is the guarantee of our inheritance until we acquire possession of it, to the praise of God's glory.

<sup>15</sup> For this reason, because I have heard of your faith in the Sovereign ⟦*or* Lord⟧ Jesus and your love toward all the saints, <sup>16</sup> I do not cease to give thanks for you, remembering you in my prayers, <sup>17</sup>that the God of our Sovereign ⟦*or* Lord⟧ Jesus Christ, the Father [*and Mother**] of glory, may give you a spirit of wisdom and of revelation in the knowledge of God, <sup>18</sup>having the eyes of your hearts enlightened, that you may know what is the hope to which you have been called, what are the riches of God's glorious inheritance in the saints, <sup>19</sup>and what is the immeasurable greatness of God's power in us who believe, according to the working of God's great might <sup>20</sup>which was accomplished in Christ when God raised Christ from the dead and made Christ sit at God's right hand in the heavenly places, <sup>21</sup>far above all rule and authority and power and dominion, and above every name that is named, not only in this age but also in that which is to come; <sup>22</sup>and God has put all things under Christ's feet and has made Christ the head over all things for the church, <sup>23</sup>which is Christ's body, the fullness of the one who fills all in all.

---

☐RSV *kings*. See Appendix.
*Addition to the text. See "Metaphor" and "God the Father and Mother" in the Appendix.

# Gospel ~ Luke 6:20-36

*Jesus begins the Sermon on the Plain.*

20 And Jesus lifted up his eyes on the disciples, and said:

"Blessed are you poor, for yours is the realm☆ of God.

21 "Blesséd are you that hunger now, for you shall be satisfied.

"Blessed are you that weep now, for you shall laugh.

22 "Blessed are you when people hate you, and when they exclude you and revile you, and cast out your name as evil, on account of the Human One!○ 23 Rejoice in that day, and leap for joy, for your reward is great in heaven; for so their ancestors did to the prophets.

24 "But woe to you that are rich, for you have received your consolation.

25 "Woe to you that are full now, for you shall hunger.

"Woe to you that laugh now, for you shall mourn and weep.

26 "Woe to you, when all speak well of you, for so their ancestors did to the false prophets.

27 "But I say to you that hear, Love your enemies, do good to those who hate you, 28 bless those who curse you, pray for those who abuse you. 29 To a person who strikes you on the cheek, offer the other also; and from a person who takes away your coat do not withhold even your shirt. 30 Give to everyone who begs from you; and of anyone who takes away your goods do not ask them again. 31 And as you wish that people would do to you, do so to them.

32 "If you love those who love you, what credit is that to you? For even sinners love those who love them. 33 And if you do good to those who do good to you, what credit is that to you? For even sinners do the same. 34 And if you lend to those from whom you hope to receive, what credit is that to you? Even sinners lend to sinners, to receive as much again. 35 But love your enemies, and do good, and lend, expecting nothing in return; and your reward will be great, and you will be children of the Most High; for God is kind to the ungrateful and the selfish. 36 Be merciful, even as [*God*] your Father [*and Mother**] is merciful."

---

☆RSV *kingdom*. See Appendix.
○RSV *Son of man*. See Appendix.
*Addition to the text. See "Metaphor" and "God the Father and Mother" in the Appendix.

# THANKSGIVING DAY

## Lesson 1 ~ Deuteronomy 26:1-11

*Israel confesses God's work in history.*

¹ When you come into the land which the SOVEREIGN [*or* LORD] your God gives you for an inheritance, and have taken possession of it, and live in it, ² you shall take some of the first of all the fruit of the ground, which you harvest from your land that the SOVEREIGN [*or* LORD] your God gives you, and you shall put it in a basket, and you shall go to the place which the SOVEREIGN [*or* LORD] your God will choose, to make God's name to dwell there. ³ And you shall go to the priest who is in office at that time, and say, "I declare this day to the SOVEREIGN [*or* LORD] your God that I have come into the land which GOD [*or* the LORD] swore to our ancestors to give us." ⁴ Then the priest shall take the basket from your hand, and set it down before the altar of the SOVEREIGN [*or* LORD] your God.

⁵ And you shall make response before the SOVEREIGN [*or* LORD] your God, "A wandering Aramean was my father, who went down into Egypt and sojourned there, few in number; and there he became a nation, great, mighty, and populous. ⁶ And the Egyptians treated us harshly, and afflicted us, and laid upon us hard bondage. ⁷ Then we cried to the SOVEREIGN [*or* LORD] the God of our ancestors, and GOD [*or* the LORD] heard our voice, and saw our affliction, our toil, and our oppression; ⁸ and GOD [*or* the LORD] brought us out of Egypt with a mighty hand and an outstretched arm, with great terror, with signs and wonders, ⁹ and brought us into this place and gave us this land, a land flowing with milk and honey. ¹⁰ And now I bring the first of the fruit of the ground, which you, O GOD [*or* LORD], have given me." And you shall set it down before the SOVEREIGN [*or* LORD] your God, and worship before the SOVEREIGN [*or* LORD] your God; ¹¹ and you shall rejoice in all the good which the SOVEREIGN [*or* LORD] your God has given to you and to your house, you, and the Levite, and the resident alien who is among you.

# Psalm 100

¹ Make a joyful noise to GOD [[or the LORD]], all the lands!
²   Serve GOD [[or the LORD]] with gladness!
    Come into God's presence with singing!
³ Know that the SOVEREIGN [[or LORD]] is God!
    It is God who made us, and to God we belong;
    we are God's people, and the sheep of God's pasture.
⁴ Enter God's gates with thanksgiving,
    and God's courts with praise!
    Give thanks to God, bless God's name!
⁵ For GOD [[or the LORD]] is good;
    God's steadfast love endures forever,
    and God's faithfulness to all generations.

## Lesson 2 ~ Philippians 4:4-9

*Paul urges Christians to set their minds on things that are excellent and praiseworthy.*

⁴ Rejoice in the Sovereign [[or Lord]] always; again I will say, Rejoice.
⁵ Let everyone know your forbearance. The Sovereign [[or Lord]] is at hand.
⁶ Have no anxiety about anything, but in everything, by prayer and supplication with thanksgiving, let your requests be made known to God.
⁷ And the peace of God, which passes all understanding, will keep your hearts and your minds in Christ Jesus.

⁸ Finally, my friends, whatever is true, whatever is honorable, whatever is just, whatever is pure, whatever is lovely, whatever is gracious, if there is any excellence, if there is anything worthy of praise, think about these things. ⁹ What you have learned and received and heard and seen in me, do; and the God of peace will be with you.

*Jesus is the bread of life.*

25 When they found Jesus on the other side of the sea, they said to him, "Rabbi, when did you come here?" 26 Jesus answered them, "Truly, truly, I say to you, you seek me, not because you saw signs, but because you ate your fill of the loaves. 27 Do not labor for the food which perishes, but for the food which endures to eternal life, which the Human One° will give to you; for that one God the Father [*and Mother**] has confirmed." 28 Then they said to Jesus, "What must we do to be doing the works of God?" 29 Jesus answered them, "This is the work of God, that you believe in the one whom God has sent." 30 So they said to Jesus, "Then what sign do you do, that we may see, and believe you? What work do you perform? 31 Our ancestors ate the manna in the wilderness; as it is written, 'God gave them bread from heaven to eat.'" 32 Jesus then said to them, "Truly, truly, I say to you, it was not Moses who gave you the bread from heaven; God gives you the true bread from heaven. 33 For the bread of God is that which comes down from heaven, and gives life to the world." 34 They said to Jesus, "Give us this bread always."

35 Jesus said to them, "I am the bread of life; whoever comes to me shall never hunger, and whoever believes in me shall never thirst."

---

°RSV *Son of man*. See Appendix.
*Addition to the text. See "Metaphor" and "God the Father and Mother" in the Appendix.

# Appendix

## Metaphor

A metaphor is a figure of speech used to extend meaning through comparison of dissimilars. For example, "Life is a dream" is a metaphor. The character of dreams is ascribed to life, and the meaning of "life" is thus extended. "Dream" is used as a screen through which to view "life." Two dissimilars are juxtaposed.

The statement "God is Father" is also a metaphor. Two dissimilars, "Father" and "God," are juxtaposed, and so the meaning of "God" is extended. Although "God the Father" has been a powerful metaphor for communicating the nature of God, like any metaphor it can become worn. It may even be interpreted literally, that is, as describing exactly. The dissimilars become similar. The metaphor becomes a proposition.

Now, if one were to say "God is Mother," the power of the metaphor would be apparent. The image "God the Mother and Father" as a lens through which to view God elicits the response of a true metaphor, just as the statement "God is Father" once did. In this lectionary, "God the Father and Mother" is used as a formal equivalent of "the Father" or "God the Father." "God the Father" is clearly a metaphor, just as "God the Mother" is. God *is* not a father, any more than God *is* a mother, or than life *is* a dream. By reading and hearing "God the Father and Mother" we provide a metaphor for God that balances the more familiar *male* imagery for God with the less familiar *female* imagery.

There are many female images for God in the scriptures. For example, God as mother is found in the Old Testament, "Now I will cry out like a woman in travail" (Isa. 42:14), and "As one whom his mother comforts, so I will comfort you" (Isa. 66:13). In the New Testament, the parable of the woman seeking the lost coin (Luke 15:8-10) functions as a female image for God. Metaphors are figurative and open-ended. Their meanings vary from hearer to hearer, but they are not dispensable, for there is no other way by which to say directly what the metaphor communicates. A metaphor provides a new way of seeing.

**(*)[*God*] the Father [*and Mother*] (RSV the Father; God the Father, God our Father)**

One of the characteristics of the Christian faith is its emphasis on the personal nature of God. While God is also described in impersonal terms (rock, light, love), personal imagery prevails. "Father" is one such personal term. The Gospels record that when Jesus prayed he called God "*Abba*" ("Father," Mark 14:36), and frequently, especially in the Gospel of John, Jesus refers to God as Father. In the Old Testament, the term "Father" is used infrequently as a designation for God.

For Jesus, "Father" was a sacred word, pointing to the mysterious intimacy Jesus had with God (Matt. 11:27), and pointing to the intimate relationship his disciples also had with God (Matt. 23:9). Jesus' own use of the word "Father" in addressing God supported the church's claim that Jesus was the "Son."

The phrase used in this lectionary, "God the Father and Mother," is offered as a way of expressing the same intimacy, caring, and freedom that is found in Jesus' identification of God as *Abba*. Jesus' use of this term to refer to God was radically nontraditional. This warrants the use of nontraditional intimate language in contemporary reference to God. Thus the use of the phrase "God the Mother and Father" is a way to affirm the important Christian belief that Jesus is the Child of God. Just as we do not create our children, but give them birth out of our very selves, we believe that God did not create Jesus, but that God "gave birth to" or "begot" Jesus.

It is also the case that Christians rejected as pagan the view that God is father of the world. For Christians, God is Father in relation to the Son. Christians are brought into this relationship of God as "Father" because they are adopted as "sons" or "heirs" (Rom. 8:15, 23; Gal. 4:6; Eph. 1:5).

That Jesus called God "Father" is the basis for the church's thinking about Jesus Christ as one of the persons of the Trinity. The relationship described by the Father/Son imagery of the New Testament opened the way for the church later to identify the Son as of the same substance as the Father. And if God the Son proceeded from God the Father alone, the procession is both a male and a female action, a begetting *and* a birth. God is the *Mother and Father* of the Child who comes forth.

The image of God as Father has been misused to support the excessive authority of earthly fathers in a patriarchal social structure. The metaphor "God the Father and Mother" points to the close relationship between language about God and language about the human community. The mutuality and coequality of the persons of the Trinity is a model for human community and especially appropriate, therefore, for readings prepared for worship. Those who worship in the Christian church are struggling to bring about a community where there is "neither male nor female," but where all are "one in Christ Jesus" and "heirs according to promise" (Gal. 3:28–29). (See also Metaphor.)

## (⊗)God (RSV my Father, the Father)

In the Gospel of John, and occasionally elsewhere, RSV "Father" is often rendered "God" where "Father" appears frequently in the lection.

## Sovereign; God, the SOVEREIGN; etc. (RSV Lord, LORD, etc.)

Sometime in the course of Israel's history the personal name of God, probably pronounced *Yahweh*, ceased to be spoken aloud for fear that it would be profaned, even though it continued to be written in the text of the scriptures. Thus, the practice was already established according to which the faith and piety of the community, shaped by the tradition of scripture itself, takes precedence over the written word in determining what is read for the divine name by the worshiping community. From that time on, the chief word read in place of the divine name was *Adonai*—an honorific title translated "Lord" or "my Lord."

In those places in the RSV where the underlying Hebrew text contains the divine name *(Yahweh)*, and not simply the word *Adonai*, the typography is changed to LORD. Where the divine name is found in the original text, the Lectionary Committee prefers to render it as "GOD" or "the SOVEREIGN." However, because of the deep commitment in the church to the word "Lord" in both Old and New Testaments, and because of a certain ambiguity about the extent to which "Lord" is heard as gender-specific, that term has been included in this lectionary text as an optional or alternative reading, set off in this manner: [[or Lord]]; [[or LORD]].

In this lectionary the Hebrew word *Elohim* is rendered "God," as in the RSV. The word "God" is also usually used for masculine pronouns referring to the "Sovereign [[or Lord]]" or to "God."

Occasionally the divine name, Yahweh, is found in combination with the word for God *(Yahweh Elohim)* or with the word for Lord *(Adonai Yahweh)*. These are rendered in the RSV as "the LORD God" and "the Lord GOD," respectively. In this lectionary the former is rendered as "the SOVEREIGN [[or LORD]] God" and the latter as "the Sovereign [[or Lord]] GOD." The following chart summarizes these various renderings.

| Hebrew Scriptures | RSV | Inclusive-Language Lectionary |
|---|---|---|
| *Elohim* | God | God |
| *Adonai* | Lord | God [[or the Lord]]; or the Sovereign [[or Lord]] |
| *Yahweh* | LORD | GOD [[or the LORD]]; or the SOVEREIGN [[or LORD]] |
| *Yahweh Elohim;* or *Elohim Yahweh* | the LORD God | the SOVEREIGN [[or LORD]] God |
| *Adonai Yahweh;* or *Yahweh Adonai* | the Lord GOD | the Sovereign [[or Lord]] GOD |

In the Greek New Testament the most frequently used words for God are *Theos* ("God") and *Kyrios* ("Lord"). It is natural that *Kyrios* occurs so often for "God" in the New Testament, because that was the word by which the Greek version of the Old Testament rendered both *Yahweh* and *Adonai;* and it was the Greek version, not the original Hebrew, that was read by the New Testament authors. *Kyrios* was also taken over by the church as a primary way of designating Jesus: "Jesus is Lord."

*Kyrios* has a wide range of other meanings. It is used for the *owner* of possessions, for the *head* of a family, or for the *master* of a house or of slaves. In the vocative it often means "Sir." *Kyrios* is usually translated into English by "Lord" (in reference to God or Jesus) or "lord" (in reference to a man). In common usage, "lord" means a man with power and authority, such as a titled nobleman.

Because "Lord" is basically a gender-specific word (despite a certain ambiguity in contemporary usage), when used of either God or Christ it connotes, for some, a male being. Since the church believes that God transcends gender and that the risen Christ is one with God, in this lectionary *Kyrios,* occasionally rendered "God" or "Christ," usually has been translated as "Sovereign." (See chart below.) This word, like "Lord," means one supreme in power and authority, but it is inclusive—women as well as men are sovereigns. This translation follows the same principle used in rendering *Yahweh* and *Adonai* as "Sovereign" in the Old Testament lections, and the word "Lord" is included in the text as an alternative reading in the New Testament lections.

| Greek New Testament | RSV | Inclusive-Language Lectionary |
|---|---|---|
| *Kyrios* | Lord | Sovereign [[*or* Lord]] |
| | | Christ [[*or* the Lord]] |
| | | God [[*or* the Lord]] |

"Sovereign" has another advantage for the translator over "Lord." It is a word in contemporary usage in the political arena, and is not confined to religious usage, as is virtually the case with the word "Lord" in the United States. Not only are there living sovereigns in monarchical societies but nations as well are said to exercise sovereignty. The designation of Jesus Christ as *Kyrios* by the early church carried precisely such a political meaning: Jesus, not Caesar, was *Kyrios.* Christians believed that Jesus Christ is supreme over all earthly authorities. Hence, the status of the authority of the *Sovereign Jesus Christ* in relation to any national sovereignty is expressed in a contemporary idiom which brings to the fore the revolutionary significance of the statement *Kyrios Iēsous* (Jesus is Lord [Sovereign]) for the history of the church.

## (◇) Child, Child of God (RSV Son, Son of God)

"Son" is used as a designation of Jesus as the Messiah (e.g., Rom. 1:3; 5:10). At Jesus' baptism there was a voice from heaven: "This is my beloved Son" (Matt. 3:17). Jesus also refers to himself as "Son" (Matt. 11:27), though seldom except in the Gospel of John, where the self-designation is common.

A son is male, and of course the historical person, Jesus, was a man. But as the Gospels depict Jesus, his maleness is not said to have any significance for salvation. It is the fact that Jesus was *human* that is crucial, both for Jesus' designation as the Christ and for Jesus' work of salvation.

If the fact that Jesus was a male has no christological significance, then neither has the fact that Jesus was a *son* and not a *daugher*. Therefore, in this lectionary the formal equivalent "Child" or "Child of God" is masculine pronouns that refer to "Child" ("Son") are rendered as "Child." Thus, all hearers of the lectionary readings will be enabled to identify themselves with Jesus' *humanity*.

In traditional language, Jesus as "the Son" makes believers "sons" and therefore heirs. In this lectionary, Jesus as the Child of God makes believers—men and women—"children" of God and therefore heirs. When Jesus is called "Son of God" it is not Jesus' male character that is of primary importance but Jesus' intimate relationship with God (see Matt. 11:25-27). Other connotations of "sonship" are divine authority (see Matt. 28:18-20) and freedom (see Rom. 8:21).

While the word "child" may imply a minor, or childishness, in the New Testament it clearly refers to "adults" in more than half of its occurrences. For example, the word "child" or "children" is used for adult descendants (Acts 13:33; Rom. 9:8); or for adults who are "children" of a teacher or an apostle (1 Cor. 4:14; 2 Cor. 6:13); or for adult Christians (2 John 1, 4); or for adults who are "children of God" (John 11:52; Rom. 8:16). In these and many other passages, "child" or "children" connotes primarily a relationship, and more often of adults than of minors. The canon, therefore, itself provides the church with a substitute for the word "son" that is not gender-specific. The two meanings of the word "child" in the New Testament are also consistent with contemporary usage where the term "child" refers not only to minors but also to a relationship to parents without reference to age.


## (○) The Human One (RSV the Son of Man)

The term "the Son of man" is found frequently in the Gospels, and almost nowhere else in the New Testament. Only Jesus uses the term (with a single exception), and the Gospel writers always intended the term to refer to Jesus. How do the Gospel authors interpret its meaning?

Much light would be shed on the meaning of the term if there were clear antecedents to its use in the Gospels, but any such antecedents are impossible to demonstrate. It cannot be shown that Jewish use of the term "Son of man" has influenced its use in the Gospels; in fact, the term does not appear to have functioned as a title prior to its application to Jesus by the church. Furthermore, its meaning varies in different contexts. The term, however, is subject to being misinterpreted as speaking about a male human being, a "son" of a "man." And so, in this lectionary, "the Human One" is used as a formal equivalent for "the Son of man." That formal equivalent is not derived from or dependent on any particular judgment as to the background of "the Son of man" in Judaism, and is not intended to prejudice in any way the ongoing discussion of that question. The Committee believes, however, that the title "the Human One" is open to the same nuances of interpretation allowed by the title "the Son of man." Many of these nuances are derived from the context in which the term is used rather than from the term itself.

In the Old Testament, Ezekiel is often addressed by God as "son of man," which is not a title, and connotes simply a "man." This lectionary renders this expression, "O mortal." In Dan. 7:13, an Aramaic expression is used which is translated "a son of man" in the RSV and "a human being" in this lectionary.

### Gender-Specific Pronouns for God and Christ

Because English pronouns are inherently gender-specific, they are not used in this lectionary to refer either to God or to the preexistent or risen Christ.

### (☆) Realm of God (RSV Kingdom, Kingdom of God, Kingship)

The Greek word used frequently in the New Testament, and usually translated by the gender-specific word "kingdom," has generally been rendered in this lectionary as "realm," though it has also been translated by other terms as well. The Greek word refers either to the activity of God (i.e., God's "kingship" or "dominion" or "reign" or "rule") or to the state of affairs brought about by God (i.e., God's "kingdom" or "dominion" or "realm"). The Hebrew root usually translated "kingdom" in the RSV is occasionally rendered "kingdom" in this lectionary, but is usually rendered by other terms, primarily "realm."

### (□) Ruler, Monarch (RSV King)

The word "king" is used in the Bible both in reference to earthly royal figures and as a metaphor for God. In this lectionary "King" as a metaphor for God is rendered as "Ruler," "Sovereign," or occasionally "Monarch." The word "king" is retained in reference to specific earthly kings, such as David, and in stories and parables about kings.

(†) **Teacher (RSV Master)**

The Greek word used only by Luke in the New Testament and rendered "Master" in the RSV is translated in this lectionary by "Teacher." It had a wide variety of connotations, such as supervisor, administrator, or governor, but no specific religious connotations. It is used for "Son" when the latter has christological significance, and the "Sovereign," "Teacher," or "Rabbi."


## Sisters and Brothers, Friends, Neighbors (RSV Brother, Brethren)

The contemporary use of such phrases as "sisters and brothers in Christ" to address members of the church is helpful in clarifying how the words "brother" and "brethren" are used in the Bible. In Hebrew and Greek usage, the same word could refer to a sibling, a more distant relative, a neighbor, or a member of one's community or race. Paul appears to reflect such a broad use of the word "brethren" in a phrase he uses in Rom. 9:3, where in the RSV "my brethren" is the equivalent of "my kinsmen by race," but in this lectionary the phrase appears as "my own people, my kinsfolk by race." In Greek, "brother" was often used to refer to a friend, or one with whom one shares a common purpose, but not necessarily a blood relative.

In the New Testament, the plural form of the word "brother" appears to have been intended to include both women and men. For example, in Luke 21:16, "brothers" is certainly intended to mean "brothers and sisters"; and when Paul addressed Christians as "brethren" (e.g., Rom. 8:12; 1 Cor. 2:1) he was surely including women as well as men. In such cases of direct address, "brethren" has been rendered in the lectionary either as "sisters and brothers" ("brothers and sisters") or as "friends." In post-resurrection sayings attributed to Jesus, "brethren" is translated as "followers" (Matt. 28:10) or "friends" (John 20:17) to make clear that the reference is to the nascent church and not to Jesus' siblings.


## (*) Addition of Women's Names to the Text

In a few instances, women's names have been added to the text in this lectionary. These names are included where generation or origin of the people is a major concern. The addition of these names is also consistent with the biblical tradition itself, where on occasion Sarah as well as Abraham is explicitly referred to as progenitor (cf. Isa. 51:1-2), or as one who along with Abraham trusted in God and God's promises (cf. Heb. 11:11). Women's names added to the text are placed in brackets and italicized. If the additional words involve a change in the verb form, the RSV rendering is in the footnotes.

261

### (▽) The Jews

The term "the Jews" occurs very frequently in the Gospel of John. Sometimes it refers in a straightforward, historical way to the ethnic people of whom Jesus was one and among whom Jesus lived out his life. Sometimes, however, it is used almost as a code word for religious leaders who misunderstand the true identity of Christ. When "the Jews" is used in the former sense in the lections from the Gospel of John, it remains unchanged in this lectionary. When it is used in the latter sense, it is rendered "the religious authorities" so as to minimize what could be perceived as a warrant for anti-Semitism in the Gospel of John.

### Other Excluding Imagery: Darkness

The New Testament imagery of light versus darkness is often used to contrast good with evil. The equation of darkness with evil, or that which is done in secret and out of the light, has unfortunately led some persons and groups to condemn and reject anything that is black or any dark-hued person as evil or somehow condemned by God. This color symbolism has its equally inaccurate and unfortunate correlative in the equation of light with white—with what is true, good, and loved of God—for example, in the verse "Wash me, and I shall be whiter than snow" (Ps. 51:7). In this lectionary the word translated "whiter" in the RSV is rendered "cleaner." While the biblical context may be free from racist intent, the too-easy misconception that dark people are also condemned and to be avoided has led to the use in this lectionary of terminology other than "darkness" and "white" as metaphors for what is either condemned or loved by God.

### Use of "They," "Them," "Themselves," "Their" as Singular Pronouns

In some cases, indefinite singular pronouns are rendered in this lectionary by "they," "them," "themselves," or "their." This usage is recognized as appropriate by the National Council of Teachers of English in its *Guidelines for Nonsexist Use of Language in NCTE Publications.* The *Oxford English Dictionary* says that "they" is "often used in reference to a singular noun made universal by *every, any,* or *no,* etc., or is applied to one of either sex ( = 'he or she')." Those grammarians who oppose this usage follow common practice established by an 1850 Act of Parliament declaring that "he" is generic and legally includes "she." That declaration in turn was based on a rule invented in 1746 by John Kirby: the male gender is "more comprehensive" than the female. This lectionary follows the precedent of St. John Fisher (1535), who wrote that God "never forsaketh any creature unless they before have forsaken themselves," and William Shakespeare, who urged "everyone to rest themselves."

## (+) Changes in the Table of Readings and Psalms

The mandate of the Inclusive-Language Lectionary Committee is to recast the language of the RSV in those places where male-biased or otherwise inappropriately exclusive language could be modified to reflect an inclusiveness of all persons. Consistent with the goal of this mandate, the Committee has determined that it is also appropriate to add certain lections about women that have not been included in the listing recommended by the North American Committee on Calendar and Lectionary. These alternate readings are:

### In Year A

| | |
|---|---|
| Easter 5, Lesson 2 | Acts 17:1-12 |
| Pentecost 25, Lesson 1 | Wisd. of Sol. 6:12-16 |
| Pentecost 26, Lesson 1 | Prov. 31:10-13, 19-20, 30-31 |

### In Year B

| | |
|---|---|
| Epiphany 2, Lesson 2 | Rom. 16:1-7 |
| Lent 4, Lesson 1 | Judges 4:4-9 |
| Pentecost 12, Lesson 1 | 2 Sam. 14:4–17 |
| Pentecost 12, Gospel | John 8:2-11 |

### In Year C

| | |
|---|---|
| Lent 3, Gospel | Luke 13:10-17 |
| Easter 5, Lesson 1 | Acts 16:11-15 |

Furthermore, where consistent with the mandate, the Committee has occasionally added or omitted some verses of a lection or substituted a reading. These alterations are:

### In Year A

| | |
|---|---|
| Pentecost 7, Lesson 1 | Ex. 1:15-21 |
| Pentecost 9, Gospel | Matt. 13:31-35 |
| Annunciation | Alternate Ps. 45 not included |

### In Year B

| | |
|---|---|
| Epiphany 2, Lesson 2 | 1 Cor. 6:12-15a, 19-20 (prescribed reading: ch. 6:12-20) |
| Pentecost 5, Lesson 2 | 2 Sam. 5:1-5 (prescribed reading: 5:1-12) |
| Pentecost 14, Lesson 2 | Eph. 6:1-4 added |
| Annunciation | Alternate Ps. 45 not included |

### In Year C

| | |
|---|---|
| Pentecost 16, Lesson 2 | Heb. 13:8-16, 20-21 (prescribed reading: Philemon 1-20) |
| Annunciation | Alternate Ps. 45 not included |

# Index of Readings for Year C

*Based on the Lectionary prepared for trial use*
*by*
*the North American Committee on*
*Calendar and Lectionary*

266